Scaling for E-Business
Technologies, Models, Performance, and Capacity Planning

What the reviewers are saying about *Scaling for E-Business:*

"Too many e-business systems have had embarrassing or even crippling episodes when they were unable to handle the amount of work they are suddenly asked to do. This book shows how to apply rigorous quantitative reasoning to one of the critical questions for a modern business—how to get satisfying performance from a complex e-business application without wasting resources. The book is a self-contained and immediately useful guide to predicting performance and capacity, and shows the reader how to analyze the critical and unusual aspects of e-commerce systems including network, crypto, and database issues."
Stuart Feldman, Director, IBM Institute for Advanced Commerce and Director, IBM Networked Computing Software Research

"E-business is transforming every element of business in many unknown ways. This book will give its readers a headstart in understanding the quantitative under-pinnings of the new environment."
Howard Frank, Dean, Robert H. Smith School of Business, University of Maryland at College Park

"This practitioner's handbook abstracts the current research articles and text-books—giving you clear advice on how to approach performance problems. The result is a very readable and useful tutorial on how to scale up a website from a single server to a site handling millions of transactions per day."
Jim Gray, Senior Researcher, Microsoft Research
1998 ACM Turing Award Recipient

ISBN 0-13-086328-9

9 780130 863287

90000

Scaling for E-Business

Technologies, Models, Performance, and Capacity Planning

Daniel A. Menascé
Virgilio A. F. Almeida

Prentice Hall PTR
Upper Saddle River, NJ 07458
www.phptr.com

Library of Congress Cataloging-in-Publication Data

Menascé, Daniel A.
   Scaling for e-business: technologies, models, performance, and capacity planning /
   Daniel A. Menascé, Virgilio A. F. Almeida
     p. cm.
   Includes bibliographical references and index.
   ISBN: 0-13-086328-9
     1. Electronic commerce. I. Almeida, Virgilio A. F.

   HF5548.32 .M46 2000
   658.8'4--dc21   00-025697

Editorial/Production Supervision: *Joan L. McNamara*
Acquisitions Editor: *Tim Moore*
Marketing Manager: *Bryan Gambrel*
Editorial Assistant: *Julie Okulicz*
Cover Design Director: *Jerry Votta*
Cover Designer: *Design Source*
Cover Illustration: *Dick Palulian*
Manufacturing Manager: *Maura Goldstaub*

© 2000 by Prentice Hall PTR
Prentice-Hall, Inc.
Upper Saddle River, New Jersey 07458

Prentice Hall books are widely used by corporations and government agencies for training, marketing, and resale. The publisher offers discounts on this book when ordered in bulk quantities. For more information, contact:
Corporate Sales Department
Prentice Hall PTR
One Lake Street
Upper Saddle River, NJ 07458
Phone: 800-382-3419; Fax: 201-236-7141; email: corpsales@prenhall.com

All product names mentioned herein are the trademarks of their respective owners.

Printed in the United States of America
10 9 8 7 6 5 4 3 2 1

ISBN: 0-13-086328-9

Prentice-Hall International (UK) Limited, *London*
Prentice-Hall of Australia Pty. Limited, *Sydney*
Prentice-Hall Canada Inc., *Toronto*
Prentice-Hall Hispanoamericana, S.A., *Mexico*
Prentice-Hall of India Private Limited, *New Delhi*
Prentice-Hall of Japan, Inc., *Tokyo*
Pearson Education Asia Pte. Ltd.
Editora Prentice-Hall do Brasil, Ltda., *Rio de Janeiro*

Contents

3 The Anatomy of E-Business Functions   67

II   Evaluating E-Business Infrastructure and Services   91

4 Infrastructure for Electronic Business   93

IV   Models of Specific E-Business Segments 375

13 Business-to-Consumer Case Studies   377

Foreword

This book teaches you how to approach website performance problems in a methodical and quantitative way. It introduces a methodology to analyze the way websites are used (behavior model graphs) and how work flows through them (interaction diagrams). The book shows you how to build these models from web logs or from a system analysis. It then shows you how to use these models to analyze your current system's behavior, and also to predict how much capacity you will need as demand grows and changes.

The book gives a very readable treatment of each step in this process, giving background tutorials on networking, web servers, server-side scripts, and database servers. It also gives quantitative measures of each of these components, telling you how to size servers and networks for each step of the interaction diagram. For example, it shows the relative cost of ordinary HTTP transactions, and then progresses to SSL/TLS secure transactions, and then SET transactions. In each case it explains the technology, then it explains the performance implications, and finally it considers the pros and cons of using hardware accelerators for the cryptographic steps. Each concept is exemplified by a specific example worked out in detail.

The web is unpredictable: it is very hard to guess what will happen next. What new technology will appear next month? What new security hole will pop up? What feature will create explosive growth on your site? This book cannot answer those questions—no book can. But, once you know what you want to do, this book gives you the quantitative tools to estimate the capacity needed to provide the new features and to estimate what they will cost, and also to estimate the new system's performance and response time.

Professors Menascé and Almeida have developed a pragmatic approach to website performance modeling. This practitioner's handbook abstracts the current research articles and textbooks—giving you clear advice on how to approach performance problems. The result is a very readable and useful tutorial on how to scale up a website from a single server to a site handling millions of transactions per day.

Jim Gray,

Microsoft Research, 301 Howard St #830, SF CA 94105

Gray@Microsoft.com

http://research.microsoft.com/~gray

Preface

Goal, Theme, and Approach

The Internet is profoundly affecting almost all businesses and commerce paradigms. Global competition, industry traditions, laws, and consumer preferences are among the many issues being impacted by e-business. Weekly magazines and newspapers have dedicated large amounts of space to discuss e-business and the new economy. Newspapers publish news about e-business almost every day. However, there is good news and bad news. The good news is many innovative people are constantly creating new and exciting ways to use the Internet to provide novel, efficient, and convenient shopping paradigms as well as streamlining ways for businesses to do business with their partners. The bad news is the most successful e-business sites are at greater risks of being overwhelmed by large numbers of customers who can potentially bring the site operation to a halt. Scalability is then a challenge to the success of e-business. Our primary goal in writing this book was to create a framework in which e-business scalability could be discussed and evaluated.

This book presents a quantitative approach to understanding and analyzing e-business scalability based on a four-level reference model. The four-level model is composed of a business model, a functional model, a customer behavior model, and an IT resource model. This framework is

3

used throughout the book to explain how e-business technologies work and how they impact performance, to characterize and forecast the workload of e-business sites, and to plan their capacity with the use of performance models.

New performance metrics for e-business are presented in the book. Models at the various levels of the reference model are used to represent and understand problems in e-business. These models include customer behavior models (e.g., Customer Behavior Model Graphs and Customer Visit Models), Client/Server Interaction Diagrams, and analytic (e.g., state transition diagrams and queuing networks) and simulation performance models. The combined use of these models provides a framework for assessing and evaluating the scalability of e-business sites.

Many examples derived from real e-business situations are used to illustrate the concepts presented in the book.

Who Should Read this Book

This book can be used by graduate and senior-level computer science students as well as students in e-commerce programs offered by business schools. Students of MBA programs with a concentration in information technology will also benefit from the concepts presented in this book.

Many professionals can use this book as a reference or as a way to learn about e-commerce technologies and the quantitative methods used to evaluate and size e-commerce sites. Examples of such professionals include Webmasters of e-commerce sites and ISPs, CIOs, system architects, project managers of e-commerce companies, e-commerce application developers, capacity planners and performance analysts, designers of Internet-based products for e-commerce, and e-commerce consultants.

Book Organization

Part I: Modeling for E-Business

Chapter 1 presents a framework for analyzing and designing e-business sites. The framework is based on a four-level model that includes a business model, a functional model, a customer behavior model, and an IT resource model. The chapter discusses various types of electronic markets including various types of business-to-business, business-to-consumer, and consumer-to-consumer markets.

Chapter 2 discusses the motivations for capturing user behavior and presents customer models at various levels. The models presented in this chapter can be used to answer what-if questions at the customer behavior level and can serve as a basis to build models at the resource level. Two types of customer models are presented in this chapter: the Customer Behavior Model Graphs and the Customer Visit Model.

Chapter 3 discusses the anatomy of e-business functions from the logical view point. The chapter describes how software servers interact to implement e-business functions and provides a graphical notation—the Client/Server Interaction Diagrams—to describe these interactions. Several numerical examples illustrate how these diagrams can be used to answer quantitative questions about the execution of e-business functions.

Part II: Evaluating E-Business Infrastructure and Services

Chapter 4 describes the various elements that comprise the IT infrastructure needed to support e-businesses. The discussion includes hardware, software, and networking issues. Multi-tier website architectures, composed of dynamic load balancers, Web servers, application servers, and database servers, are described.

Chapter 5 presents a quantitative analysis of authentication services used in e-business. The chapter shows how the mechanisms and protocols used to support security may impact system performance. Many quantitative examples illustrate the tradeoffs between performance and security. In particular, the chapter analyzes how authentication protocols such as the Transport Layer Security (TLS) protocol, a successor of the Secure Sockets Layer (SSL) protocol, affects performance.

Chapter 6 provides an overview of what happens when one uses a credit card for payment in the physical world. Then, it discusses how Secure Electronic Transaction (SET) allows for credit card payments to take place over the Internet. The chapter describes SET at a high enough level of detail to provide the reader with an overall picture of the protocol as well as its performance implications. The performance of SET transactions is then discussed through various numerical examples. The chapter concludes with a brief discussion of other payment services.

Part III: Capacity Planning for E-Business

Chapter 7 contains an example-driven description of a capacity planning methodology for e-businesses. The methodology is composed of three planning activities: business and functional planning, customer behavior planning, and IT resource planning. Each of these activities is described in detail and illustrated with examples.

Chapter 8 provides insight and intuition regarding how simple performance models can be constructed, solved, and used in the context of electronic business environments. The fundamentals of performance models are then introduced. These include concepts such as service time, service demand, waiting time, response time, throughput, and performance laws. Scalability analysis techniques based on the study of performance bounds is presented here.

Chapter 9 starts by introducing very simple models. Complexity is progressively introduced and the solution to each model is presented using first principles and intuitive concepts. Two broad categories of models are covered in this chapter: system- and component-level models. System-level models treat the actual system as a black box that receives requests, processes them, and returns the results. Component-level models, based on queuing networks, in which components are represented by queues, allows one to explicitly represent processors, storage subsystems, networks, and routers.

Chapter 10 uses several examples to illustrate the performance impacts of contention for software resources (e.g., threads of a software server, database locks, and semaphores). Performance models that deal with software contention may be based on approximate analytic models or on simulation models. This chapter gives an overview of the techniques used to solve approximations that represent the effects of software contention. To show the impact of software contention, we discuss various results obtained by a combination of simulation and analytic models.

Chapter 11 presents a methodology for characterizing e-business workloads. In particular, the chapter shows how Customer Behavior Model Graphs (CBMGs) and Customer Visit Models (CVMs) can be obtained from HTTP logs and describes methods, based on clustering analysis, to derive small groups of CBMGs or CVMs that accurately represent the workload. The chapter also shows how the parameters for the resource models (e.g., queuing network models) can be derived from customer behavior models.

Chapter 12 discusses techniques that can be used to analyze and forecast the demand for e-business sites. The chapter discusses traffic burstiness, traffic patterns in e-business, and forecasting techniques including regression methods, moving averages, and exponential smoothing. Logs of a real e-tailer are used to illustrate the traffic characteristics of an e-business site.

Part IV: Models for Specific E-Business Segments

Chapter 13 illustrates the use of the quantitative methods presented in the book through several examples in the business-to-consumer segment. A hypothetical electronic retailer is described. Then, different planning situations are discussed. In light of the models introduced throughout the book, we show how to tackle the problems and we present their solutions. The goal of the chapter is to guide the reader, in a step-by-step manner, through the model-based solution of a number of e-commerce examples.

Chapter 14 illustrates the use of the quantitative methods presented in the book through several examples in the business-to-business segment. An example of supply-chain integration and made-to-order computers is used to illustrate how capacity planning can be carried out in business-to-business environments. The chapter also shows how business-to-consumer transactions generate business-to-business transactions.

Part V: Summary, Challenges, and Perspectives

Chapter 15 concludes the book with a summary of important points covered in the book, challenges for e-business, and future perspectives.

Appendix A contains a glossary of the important terms introduced in the book.

Acknowledgments

The authors would like to thank their many colleagues for discussions that contributed substantially to this book. Special thanks go to our co-author in the first book of this series, Larry Dowdy of Vanderbilt University, for his enthusiasm and dedication to the field of performance evaluation. Thanks go to Rodrigo Fonseca, Wagner Meira Jr., Marco Aurelio Mendes, Goedson Paixão, Adriano Pereira, and Flavia Peligrinelli Ribeiro, who collaborated on several papers on e-commerce with the authors of this book, to Ross Lumley who pointed to information on SET, and to Krysztof Gaj for providing useful literature on cryptography. Particular thanks go to Stuart Feldman of the IBM Institute for Advanced Commerce, Howard Frank of the Robert H. Smith School of Business at the University of Maryland at College Park, and to Jim Gray of Microsoft Research for their praise of our work and permission to quote them in the book. The authors would like to express their most sincere appreciation to Jim Gray for writing the foreword for the book and for providing useful references to papers and reports.

Working with the team at Prentice Hall PTR was a real pleasure. We would like to thank our editor, Tim Moore, for his enthusiasm and continued support throughout this project, for being always available to discuss issues and problems, and for his ideas regarding the packaging of the book. The competence of our production manager, Joan L. McNamara, was essential in making it possible to produce this book in such a short time. We would like to thank Lori Hughes for her superb job as copyeditor and for designing the LaTeX macros we used to prepare the book. Thanks also go to the art department for their work on the cover of the book and to many others at PTR who made this project possible.

Daniel Menascé would like to thank his students and colleagues at George Mason University for providing a stimulating work environment. He would also like to thank the Office of the Provost and the Chair of the Computer Science Department, Henry Hamburger, at George Mason University for awarding him a study leave during the Fall of 1999, which allowed him to dedicate more time to this book. Daniel would like to recognize his mother and the much cherished memory of his father for all the love and direction in life he received from them. Special thanks go to his wife Gilda for a life full of love, dedication, companionship, encouragement, and support, and for having given him two real treasures, his children Flavio and Juliana, whose love, friendship, and positive attitude in life have been a continuous delight.

Virgilio Almeida would like to thank his colleagues, students, and staff at the Computer Science Department of the Federal University of Minas Gerais (UFMG). He would also like to thank CNPq (the Brazilian Council for Scientific Research and Development) and the SIAM/Finep Project, which provided partial support for his work on this book. Virgilio would also like to thank his wife Rejane and sons Pedro and Andre for their joy, patience, and encouragement during the many nights and weekends he worked on this book.

From the Same Authors

Menascé and Almeida co-authored the following books:

- *Capacity Planning for Web Performance: Metrics, Models, and Methods*, D. A. Menascé and V. A. F. Almeida, Prentice Hall, 1998.
- *Capacity Planning and Performance Modeling: From Mainframes to Client-Server Systems*, D. A. Menascé, V. A. F. Almeida, and L. W. Dowdy, Prentice Hall, 1994.

Book's Website and Authors' Addresses

Readers of this book can download the various MS Excel workbooks referenced in the various chapters from www.cs.gmu.edu/~menasce/ebook/. This website will also be used to keep the readers informed about new developments related to the book. The authors' e-mail and postal addresses and websites are:

Prof. Daniel A. Menascé
Department of Computer Science, MS 4A5
George Mason University
Fairfax, VA 22030-4444
+1 703 993-1537
menasce@cs.gmu.edu
http://www.cs.gmu.edu/faculty/menasce.html

Prof. Virgilio A. F. Almeida
Department of Computer Science
Universidade Federal de Minas Gerais
P.O. Box 920
31270-010 Belo Horizonte, MG
Brazil
+55 31 499-5887
virgilio@dcc.ufmg.br
http://www.dcc.ufmg.br/~virgilio

Part I

Modeling for E-Business

Chapter 1: Models for E-Business
Chapter 2: Customer Behavior Models
Chapter 3: The Anatomy of E-Business Functions

Chapter 1

Models for E-Business

1.1 Introduction

As electronic business expands all around the world, so do technical problems associated with it. Consequences of surges in volumes of e-business transactions, delays and outages occur as systems and networks become overloaded. Surveys and studies [6] indicate that slow downloading time is one of the most often cited reasons that an online customer leaves a site and looks for another vendor's website instead. Since online companies' entire business depends on the behavior of their sites, long waiting times and unavailability can be disastrous.

Online companies must continuously offer good quality electronic service to avoid losing sales and customers. In any e-business site, whether online brokerage service, merchant, or auctioneer, it is necessary to guarantee the quality of service, represented by key issues such as security, performance, and availability. Frequently, technical literature and newspapers report cases of online companies that have experienced tremendous performance and availability problems. Customers on the Web are increasingly demanding faster response times and higher availability from e-business sites. Failure to provide high-quality services results in lost "eyeballs." For instance, e-business sites try to follow the "eight-second rule," an unsubstantiated but widely held belief that after eight seconds of waiting for a Web page to be downloaded, a customer becomes impatient and will likely abandon the site. Therefore, for most electronic businesses, poor performance and low availability almost always mean lost revenue, bad press, bad public perception, and a drop in the company's stock price.

The purpose of this book is to provide the fundamental analytic techniques, methods, and models to understand the behavior of e-business systems and their customers. This chapter is organized around models that highlight the different levels of service involved in electronic business. It introduces concepts and models associated with various types of electronic businesses. Some simple quantitative examples associated with quality of service of electronic business are discussed in the chapter. Finally, it provides an overview of a systematic approach to identifying and planning architectures and systems for electronic business.

1.1.1   Quantitative Approach

The quality of service of e-business sites depends on many interrelated factors such as site architecture, network capacity, and system software structure. The complexity of an e-business site is compounded by unpredictable public behavior. Usage patterns can change overnight with spikes in demand occurring for several reasons. For instance, breaking news always causes bursts of traffic on online editions of major newspapers. When a company runs a marketing campaign, the capacity of its site may be inadequate to support the huge number of visitors who react to the campaign. All these characteristics of e-business clearly indicate that quantitative techniques are needed to manage the behavior of online companies and to guarantee quality of service. These techniques should help management answer the following typical questions.

- Is the online trading site prepared to accommodate the surge in volume that may increase the number of trades per day by up to 75%?

- How can IT people justify to higher levels of management an enormous dollar amount for site expansion without showing any analytics?

- Is the number of servers enough to handle a peak of customers ten times greater than the monthly average?

- How can we guarantee the quality of electronic customer service for different scenarios of traffic growth?

- In a business-to-business environment, sending and receiving sensitive data, conducting financial transactions, and exchanging credit and production data depend on the secure and fast transmission of information. How can our company guarantee the quality of service required for implementing a supply-chain integration?

- E-business sites may become popular very quickly. How fast can the site architecture be scaled up? What components of the site should be upgraded? Database servers? Web servers? Application servers? Network link bandwidth?

- How can a small- or medium-sized company that cannot afford frequent hardware and software updates determine the adequate capacity of its e-business site?

1.1.2   Electronic Business Challenges

Electronic business brings a unique set of challenges to the information technology infrastructure. Some of the most important e-business infrastructure issues are adequate site capacity, scalability, and fault-tolerance. The viability of electronic business depends on the ability of the underlying systems to offer timely and reliable services.

As computers become more pervasive, performance and availability problems tend to aggravate. Personal digital assistants (PDAs) and embedded computers in home appliances [5] attached to the Internet will add at least an order of magnitude to the number of traffic sources and will change the characteristics and intensity of Internet traffic. In addition, local access technologies like Universal Mobile Telecommunications System (UMTS), cable modems, Digital Subscriber Lines (DSL), and novel interfaces (e.g., Voice User Interface) will change workloads arriving from traditional end systems. Furthermore, software agents have become very popular in the Web [9]. Personalized software agents can be used to automate several of the most time-consuming phases of the negotiation process, either selling or buying goods. As a consequence, the popularity of agents will generate more commercial transactions and more load on e-business servers.

Understanding the impact of these changes, in terms of customer behavior, workload characteristics, and system performance, is challenging. Performance, availability, and capacity modeling techniques can help solve problems in advance. Internet Service Providers (ISP), network providers, and e-business companies will need to understand the impacts of new workloads to properly design and operate their systems.

1.2   Electronic Markets

Electronic commerce can be loosely defined as any form of business transaction in which the parties interact electronically. A transaction in an electronic market represents a number of interactions between parties. For instance, it could involve several trading steps, such as marketing, ordering, payment, and support for delivery. An electronic market allows participating sellers and buyers to exchange goods and services with the support of information technology. Electronic markets have three main functions: i) matching buyers and sellers, ii) facilitating commercial transactions, and iii) providing legal infrastructure [2]. Information technology permeates all three functions and helps to increase market efficiency and reduce transaction costs. The interaction between participants is supported by electronic trade processes [7] that are basically search, valuation, payment and settlement, logistics, and authentication, as shown in Fig. 1.1. The Internet and the World Wide Web allow companies to efficiently implement these key trading processes. For instance, many search services and brokers are available to help buyers find information, products, and merchants in electronic markets [1].

Businesses, individuals, and government organizations are the main players in an electronic market. The relations between these players is depicted in Fig. 1.2 and can be grouped into the following categories of electronic business.

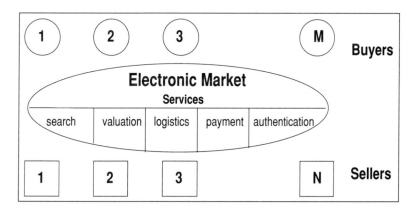

Figure 1.1. Representation of an Electronic Market.

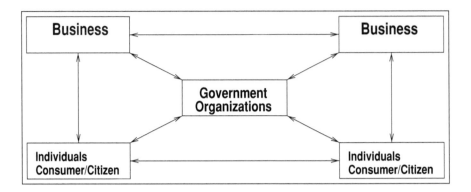

Figure 1.2. Business Relations in the Electronic Market.

- *Business-to-Business (B2B)*: the business-to-business category includes all transactions made by a company with its suppliers or any other companies. Business-to-business applications have been well established for several years, particularly using Electronic Data Interchange (EDI) over private or value-added networks (VANs).

- *Business-to-Consumer (B2C)*: this category is mainly represented by electronic retailing and covers a large range of commercial sites from online retailing to online financial services to online publishing.

- *Consumer-to-Consumer*: consumer-to-consumer electronic markets are formed basically by Web-based auctions. Collectible items, used cars, and any type of item usually found in classified sections of local newspapers can be negotiated between consumers through auction sites available on the Web.

- *Government-to-Business*: the government-to-business category covers all transactions between companies and government organizations. It includes government electronic procurements and other government to business communications. In addition to public procurement, government organizations may also offer the option of electronic transactions such as payment of corporate taxes.

- *Government-to-Citizens*: the government-to-citizens category covers electronic interactions between citizens and government in areas such as welfare payments and tax returns.

Electronic markets are emerging in various fields. Different industries have markets with different characteristics. For example, an information B2C market differs in many respects from the automotive B2B market [3]. The former represents companies that sell digital information goods, such as news, articles, music, books, or digital videos. In the information B2C market, the electronic infrastructure not only helps match customers and sellers, but also acts as the distribution channel, delivering products to customers. In this case, the infrastructure, such as servers and networks, must support the delivery of large files, streaming media, and other types of digital goods in an efficient way. This B2C market over the Internet can be viewed as an open system, where the number of participants is unknown. In the automotive B2B market, the products traded have a high degree of specificity, such as parts and components of cars. The market infrastructure used to be mainly based on Electronic Data Interchange (EDI) over expensive VAN services. EDI involves the exchange of standardized, structured information between organizations, permitting direct communication between computer systems. Now, the automotive B2B market is using the Internet for many of its activities. At the heart of B2B applications is the strong integration of different applications. Servers, networks, and software should provide the infrastructure to integrate Web-based applications with mainframe and legacy systems. B2B is also a closed market in the sense that the number of participants involved in trading is limited and known a priori.

Understanding the nature of the market's requirements is critical for creating the underlying e-business infrastructure. The relation between B2B and B2C models is clearly shown in Fig. 1.3. B2B covers business transactions along the various interactions existing in the value chain from producers of raw materials to retailers, including manufacturers and distributors. On

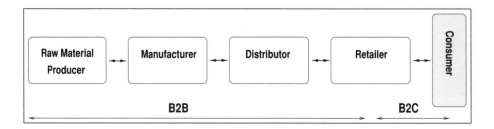

Figure 1.3. Electronic Business Value Chain.

the other hand, B2C reflects only the interactions between a customer and a retailer. Basically, B2C transactions include the following steps: i) account acquisition, ii) product discovery through search and browse, iii) price negotiation, iv) payment, and v) product delivery. In some cases, dispute resolution and customer services may also exist.

1.2.1   Business-to-Business Transactions and Models

B2B interactions involve much more complexity than B2C. For instance, typical B2B transactions include, among others, the following steps: i) review catalogs, ii) identify specifications, iii) define requirements, iv) post request for proposals (RFP), v) review vendor reputation, vi) select vendor, vii) fill out purchase orders (PO), viii) send PO to vendor, ix) prepare invoice, x) make payment, xi) arrange shipment, and xii) product inspection and reception. Due to the large number of transactions involved, business-to-business operations can be too risky if e-business sites cannot guarantee adequate quality of service in terms of performance, availability, and security.

Several models and classifications have been proposed for B2B commerce [4] [12]. Figure 1.4 illustrates an electronic marketplace for B2B trading. The model could be oriented to a vertical market (e.g., wholesale trade, chemicals, construction, and electronics) or to a horizontal approach (e.g., office supply, and logistics). The various models are described below.

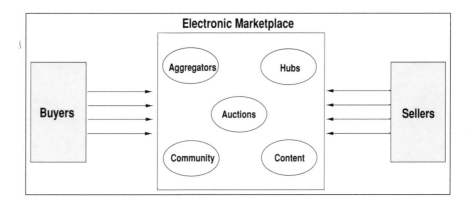

Figure 1.4. Business-to-Business Marketplace.

- *Aggregators.* In the aggregation model, one company aggregates buyers in order to form a virtual buying entity and/or aggregates suppliers to constitute a virtual distributor. For example, in the science marketplace, one company became the central buying location for thousands of buyers to implement their own purchasing rules and obtain volume discounts. The aggregator takes the responsibility for selection and fulfillment, pricing, and marketing segmentation. Another example is an electronic company that offers a total home buying service, from search to financing, under one site.

- *Hubs or Process Integration.* Hubs or process integration focuses on producing a highly integrated value proposition through a managed process. Hubs have been defined as neutral Internet-based intermediaries that focus on a specific industry or a specific business process [12]. Hubs host electronic markets and create value by reducing costs of transactions between sellers and buyers. There are examples of vertical hubs that serve a vertical market or a specific industry, such as energy, steel, telecommunications, and plastic. On the contrary, functional hubs specialize in horizontal markets across different industries. Functional hubs focus on business processes such as project management and MRO, i.e., maintenance, repair and operating, procurement.

For instance, an electronic business company that provides office supplies to many industries is a good example of a functional hub in a B2B commerce.

- *Community or Alliance.* In the community model, alliances are used to achieve high value integration without hierarchical control. Members and end users play key roles as contributors and customers. Basically, communities produce knowledge with economic value, such as Linux, MP3, and Open Source.

- *Content.* Content is the end product of this model of B2B commerce. It has the purpose of facilitating trading. Revenue can be generated from subscriptions, membership, or advertising. For example, there are e-companies that sell information about contracts to bid, market intelligence and analysis, and jobs by industry.

- *Auctions or Dynamic Pricing Markets.* Auctions or dynamic pricing markets handle complex exchanges between buyers and sellers in B2B commerce. Auctions [8] (e.g., English, Dutch, Vickrey, Reverse) are dynamic and efficient mechanisms for mediating and brokering in complex marketplaces, like supply-chain and procurement systems. Bundle auctions [11] allow agents to bid for bundles of items and are useful for B2B applications such as automatic supply-chain or procurement.

1.3   Reference Models for Electronic Business

The reference model for electronic business, shown in Fig. 1.5, creates a framework for the quantitative approach developed in this book. It also provides a basis for defining conceptual activities in the electronic business and for identifying improvement opportunities. The reference model consists of four layers grouped into two main blocks. The upper block focuses on the nature of the business and the processes that provide the services offered by the electronic business site. The lower block concentrates on the way customers interact with the site and the demand they place upon the

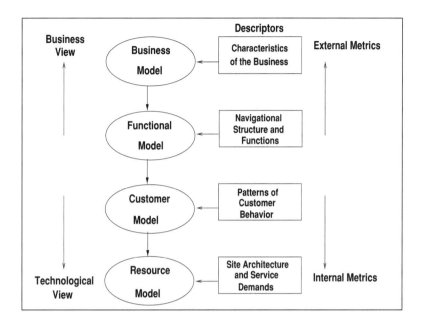

Figure 1.5. Reference Models for Electronic Business.

resources of the site infrastructure. Each layer of the reference model is associated with two broad classes of descriptors and metrics used to provide a quantitative characterization of the layer.

External metrics and descriptors cover the nature of the business and are visible to management and customers. These metrics are used to assess the performance of the business processes. For instance, one could use a metric for e-business that reflects at the same time the behavior of the online store and its customers. One such metric is revenue throughput, measured in dollars/sec generated by completed online transactions [10]. Other external metrics could be availability, download times, page views/day, and unique visitors/day. External descriptors give a quantitative overview of the business. For example, external descriptors include information such as the number of registered customers, number of potential customers, maximum number of simultaneous customers in the store, number of items, estimated operational cost, and services available to customers.

Internal descriptors and metrics characterize the site infrastructure and the way services and resources are used by customers. Internal metrics are oriented to measure the performance of applications and of the information technology infrastructure. Examples of such metrics include HTTP requests/second, database transactions/second, server response time, transaction response time, and processor, disk and network utilization. Internal descriptors also include application and architecture information, such as navigational structure, customer's navigation patterns, and characteristics of the components that make up the site.

1.3.1   Business and Functional Models

A business model [14][15] can be defined as an architecture for product, service, and information flow, including a description of business players, their roles, and revenue sources. For example, some of the most popular revenue-generating models adopted by companies are: i) charge fees for advertising, ii) sell goods and services, iii) sell digital contents, and iv) charge for processing the transactions that occur between two parties on the Web. There are several electronic business models, as exemplified by the following.

- *Online retailing.* Electronic stores use the Web to sell physical goods (e.g., books, CDs, computers, and clothing) to consumers. Sophisticated electronic catalogs, including pictures, detailed product descriptions, pricing, and sizing information, are available to customers.

- *Online auction.* Electronic auction sites offer a variety of items that range from collectibles, such as antiques, sports memorabilia, coins, stamps, and books, to more general items, such as real state, airline tickets, and computers. In the most popular form of electronic auction, buyers and sellers can access auctions through an intermediary, i.e., an electronic auctioneer. Electronic auctions are a very popular way of selling and buying products. Their popularity is attributed to

i) reduced search costs for the participants in electronic markets, ii) availability of a worldwide communication infrastructure with trading partners, and iii) availability of efficient search engines and diffusion of the WWW standard protocols and hypermedia representation of trade objects.

- *Content portal.* Sites that are the major gateways to the Web or to a set of Web pages addressing specific topics are called portals. To attract traffic, portals provide value-added services to users, such as consistent interface to the Web, prioritization of links, and timely information.

- *Distribution.* Some B2B sites provide components and production supplies. For example, in the industrial electronics market, online distributors offer products such as semiconductors, connectors, components, computer systems and peripherals, and production supplies.

- *Services.* Many companies use the B2C model to sell services. Examples can be found in the travel, financial, banking, and insurance industries. Using their e-business sites, online companies offer services twenty-four hours a day, seven days a week.

- *Publishing.* Newspapers, magazines, survey reports, and encyclopedias are examples of contents made available on the Internet by online publishing companies. Some companies charge subscription fees while others offer information for free and adopt advertising as the revenue-generating model.

Answers to the following types of questions help build a business model of an online company [13]. What is the purpose or mission of the business? What are the business goals? What are the measurable objectives? Is the electronic market open or is it restricted to certain groups? What is the potential size of the market? What business policies do participants follow? What are the revenue models? What value-added services offered to customers could be considered critical success factors?

The functional model depicts the trading processes that deliver services to customers of an electronic business company. The processes are sets of interlinked activities that directly deliver business outcomes. Functional models can be obtained from a top-down analysis of the electronic business. They can be represented by many techniques, such as process flow models, hierarchical activity models, data flow diagrams, and entity relationship models [15]. In the context of electronic business, the activities of a process can be further decomposed into services a customer can request from a Web site. Thus, a functional model provides the framework to identify the navigational structure of a site and to analyze different possible paths taken by customers.

Consider the case of XYZ, a Web-based auction company. Let us describe some information that would be part of the two upper layers of the reference model. Customers use the XYZ auctions to sell and buy items such as coins, stamps, CDs, pottery, glass, photography, computers, and electronics. Items are grouped into categories. There is no charge to browse, bid on, or buy items at the XYZ auction site. But sellers do pay fees to list and sell items. The XYZ trading site on the Web is available twenty-four hours a day and seven days a week and provides fast response time to any request. The business model of XYZ could be quantified by the following descriptors.

- number of item categories: 1100;

- number of new items "for sale" added daily to the site: 120,000;

- number of auctions per day: 45,000;

- number of registered users: 1.9 million;

- number of page views per day: 4.8 million.

Figure 1.6 depicts the functional model of a typical online auction company with its six basic processes [8]. For instance, the "Bidding" process is responsible for collecting the bids from buyers and implementing the rules

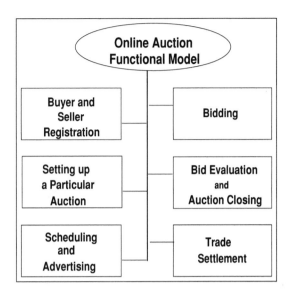

Figure 1.6. Functional Model of an Online Auction.

for the auction. In the case of a Dutch auction, the site lowers the starting price in each time interval until the first buyer bids. The functional model can be used as a starting point to design or identify the navigational structure of the auction site. For example, when a customer arrives at the home page, the site either authenticates the customer, using a login name and password, to initiate a secure session or offers the customer the opportunity to register with the XYZ company. After the registration or authentication step, the customer can visit typical pages such as 1) Browse, 2) Search, 3) Display Item Description, 4) Bid on an Item, 5) List Auction Rules, 6) Bid, and 7) Pay. From this functional model, one could draw representations for the navigational structure.

1.3.2 Customer and Resource Models

The two lower layers of the reference model are extensively treated throughout the book. Therefore, just a brief description of these layers is provided here. Customers interact with an e-business site through sequences of requests to execute the various services available at the site. The customer model captures the navigational pattern of a customer during a visit to an e-business site. This model describes how customers navigate through the site and allows one to derive behavior metrics such as how many times a certain function is invoked during a shopping session or the average length of a typical session. Each service requested by a customer exercises the resources of the e-business site infrastructure in a different way. Some services may use only the application server, others may request many operations from the database server. For example, a *Display Product Information* button of a multimedia catalog could require a large amount of network time and disk operations to send out large files of video and sound associated with the product. Thus, the performance of an e-business site depends on i) the pattern of services requested by customers, as described by the customer model, ii) the demands that each service places on the site's resources, and iii) the intensity at which customers arrive at the site.

The resource model combines these three aspects and calculates the site performance. In order to do that, the resource model contains two key elements: the workload model and the performance model. The former captures the pattern of services requested by customers and the demands that each service requires from the site's resources in terms of time. The workload model also characterizes the workload intensity as described by the customer arrival process within a representative time frame, such as the peak hours. The performance model is used to calculate performance metrics for an e-business site as a function of the site architecture and workload description. This model is used to compute metrics for different views of the site. Examples of resource usage metrics include processor utilization and average number of requests waiting for the database service. Higher level metrics, such as customer response time or site revenue per second, can also be obtained by the resource model.

1.4 Quality of Service Requirements

This section analyzes the system requirements in light of the models for e-business. Regardless of the type of e-business model adopted, there are some issues that have to be carefully considered during the design and implementation of an electronic business site. These include the reliability, security, capacity, scalability, and cost of the system and network. E-business activities and Web services are essentially real time processes in which performance and availability problems have a high cost. Frustrated users can translate into lost customers and lost revenue. The cost of not doing business may be too high for an online company. Therefore, capacity planning methodologies should be able to anticipate problems for electronic business environments. Performance, availability, and security goals need to be set very early in the projects because they are closely related to the design of the applications.

Example 1.1

Consider again the auction example and examine the quality of service requirements for this kind of business. In auction markets, where products are traded electronically, customers may want to be able to look at the product and its features. Therefore multimedia capabilities should be part of the system design, which implies adequate bandwidth capacity and fast processors and disks. Also, the load of an auction site depends on the time of day, day of the week, items for sale, and advertising campaigns. As a consequence, the load of an auction site can easily vary by a factor of ten [16]. Let us consider that during the peak hour the ratio between peak and average page request equals ten. Management wants to know what network bandwidth increase will be needed to support the multimedia capabilities during the peak hour?

From the business model, we know that the number of page views per day is 4.8 million. Based on the navigational patterns, analysts identified that three out of each ten page requests are "Display Item Description." In order to add multimedia features, analysts calculated that the average size of the pages would increase by ninety thousand bytes. Therefore, the increase in bandwidth is calculated as follows.

$$
\begin{aligned}
\mathrm{AveragePageRequest/Hour} &= \mathrm{PagesPerDay}/24 \\
&= 4,800,000/24 \;=\; 200,000 \text{ pages/hour} \\
\mathrm{PeakPageRequest} &= \mathrm{AveragePageRequest} \times \mathrm{PeakLoadFactor} \\
&= 200,000 \times 10 \;=\; 2,000,000 \text{ pages/hour} \\
\mathrm{NumberOfDisplayPagesOnPeak} &= \mathrm{PeakPageRequest} \times 0.3 \\
&= 2,000,000 \times 0.3 \;=\; 600,000 \\
\mathrm{PeakBandwidthIncrease} &= \mathrm{NumberOfDisplayPagesOnPeak} \times \\
&\quad\;\; \mathrm{PageSizeIncrease} \\
&= 600,000 \times 90,000 \text{ bytes} \\
&= 54,000 \text{ Mbytes/hour} = 120 \text{ Mbps}
\end{aligned}
$$

∎

Example 1.2

Consider the auction company example. In determining the service levels, management established an availability goal of 99% for the company services. What is the maximum number of hours of downtime allowed per year in order to achieve the availability goal?

The downtime period is the time available to repair the application if damaged, repair the database if damaged, do maintenance on the system, restart the system, etc. The maximum number of downtime hours is:

$$
\mathrm{\%ofAvailabilityPerYear} = \frac{\mathrm{HoursPerYear} - \mathrm{HoursOfUnavailability}}{\mathrm{HoursPerYear}}
$$

$$
99\% = \frac{8760 - \mathrm{HoursOfUnavailability}}{8760}
$$

$$
\mathrm{HoursOfUnavailability} = 8760 - (0.99 \times 8760) = 87.6 \text{ hours.}
$$

∎

Example 1.3

Consider a company that does one million dollars a day in online revenue. Its site crashed at 8:00PM and stayed unavailable for two hours. What is the cost of the site unavailability?

Considering that 30% of daily transactions occur during a four-hour period, from 8:00PM to midnight, we can estimate the lost transaction revenue as follows.

$$\%ofLostTransactions = \%ofTransactions \times DurationOfUnavailabilityPeriod$$
$$= 30\% \times 2/4 = 0.15$$
$$LostRevenue = \%ofLostTransactions \times AverageDailyRevenue$$
$$= 0.15 \times \$1 \text{ million} = \$150,000$$

■

Example 1.4

Suppose that during the peak period, the site of an online retailer exhibits a poor performance. The average number of consumers that visit the site per hour is twenty thousand. However, during the peak hour, the visitors rate is three times higher than the average. During this period, 90% of the customers that visited the site experienced a page download time exceeding eight seconds. What is the cost of poor performance during the peak hour?

Some analysts consider that after eight seconds of waiting for a Web page to load, consumers become frustrated and abandon the site. Examining the logs of the e-business site, management found that 6% of the visitors purchased something and the average value of a purchase was $45. The lost revenue during peak hours is the metric used to assess the cost of poor performance. Therefore, lost revenue due to the site's poor performance is calculated as follows.

$$HourlyRevenue = VisitorRate \times BuyingPercentage \times$$
$$AverageAmountOfPurchase$$

$$= 20,000 \times 3 \times 0.06 \times 45 = \$162,000.00$$

$$\text{LostRevenue} = \text{HourlyRevenue} \times \text{AbandonRate}$$

$$= 162,000.00 \times 0.90 = \$145,800.00$$

∎

1.5   Overview of the Quantitative Approach

Speed, around-the-clock availability, and security are the most common indicators of quality of service of an electronic business site. Management faces a twofold challenge. On one hand, companies must meet customer expectations in terms of quality of service. On the other hand, companies have to keep site costs under control to stay competitive. Therefore, capacity, reliability, scalability, and security are key issues to e-business site managers. E-business sites are complex computer-system architectures, with multiple interconnected layers of software and hardware components, such as networks, caching proxies, routers, high speed links, and mainframes with large databases. The nature of e-business workload is also complex due to its transactional nature, secure requirements, payment protocols, and the unpredictable characteristics of service requests over the Internet. Planning the capacity of e-business sites requires more than just adding extra hardware. It requires more than intuition, ad hoc procedures, and rules of thumb. There are many possible alternative architectures and one has to be able to determine the most cost-effective architecture. This is where the quantitative approach of this book and capacity planning techniques for electronic business come into play.

Figure 1.7 gives an overview of the main steps of the quantitative approach to analyze electronic business sites. The approach is represented by a cycle with a series of steps that are discussed in detail throughout the chapters of this book. The starting point is the business model and its measurable objectives, which are used to establish service level goals and

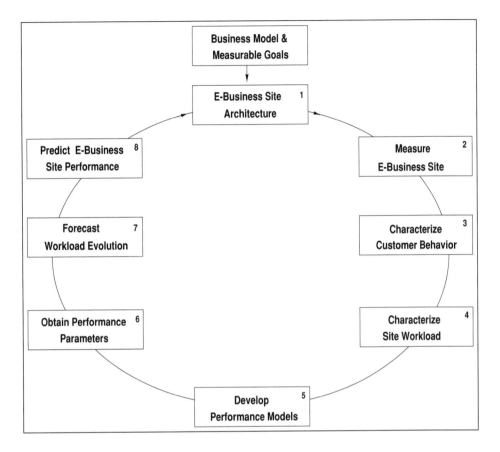

Figure 1.7. Quantitative Analysis Cycle of an E-business Site.

determine what applications are central to the goals. Once the business
model and its quantitative objectives have been understood, one is able to
go through the quantitative analysis cycle.

1. The first step entails obtaining an in-depth understanding of the e-
   business site architecture. What are the system requirements of the
   business model? What is the configuration of the site in terms of
   servers and internal connectivity? How many internal layers are there
   in the site? What types of servers (i.e., HTTP, database, or authentication) is the site running? What type of software (i.e., operating

system, HTTP server software, transaction monitor, DBMS) is used in each server machine? How reliable and scalable is the architecture? This step should yield a systematic description of the website environment, its components, and services.

2. The second step consists of measuring the performance of the systems that make up the e-business site. This is a key step in the process of guaranteeing quality of service and preventing problems. Performance measurements should be collected from different reference points, each point carefully chosen to observe and monitor the environment under study. For example, logs of transactions and accesses to servers are the main source of information. Further information, such as downloading times from different points of the network, may help to follow the service level perceived by customers. The information collected should be capable of answering questions like the following. What is the number of customer visits per day? What is the site revenue for a specific period of time? What is the average and peak traffic to the site? What characterizes the shoppers of a particular set of products?

3. The third step focuses on understanding the customer behavior. Customers interact with an electronic business site through sequences of requests to invoke the various services available in the site. Some customers may be considered as heavy buyers while others, considered occasional buyers, spend most of their time browsing and searching the site. These two examples of classes of customers exhibit different navigational patterns and, as a consequence, invoke services in different ways with different frequencies. The point is that each service may exercise the site's resources in a different manner. Some services may use a large amount of processing time from the application server while others may concentrate on the database server. Understanding customer behavior is critical for achieving the business objectives as well as for adequately sizing the resources of the site.

4. The fourth step characterizes the workload of an e-business site. E-business workloads are composed of sessions, sequences of requests of different types made by a single customer during a single visit to a site. Examples of requests from an online shopper are browse, search, select, add to the shopping cart, user registration, and pay. An online trader would have different operations, such as enter a stock order, research a fund, obtain real-time quotes, retrieve company profiles, and compute earning estimates. This step uses the representations generated by the previous step. Another aspect of the nature of the e-business workload is its intensity, which measures how often customers arrive to the site.

5. In the fifth step, quantitative techniques and analytical models based on queuing network theory are used to evaluate the performance of electronic business sites. Performance models can be used to predict performance when any aspect of the workload or the site architecture is changed.

6. The sixth step aims at obtaining the input parameters for performance models. These parameters describe the architecture of the e-business site and the workload under study. A site architecture typically includes Web servers, application servers, and database servers organized in layered groups. Each server consists of many basic components that contribute to the system performance, such as processors, disks, and network interfaces. Some parameters can be directly derived from measurement data while others must be estimated according to specific features of the site.

7. The seventh step forecasts the expected workload for an e-business site. The techniques and strategies for forecasting demand in the electronic marketplace should provide answers to questions: What is the expected workload of the e-business website of an electronic bookstore during

the holiday season? How will the number of users of an online auction vary during the next six months?

8. Using the performance models and workload forecasts, the last step of the cycle analyzes many possible alternative architectures to determine the most cost-effective one. The future scenarios should take into consideration the expected workload, the site cost, and the quality of service perceived by customers.

1.6   Summary

For online companies, whose entire business depends on the behavior of their sites, long waiting times and unavailability can be disastrous. Electronic businesses must continuously guarantee quality of service to avoid losing sales and customers. Security, performance, and availability are key issues for any e-business site. This chapter introduced a reference model for electronic business that creates a framework for the quantitative approach developed in the book. It also gives an overview of the main steps required to analyze the behavior and performance of electronic business sites.

Bibliography

[1] V. Almeida, W. Meira, V. Ribeiro, and N. Ziviani, "Efficiency Analysis of Brokers in Electronic Marketplace," *Computer Networks*, vol. 31, 1999.

[2] Y. Bakos, "The Emerging Role of Electronic Marketplaces on the Internet," *Comm. ACM*, vol. 41, no. 8, Aug. 1998.

[3] J. Bailey and Y. Bakos, "An Exploratory Study of the Emerging Role of Electronic Intermediaries," *International J. Electronic Commerce*, vol. 1, no. 3, Spring 1997.

[4] S. Boll, A. Gruner, A. Haaf, and W. Klas, "A Database-Driven Electronic Market Place for Business-to-Business Commerce on the Internet," *Distributed and Parallel Databases*, vol. 7, no. 2, Apr. 1999.

[5] K. Eustice, T. Lehman, A. Morales, M. Munson, S. Edlund, and M. Guillen, "A Universal Information Appliance," *IBM Systems J.*, vol. 38, no. 4, 1999.

[6] GVU, "GVU's WWW User Surveys," http://www.gvu.gatech.edu.

[7] A. Kambil, "Doing Business in the Wired World," *IEEE Computer*, vol. 30, no. 5, May 1997.

[8] M. Kumar and S. Feldman, "Internet Auctions," *Proc. 3rd USENIX Workshop On Electronic Commerce*, USENIX Association, Boston, Aug. 1998.

[9] P. Maes, R. Guttman, and A. Moukas, "Agents that Buy and Sell: Transforming Commerce as We Know It," *Comm. ACM*, vol. 42, no.3, March 1999.

[10] D. A. Menascé, V. A. F. Almeida, R. C. Fonseca, and M. A. Mendes, "Resource Management Policies for E-commerce Servers," *Proc. Second Workshop on Internet Server Performance* (WISP'99) held jointly with ACM Sigmetrics'99, Atlanta, GA, May 1st, 1999.

[11] D. Parkes, "iBundle: An Efficient Ascending Price Bundle Auction," *Proc. ACM Conference on Electronic Commerce*, Denver, CO, Nov. 3-5, 1999, pp. 148–157.

[12] M. Sawhney and S. Kaplan, "Let's Get Vertical," *Business 2.0*, Sep. 1999.

[13] B. Schmid and M. Lindermann, "Elements of a Reference Model for Electronic Markets," *Proc. 31st Annual Hawaii International Conference on Systems Sciences, HICCS98*, Jan. 1998.

[14] P. Timmers, "Business Models for Electronic Market," *International J. Electronic Markets*, vol. 8, no. 2, Jul. 1998.

[15] J. Ward and P. Griffiths, *Strategic Planning for Information Systems*, John Wiley & Sons, 1997.

[16] C. Wrigley, "Design Criteria for Electronic Market Servers," *International J. Electronic Markets*, vol. 7, no. 4, Dec. 1997.

Chapter 2

Customer Behavior Models

2.1   Introduction

Customers of an e-commerce site interact with it through a series of consecutive and related requests made during a single visit, which is called *session*. Within a session, customers can issue requests of different types, such as Login, Browse, Search, Add to Shopping Cart, or Pay. Different customers may exhibit different patterns of navigation through an e-commerce site and therefore may invoke the different functions provided by the site in different ways and with different frequencies. Some customers may be heavy

41

buyers while others may be occasional buyers who do extensive searching and browsing but very seldom buy from the site. The customer's behavior while interacting with an e-commerce site has impacts on the IT resources of the site and on the revenue of the e-store. Thus, it is important to be able to characterize the behavior of customers or groups of customers of an e-commerce site.

This chapter discusses the motivations for capturing user behavior and presents customer models at various levels. The models presented here can be used to answer what-if questions at the customer behavior level as well as to serve as a basis to build models at the resource level.

2.2   Why Model Customer Behavior?

Figure 2.1 shows the relationship between the customer model, the workload model, and the resource model. This chapter concentrates on the customer model. The other models will be discussed in detail in other chapters of the book.

The *customer model* captures elements of user behavior in terms of navigational patterns, e-commerce functions used, frequency of access to the various e-commerce functions, and times between access to the various services offered by the site. A customer model can be useful for navigational and workload prediction.

- Model User Navigational Patterns for Predictive Purposes. By building models, such as the Customer Behavior Model Graph (CBMG) described in Section 2.4, one can answer what-if questions regarding the effects on user behavior due to site layout changes or content redesign. Such models could potentially be used to predict future moves of a user and pre-fetch objects in order to improve performance.

- Capture Workload Parameters. If the only purpose of a customer model is to generate a workload model to be used as input to a re-

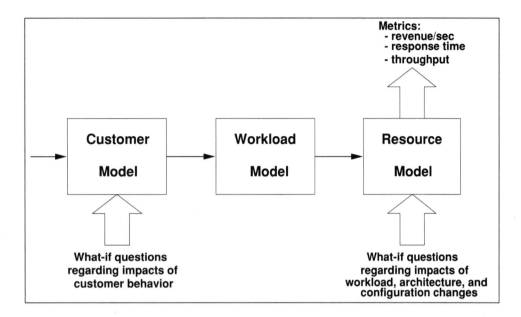

Figure 2.1. Customer, Workload, and Resource Models.

source model, then it is not necessary to use a detailed model such as the CBMG. Less detailed models, such as the Customer Visit Model (CVM), described in Section 2.8, capture the information needed to build a workload model. The CVM, unlike the CBMG, has no predictive capability to answer what-if questions regarding the impact of customer behavioral changes.

The *workload model* describes the workload of an e-business site in terms of workload intensity (e.g., transaction arrival rates) and service demands on the various resources (e.g., processors, I/O subsystems, networks) that make up the site. The workload model can be derived from the customer model as we will discuss later in the book.

The *resource model* represents the various resources of the site and captures the effects of the workload model on these resources. The resource model can be used for predictive purposes to answer what-if questions regarding performance impacts due to changes in configuration, software and hardware architecture, and other parameters. The resource model is used to compute the values of metrics such as response time, throughput, and business-oriented metrics such as revenue throughput (see Section 2.6).

Most of the sections that follow deal with the more detailed Customer Behavior Model Graph as an example of customer model. The Customer Visit Model is introduced in Section 2.8.

2.3   A Customer Behavior Model of an Online Bookstore

In this section, we use an example of an online bookstore to give an informal introduction to the user behavior model of an e-commerce site. Consider an online bookstore in which customers can perform the following functions.

- Connect to the home page and browse the site by following links to bestseller books and promotions of the week per book category.

- Search for titles according to various criteria including keywords, author name, and ISBN.

- Select one of the books that results from a search and view additional information such as a brief description, price, shipping time, ranking, and reviews.

- Register as a new customer of the virtual bookstore. This allows the user to provide a user name and a password, payment information (e.g., credit card number), mailing address, and e-mail address for notification of order status and books of interest.

- Login with a user name and password.

- Add items to the shopping cart.

- Pay for the items added to the shopping cart.

Thus, during a visit to the online bookstore, a customer issues several requests that will cause the functions above to be executed. For example, a customer may cause a search to be executed by submitting a URL that specifies the name of an application to be run at the server through a server API (e.g., CGI and ASP) and the keywords to be used in the search. The application will then execute a search in the site database and return an HTML page with all the books that match the search criteria. Remember that the sequence of consecutive requests issued by the same customer during a single visit to an e-commerce site is called a *session*.

During a session, a customer may be classified as being in different states according to the type of function (i.e., request) requested. For example, the customer may be browsing, searching, registering as a new customer, logging in, adding books to the shopping cart, selecting the result of a search, and paying for the order. The possible transitions between states depend on the layout of the site. For example, one customer may go from the home page to search, from search to select, from select to add to cart, and from there to pay. Another customer may go from the home page to the browse state before doing a search and leaving the online bookstore without buying anything.

To capture the possible transitions between the states in which a customer may be found, we need a model that reflects the navigational pattern of a user during a visit to an e-commerce site. This model is in the form of a graph and is called the Customer Behavior Model Graph (CBMG) [4] [5]. The nodes of the CBMG, represented by squares, depict the states a customer is in during a visit to the e-commerce site. Arrows connecting states indicate possible transitions between them.

Figure 2.2 shows the states and transitions of the CBMG for the virtual bookstore example. The states of this CBMG and their descriptions follow.

- *Entry*. This is a special state that immediately precedes a customer's entry to the online store. This state is part of the CBMG as a modeling convenience and does not correspond to any action started by the customer.

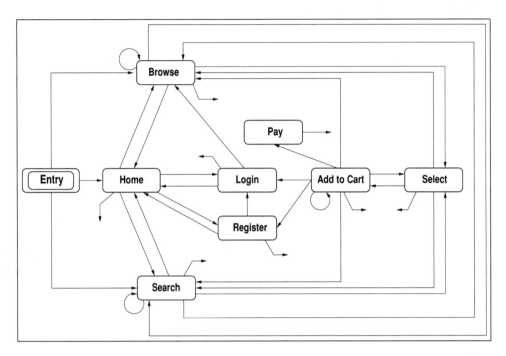

Figure 2.2. States and Transitions of the Customer Behavior Model Graph (CBMG) for the Virtual Bookstore Example.

- *Home.* This is the state a customer is in after selecting the URL for the site's home page.

- *Search.* A customer goes to this state after issuing a search request.

- *Browse.* This is the state reached after a customer selects one of the links available at the site to view any of the pages of the site. These links include the list of bestsellers and weekly promotions.

- *Select.* A search returns a list of zero or more links to books. By selecting one of these links, a customer moves to state Select.

- *Login.* A customer moves to this state after requesting to login to the site.

- *Register.* To have an account created by registering with the online bookstore, the customer selects the proper link for the registration page, thus making a transition to the Register state.

- *Add to Cart.* A customer moves to this state upon selecting the button that adds a selected book to the shopping cart.

- *Pay.* When ready to pay for the items in the shopping cart, the customer moves to the Pay state.

- *Exit.* Customers may leave the site from any state. Thus, there is a transition from all states, except the Entry state, to the Exit state. The Exit state is not explicitly shown in Fig. 2.2 to improve its readability. However, the transitions to the Exit state are shown as dangling arrows leaving the state.

In the case of Fig. 2.2, customers can enter the virtual bookstore at only three states: Home, Browse, and Search. From the Home state, they can visit the Register, Login, Browse, and Search states as well as exit the site.

Note that Fig. 2.2 reflects all possible transitions between states. However, during a single visit to the e-store, a customer may not visit all states, and different visits by the same customer or by a different customer may differ in terms of the frequency by which states are visited. Thus, to characterize the user behavior during a visit to the site, one must also capture the frequency with which transitions occur. Consider that during a visit to the e-commerce site, a customer visits the Select state twenty times. Out of these, the customer moves to the Search state seven times, to the Browse state eight times, to the Add to Cart state four times, and once to the Exit state (see Fig. 2.3). We can then say that the transition frequencies out of the state Select are 0.40 (= 8/20) to state Browse, 0.35 (= 7/20) to state Search, 0.2 (= 4/20) to state Add, and 0.05 (= 1/20) to state Exit.

In general, we label each transition in the CBMG with the frequency with which a customer follows the path between two states. Since we will be using CBMGs to characterize the behavior of many similar visits to the site, we will refer to the transition frequencies as transition probabilities.

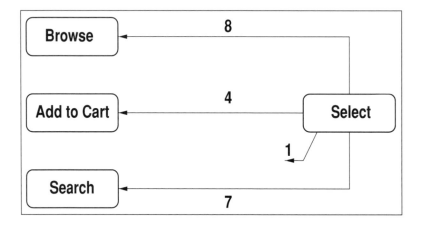

Figure 2.3. Transitions Out of the Select State.

Figure 2.4 shows a complete CBMG for the bookstore example with all transition probabilities. Chapter 11 discusses the approach for determining these transition probabilities from HTTP logs.

For example, according to the CBMG of Fig. 2.4, customers have a 10% probability of leaving the site after performing a search. This is indicated by a transition from the Search state to the Exit state. From the Search state, customers have a 20% probability of going to the Home state, a 25% probability of doing another search, a 20% probability of selecting one of the books that resulted from the search, and a 25% probability of going to the Browse state.

Different types of users may be characterized by different CBMGs in terms of the transition probabilities. As an example, consider two customer profiles: occasional and heavy buyers. The first category is composed of customers who use the Web store to find out about existing products, such as new books or best fares and itineraries for travel, but end up not buying, most of the time, at the Web store. The second category is composed of customers who have a higher probability of buying if they see a product that interests them at a suitable price. Thus, workload characterization for e-commerce entails in determining the set of CBMGs that best characterize

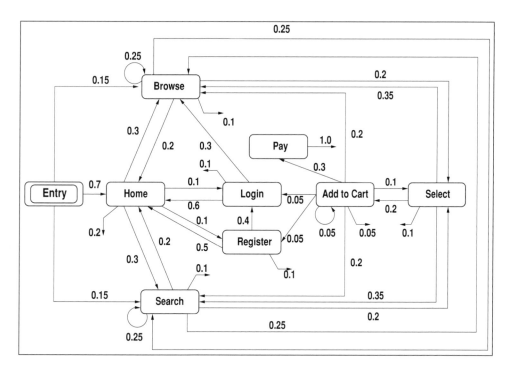

Figure 2.4. Customer Behavior Model Graph (CBMG) for the Virtual Bookstore Example.

customer behavior, as explained in Chapter 11. Note that it is possible for the same customer to exhibit different types of behavior during each visit to the site. Thus, a CBMG is in fact associated to a visit to the site and not necessarily to a specific customer. The next section generalizes the concept of Customer Behavior Model Graph and provides a more formal definition.

2.4   The Customer Behavior Model Graph (CBMG)

A Customer Behavior Model Graph (CBMG) has n states, where state 1 is always the Entry state and state n is always the Exit state. The actual number of states and the type of states of a CBMG vary among e-commerce sites. For example, online trading sites may have other types of states such as Obtain Quote, Trade Stock, Trade Mutual Fund, View Chart (of stock value variation), Access Portfolio, and Get Press Releases (on a company).

A CBMG is a characterization of the navigational pattern of a group of customers, as viewed from the server side. This means that a transition from state i to state j is said to occur when the request to go to state j arrives at the server. In Fig. 2.4, the transition from state Search to Select is said to occur when the e-commerce server receives a request to display additional information about one of the books that resulted from a previous search. User requests that are resolved at the browser cache or at a proxy server cache are not seen by the e-commerce server and therefore are not reflected in the CBMG. This is not a problem when the purpose of the workload characterization is for server sizing and capacity planning. In these cases, it is important to capture the load imposed on the server resources by the various requests submitted by a customer. It should also be noted that, in the case of e-commerce, many pages that are intrinsically static are generated dynamically and therefore are not cached because they contain advertisement. Zaiane et al discuss the problem of relying solely on server side information in the context of using data mining and online analytic processing techniques (OLAP) on HTTP logs [9]. The authors conclude that although server side information is not 100% complete, much useful information can be discovered from it.

So, a CBMG can be more formally characterized by a set of states, a set of transitions between states, and by an $n \times n$ matrix, $P = [p_{i,j}]$, of transition probabilities between the n states of the CBMG. A similar matrix exists in which Online Analytical Processing (OLAP) and Data Mining techniques are used to analyze Web logs [9]. Table 2.1 shows the transition probability matrix P for the CBMG of Fig. 2.4. Note that the elements of the first column and last row of the matrix P for any CBMG are all zeroes since, by definition, there are no transitions back to the Entry state from any state nor any transitions out of the Exit state.

A CBMG has two aspects: a static and a dynamic one. The static aspect reflects the structure of the e-commerce site and does not depend on the way users access the site. The static aspect of the CBMG is composed

Table 2.1. Matrix P for the CBMG of Fig. 2.4.

	y	h	b	s	l	p	r	a	t	x
Entry (y)	0.00	0.70	0.15	0.15	0.00	0.00	0.00	0.00	0.00	0.00
Home (h)	0.00	0.00	0.30	0.30	0.10	0.00	0.10	0.00	0.00	0.20
Browse (b)	0.00	0.20	0.25	0.25	0.00	0.00	0.00	0.00	0.20	0.10
Search (s)	0.00	0.20	0.25	0.25	0.00	0.00	0.00	0.00	0.20	0.10
Login (l)	0.00	0.60	0.30	0.00	0.00	0.00	0.00	0.00	0.00	0.10
Pay (p)	0.00	0.00	0.00	0.00	0.00	0.00	0.00	0.00	0.00	1.00
Register (r)	0.00	0.50	0.00	0.00	0.40	0.00	0.00	0.00	0.00	0.10
Add to Cart (a)	0.00	0.00	0.20	0.20	0.05	0.30	0.05	0.05	0.10	0.05
Select (t)	0.00	0.00	0.35	0.35	0.00	0.00	0.00	0.20	0.00	0.10
Exit (x)	0.00	0.00	0.00	0.00	0.00	0.00	0.00	0.00	0.00	0.00

of the set of states and the set of possible transitions between these states. The matrix of transition probabilities, P, is part of the dynamic aspect of the CBMG. Figure 2.2 is the static aspect of the CBMG of Fig. 2.4. All groups of customers share the same static aspect of the CBMG since this is a characteristic of the functions provided by the e-commerce site, of the organization of the pages, and of the ways of invoking the various functions from the several pages.

We can now view an e-commerce site as a business that provides to its customers several Web-based functions such as Browse, Search, Select, and Pay. These functions use the IT infrastructure of the site, i.e., its processors, internal networks and routers, and storage subsystems. Different visits by the same customer or by different customers invoke these functions in different patterns as described by a CBMG (see Fig. 2.5).

2.5   Building a CBMG

We describe in this section the approaches that can be followed to build the static portion of a CBMG. The dynamic portion is obtained as part of a

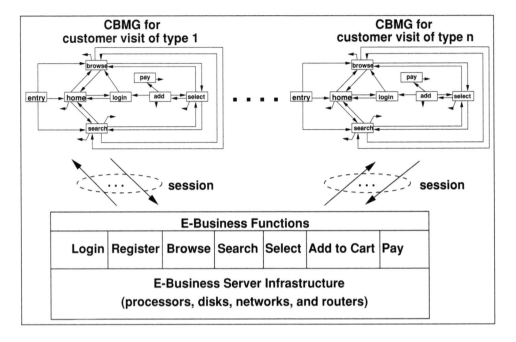

Figure 2.5. E-business Site View from the User Perspective.

workload characterization process, as described in Chapter 11.

To determine the static portion of the CBMG, the following steps should be followed.

1. *Determine the set of functions provided to the customers of the e-commerce site.* While some of the functions (e.g., Search, Login) may be found in most e-commerce sites, there are functions that are characteristic of certain e-commerce sites or of specific types of e-commerce sites. Table 2.2 gives some examples of functions common to most sites and functions characteristic of types of e-commerce sites. The first part of the table lists some functions, such as Login, Register, Select, and Browse, that are common to most sites. Then, the table presents some examples of functions commonly found in retail, online trading, and information distribution e-commerce sites. Each function should be associated with a state of the CBMG.

2. *Refine the set of functions according to resource consumption.* Each function requires a certain amount of processing by the IT infrastructure of the e-commerce site. Therefore, it is important to separate functions that may require significantly different types of processing. For example, in the online trading case, it may be necessary to separate the Trade function into Trade Stock, Trade Mutual Fund, and Trade Bonds since they may require very different workflows. Similarly, a site that sells multimedia presentations may want to distinguish Download Audio from Download Video due to the significantly different bandwidth requirements imposed by each type of multimedia product.

3. *Determine the transitions between states.* At this step, one needs to examine all possible transitions between states of the CBMG. This can be done by analyzing the layout of the pages offered to customers of the e-business site. For example, consider that the home page of an online trading site makes available the following functions: Open Account, Get Quotes, Login, Trade, Asset Planner. Then we know that from the state Home, there are transitions in the CBMG to each of these states. Then, one has to look at the possible functions available at each of the pages that are used when invoking these functions. For example, the Trade function may be accessible from the Get Quotes page.

The next section describes metrics for Web and e-business sites aggregated over many visits to a site. Section 2.7 shows how the CBMG, with its static and dynamic aspects, can be used to obtain metrics related to customer behavior during each visit.

2.6   Aggregate Metrics for Web and E-Business Sites

Since the Web became a widely used vehicle to support all sorts of applications, including e-business, the need arose to devise metrics to measure a

Table 2.2. Examples of E-Business Functions.

Category	Function	Description
Common	Login	Login to the site.
	Register	Register as a new user.
	Search	Search site database.
	Select	View one of the results of a search.
	Browse	Follow links within the site.
Retail	Add Item	Add item to shopping cart.
	Remove Item	Remove item from shopping cart.
	See Shopping Cart	Check contents and value of shopping cart.
	Create Registry	Create a gift registry.
	Add to Registry	Add item to gift registry.
	Check Status	Check status of previous order.
	Pay	Pay for items in shopping cart.
Trading	Open Account	Open account for trading.
	Get Quotes	Get delayed or real-time quotes.
	Get Report	Get performance report on companies.
	View Chart	View charts of closing prices.
	View Indexes	View values of indexes (e.g., DJI, SP500).
	Trade	Buy/sell/exchange stocks or mutual funds.
	Create Portfolio	Create stock/funds portfolio.
	Add to Portfolio	Add stocks/funds to portfolio.
	Delete from Portfolio	Delete stock/fund from portfolio.
	Asset Planning	Plan allocation of assets.
Information	Download	Download software/report/music.
	Subscribe	Subscribe to regular downloads.
	Listen	Listen to real-time audio (e.g., lecture).
	Watch	Watch real-time movie.

site's efficiency in attaining its goals. Many metrics have been used to assess the success of sites in terms of popularity and/or revenue generated.

- *Hits/sec* measures the number of requests for objects served in each second by a website. Note that a page is usually composed of one HTML file and several other embedded image files that are automatically requested from the Web server when a user requests the HTML document. So, hits/sec counts not just the HTML pages but all embedded objects in a page as separate requests, which does not give a precise idea of the number of times a specific page, with its advertisement banners, was viewed.

- *Page Views/Day* reflects the number of individual pages served per day. A company paying for a banner ad to be posted on a page may be interested in the number of times its ad is being seen. Very popular sites can display a few hundred million page views per day [3].

- *Click-throughs* measures the percentage of users that not only view an online ad but also click on it to get to the Web page behind it. This metric is oriented more toward assessing the impact of online ads. However, this measure can be misleading [3]. If the message in the banner ad is too general, it may draw a larger number of clicks than a more specific message. However, users who respond to the more specific message are more likely to be interested in the product being advertised than those who react to the more general message.

- *Unique Visitors* indicates how many different people visited a website during a certain period of time. Many times it is more important to know how many different people visited your site than the total number of visits received during a certain period.

- *Revenue Throughput* is a business-oriented metric that measures the number of dollars/sec derived from sales from an e-commerce site [5]. This measure implicitly represents customer and site behavior. A customer who is happy with the quality of service (e.g., response time) of an e-business site will shop at the Web store, and the revenue throughput will increase.

- *Potential Loss Throughput* is another business-oriented metric that measures the amount of money in customers' shopping carts that is not converted into sales because the customer leaves the site due to poor performance or other reasons [5].

2.7   Metrics Derived from the CBMG

We explore here how the CBMG can help in providing quantitative insight into how customers interact with an e-commerce site. For example, we would like to be able to answer the following types of questions with the help of the CBMG.

- How many times on average is each e-business function (e.g., Search, Browse, Select, Add) invoked per visit to the e-commerce site?

- On average, how often customers buy something each time they visit the e-commerce site?

- What is the average number of e-commerce function executions requested by a customer during his/her visit to the store?

Answers to these and other questions can be obtained through the solution of a set of linear equations derived from the CBMG. We defer to Chapter 11 the formal treatment and discussion of these equations. In this chapter, we provide a more informal and intuitive view of these equations. For this purpose, in the numerical examples that follow, we use the MS Excel workbook, called `CBMG.XLS`, that can be downloaded from the Web site associated with the book (see Preface) by following the link to `Chapter 2`.

Example 2.1

Consider the CBMG of Fig. 2.4. What is the average number of visits to each state of the CBMG?

To answer this question, we used the MS Excel workbook `CBMG.XLS`. The worksheet `TransitionProbabilities` of this workbook has the transition matrix P shown in Table 2.1. The worksheet `Visit Ratios` shows, in blue in line 7, the average number of times that each state of the CBMG is visited per visit to the site. Table 2.3 shows the results displayed in the worksheet.

Instructions in the worksheet indicate how to obtain the visit ratios in Table 2.3. These numbers give us some interesting insight into the behavior of the customers who visit our virtual bookstore as described in the examples that follow. ∎

Table 2.3. Average Number of Visits per State of the CBMG of Fig. 2.4.

State	Visit Ratio
Entry	1.000
Home	1.862
Browse	2.303
Search	2.193
Login	0.274
Pay	0.058
Register	0.196
Add to Cart	0.193
Select	0.919
Exit	1.000

Example 2.2

Consider again the CBMG of Fig. 2.4 and the solution to the average number of visits per state of the CBMG given in Ex. 2.1. Suppose the site receives 100,000 visitors per day. What is the fraction of visitors that end up buying from the virtual bookstore? What is the average number of sale transactions performed per day? What percentage of customers leave the site after having added at least one item to their shopping cart?

Since the average number of visits to the Pay state per visit to the site is 0.058, 5.8% of the visitors end up buying from the bookstore. Since 100,000 customers visit the store per day, the site has to be able to process 5,800 sale transactions per day. However, 19.3% (i.e., 0.193) of the visitors add at least an item to their shopping carts, but only 5.8% buy. So, 13.5% (=19.3% - 5.8%) leave the site without buying while having at least an item in their shopping carts. This could be caused by a high response time at the site, which causes customers to become frustrated with the site and move their business to other e-stores. The survey "GVU's WWW User Surveys" showed that around 19% of the people surveyed attribute bad experiences they had with e-business sites to bad performance [2]. Customers who have items in their shopping carts and leave the site represent a potential loss in revenue to the e-business. This type of situation should be avoided.   ■

An important metric for e-business sites is the *buy to visit ratio (BV)*, defined as the average number of sale transactions per visit to the site. As we can see from Ex. 2.2, this ratio is simply given by the average number of visits to the Pay state.

Example 2.3

Consider again the CBMG of Fig. 2.4. What is the average number of requests submitted to the e-commerce server per session?

That is, what is the average session length? This can be easily obtained by adding the average number of visits to the states Home, Browse, Search,

Login, Pay, Register, Add to Cart, and Select. So, the average session length is equal to $1.862 + 2.303 + 2.193 + 0.274 + 0.058 + 0.196 + 0.193 + 0.919 = 7.998$ ■

In general, the *average session length* is given by the sum of the visit ratios for all states of the CBMG, except the Entry and Exit states.

Example 2.4

Consider again the CBMG of Fig. 2.4. What is the new buy to visit ratio if the following changes are made to the transition probabilities: $p_{\text{Select,Browse}} = 0.4$, $p_{\text{Select,AddtoCart}} = 0.1$, $p_{\text{Select,Search}} = 0.4$? These changes indicate a smaller probability that customers will add an item to their shopping carts after they have selected it.

To answer this question, we use again the workbook CBMG.XLS, make the proper changes in the probability values in the worksheet Transition-Probabilities, and use the solver again to obtain the new values of the visit ratios. The new value of the buy to visit ratio is the new value of the average number of visits to the Pay state, which is 0.030. In other words, now only 3.0% of the customers who visit the site buy as opposed to 5.8% in the previous case.   ■

2.8 The Customer Visit Model (CVM)

As we discussed in the previous sections, one can obtain the average number of visits to each state of the CBMG from the transition matrix P associated to the CBMG. An alternate and less detailed representation of a session would entail representing a session as a vector of visit ratios to each state of the CBMG. The visit ratio is the number of visits to a state during a session.

Table 2.4 shows an example of three sessions described by the number of visits to each state. Note that states Entry and Exit are not represented in the CVM since the number of visits to these states is always one. Session 1 in the table represents a session of a customer who browsed through the site, did a few searches, but did not login or buy anything. In Session 2, the

Table 2.4. Example of Session Characterization Using the CVM.

	Session 1	Session 2	Session 3
Home	1	2	3
Browse	4	8	4
Search	5	5	3
Login	0	1	1
Pay	0	0	1
Register	0	0	1
Add to Cart	0	2	1
Select	3	3	2

customer logged in but did not need to register because it was an already registered customer. This customer abandoned the site before paying even though two items had been added to the shopping cart. Finally, Session 3 represents a new customer who registers with the site, adds one item to the shopping cart, and pays for it.

The CVM is then a set of vectors (columns in Table 2.4) that indicate the number of times each of the functions supplied by the e-business site are executed. For example, Session 1 would be represented by the vector (1, 4, 5, 0, 0, 0, 0, 3) and Session 2 by the vector (2, 8, 5, 1, 0, 0, 2, 3).

Note that the CVM is less detailed than the CBMG in the sense that it does not provide information on the number of times a customer moves from one state to another. Thus, the CVM cannot be used to answer what-if questions of the type illustrated in Ex. 2.4.

Example 2.5

Consider the three sessions of Table 2.4. Assume that each Search request performs an average of three I/Os to the disk containing the index to the catalog of items and that each Select function performs an average of two

I/Os to the disk containing the product descriptions. What is the average number of I/Os generated by the three sessions on each of these two disks?

The three sessions perform a total of 13 (=5+5+3) Searches and 8 (=3+3+2) Selects. Thus the average number of I/Os to the index disk is 39 (=13×3) and the average number of I/Os to the catalog disk is 16 (=8×2). ■

This example illustrates how the CVM can be used to obtain workload information to be used by the resource model. Chapter 11 discusses these issues in more detail.

2.9   Session Identification

As we saw in the above discussion, characterizing the user behavior hinges on being able to identify user sessions. Remember that a *session* is a sequence of consecutive requests from the same customer during the same visit to an e-commerce site. There are two relevant issues to be discussed with respect to this definition:

1. How does one identify requests as coming from the same customer?

2. How does one determine if requests coming from the same customer belong to the same or to a different session?

Before we answer the above questions, it is important to remember that HTTP is a stateless protocol. This means that the HTTP server does not store information about a request after that request has been serviced. Even though the HTTP server generates an entry in the HTTP log for each completed request, this information is not used to process the next request.

Let us now turn our attention to question 1. A possible solution to this question lies in the technology known as *cookies*, pieces of information sent by the server to the browser and stored there [8]. The information is sent back to the server on every subsequent request to the server. This way, cookies can be used to store customer and/or session identifiers. This idea

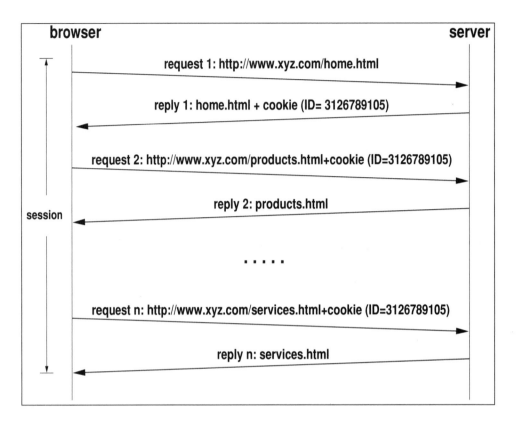

Figure 2.6. Session Identification with Cookies.

is illustrated in Fig. 2.6, which shows a session composed of n requests. The first request asks the server to send file home.html. Before sending the file, the server generates an identification for the session, ID=3125789105 in this case. This ID is sent back to the browser as a cookie, along with the requested file. As seen in the figure, all subsequent requests sent by the browser to the server carry with them the same ID. This way, the server can identify all of the n requests as coming from the same browser.

Cookies can also be used to store the state of an application. For example, as customers add items to their shopping carts, the state of their interaction with the site changes. This information can be stored at a server's database or at an in-memory data structure. At any rate, the session ID can be used to retrieve the information for check-out purposes. Cookies can also be used to send state information to the browser. In this case, instead of storing state information (e.g., the contents of the shopping cart) at a server's database, this information is stored at the client side. This strategy brings a performance benefit: it reduces the number of database accesses during an online shopping session. Besides cookies, other techniques can be used to identify sessions, including authentication mechanisms, hidden fields in HTML forms, and dynamic URLs [8].

Let us now discuss the second question posed. Suppose that a customer interacts with an e-commerce site with the purpose of buying some books. A few hours later, the same customer returns to the site. This second interaction with the site is clearly a different visit, and therefore two different sessions are involved. One way of determining when a request belongs to the same or to a different session is by establishing a time threshold after which a request from the same browser is considered to belong to a different session, and this will be discussed in Chapter 11.

2.10 Concluding Remarks

Understanding the behavior of customers is paramount to the proper sizing of the resources of an e-commerce site as well as for achieving the business goals of the virtual store. Customers interact with an e-commerce site through sequences of requests to execute various functions. Each of these functions exercise the resources of the e-commerce server in a different way. Some may be more CPU intensive, others more I/O intensive, and others may demand a lot of network resources. Understanding how customers interact with a site allows us to determine how often these functions are used per visit to a site, the average number of functions executed per visit, and how often customers buy when they visit the site.

The Customer Behavior Model Graph (CBMG) introduced in this chapter is the basis for capturing and understanding user behavior. The CBMG can be useful for capacity planning and business reporting purposes. The use of CBMGs for capacity planning is explored in detail in Chapter 11 where workload characterization is discussed. The CBMG can be used for business and marketing analysis purposes. For example, states visited very seldom point to functions and site features not explored by customers, perhaps due to poor site design. A high probability of spontaneous transitions to the Exit state may be worrisome since it may indicate that customers are not being retained either because they are not interested in what they are seeing or because of poor response time. Business metrics obtained from the CBMG, such as the buy to visit ratio, are useful in determining the site's efficiency in converting visits to sales.

Graph notations are useful for analyzing user interactions with interactive systems and to evaluate their performance. Interaction and user behavior graphs [1] [7], capture both user and system states and are used to obtain bounds on performance metrics of interactive systems. We use CBMGs to model user behavior and client/server interaction diagrams (CSIDs), discussed in the next chapter, to model the interaction between software components when satisfying customer requests.

When the purpose of the customer model is to obtain parameters for a workload model, less detailed customer models, such as the Customer Visit Model, can be used.

Understanding customer behavior is also very important for marketing purposes. Some companies offer software for doing real-time marketing based on predicting a customer's next move from past behavior [6].

Bibliography

[1] D. Ferrari, "On the Foundations of Artificial Workload Design," *Proc. 1984 ACM Sigmetrics Conf.*, Cambridge, MA, August 21-24, 1984, pp. 8–14.

[2] GVU, GVU's WWW User Surveys,www.gvu.gatech.edu/user_surveys/.

[3] S. V. Haar, "Web Metrics: Go Figure," *Business 2.0*, June 1999.

[4] D. A. Menascé, V. A. F. Almeida, R. C. Fonseca, and M. A. Mendes, "A Methodology for Workload Characterization for E-commerce Servers," *Proc. 1999 ACM Conference in Electronic Commerce*, Denver, CO, Nov. 3-5, 1999, pp. 119–128.

[5] D. A. Menascé, V. A. F. Almeida, R. C. Fonseca, and M. A. Mendes, "Resource Management Policies for E-commerce Servers," *Proc. Second Workshop on Internet Server Performance (WISP'99)* held in conjunction with ACM Sigmetrics'99, Atlanta, GA, May 1st, 1999.

[6] C. Pickering, "They're Watching You," *Business 2.0*, February 2000.

[7] E. A. Stohr and Y. Kim, "A Model for Performance Evaluation of Interactive Systems," *Proc. 31st. Annual Hawaii International Conference on System Sciences*, Vol. 4: Internet and the Digital Economy, Kahala Coast, HI, Jan 6-9, 1998.

[8] G. W. Treese and L. C. Stewart, *Designing Systems for Internet Commerce*, Addison Wesley, Reading, MA, 1998.

[9] O. R. Zaiane, M. Xin, and J. Han, "Discovering Web Access Patterns and Trends by Applying OLAP and Data Mining Technology on Web Logs," *Proc. Advances in Digital Libraries Conf. (ADL'98)*, Santa Barbara, CA, April 1998, pp. 19–29.

Chapter 3

The Anatomy of E-Business Functions

3.1 Introduction

Chapter 2 presented a model, the CBMG, for understanding how a customer interacts with an e-business site. The states of the CBMG, except for the Entry and Exit states, correspond to an e-business function. These functions are implemented by various software entities, called *servers*, which communicate with one another to implement the required e-commerce functions. These software servers run on machines interconnected through Local Area Networks (LANs) and sometimes Wide Area Networks (WANs).

This chapter discusses the anatomy of e-business functions from the logical view point. In other words, the chapter describes how software servers interact to implement e-business functions and provides a graphical notation to describe these interactions.

The interaction between servers is described independently of the underlying physical architecture used to support the execution of e-business functions. This distinction is important because the same software architecture can be mapped into many different physical configurations. The performance characteristics of an e-commerce site are determined by its software architecture, by its physical configuration, and by the mapping between software and hardware elements.

The graphical notation used in this chapter is called *Client/Server Interaction Diagrams (CSIDs)* and is used to describe the logical architecture of e-business functions. This notation is an extension of a previous graphical notation [6]. This chapter illustrates, through several numerical examples, how CSIDs can be used to answer quantitative questions about the execution of e-business functions.

3.2   Requests and Services

Customers interact with an e-business site by requesting the execution of an *e-business function*. Examples of these functions include Search, Browse, Login, Register, and Pay, as discussed in Chapter 2. The execution of such functions starts with a request coming from the customer browser, acting as a *client* to a software entity that fulfills the request. This is called a client/server (C/S) interaction. There are two models for implementing C/S interactions: the server-oriented model and the object-oriented model.

In the server-oriented model, the client process communicates with a *server* process through a Remote Procedure Call (RPC) mechanism [1] [9] (see Fig. 3.1 (a)). The server process (e.g., a database server, an HTTP server, a file server) implements a set of related functions. Requests for ser-

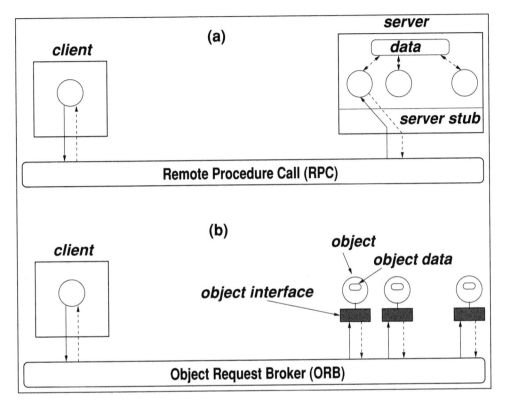

Figure 3.1. (a) Server-Oriented C/S Interaction. (b) Object-Oriented C/S Interaction.

vice (i.e., execution of one of the server functions) are handled by a common piece of software, called the server stub, responsible for determining which function is being invoked, retrieving the parameters for the function from the request, making any necessary parameter conversion, invoking the function, and sending the result back to the client. The server may also host data areas, in either main memory (e.g., a cache) or disk (e.g., a database), to be shared by the functions that run at the server. Other functions executed by the server include queuing and scheduling of requests and thread management functions.

In the object-oriented model, services are performed by methods of objects and invoked remotely by clients (see Fig. 3.1 (b)). Objects must export the interface to be used by any client that invokes its methods. In networked environments, objects could be anywhere, and it should be possible for a client to invoke a method of an object by providing a location-independent name for the object along with the arguments for the method invocation. This transparency can be achieved by an *Object Request Broker (ORB)*. An ORB allows objects to discover each other at run time and invoke each other's services [9]. An architecture for object-oriented services was defined by the Object Management Group and is called CORBA (Common Object Request Broker Architecture). Distributed CORBA objects can be thought of as components that can be used to put together distributed applications. Components can be written in any language, can run on any platform, and can be easily integrated into any application since they can be located through an ORB and their methods invoked by other objects through an advertised interface. Microsoft's version of an ORB is called DCOM (Distributed Component Object Model). See Orfali et al [9] for a comprehensive discussion of the various client/server technologies.

Our interest in making the distinction between the two approaches to client/server interaction is on their performance impact. While an ORB-based approach provides substantial flexibility, it adds another level of indirection between the client and the entity performing the service (an object or a server process). This may have an impact on performance. There is no such thing as a free lunch.

In what follows, we refer to a *server* as a software entity that performs some service upon request from a client. The service can be executed by a function invoked through an RPC mechanism as in Fig. 3.1 (a) or by a method of an object as in Fig. 3.1 (b). Section 3.4 provides a performance-annotated notation to specify client/server interactions.

3.3   E-Business Servers

This section discusses some of the common software servers that are used to support e-business functions. An e-business function is processed by several servers in an e-business site. Requests arrive from browsers in the case of customer to individual e-commerce or are generated by computers as is the case in many business-to-business applications. In any case, we say that the source of the requests are clients of the services provided by the servers of the e-business site.

Figure 3.2 illustrates a typical logical configuration of an e-business site. The front-end server is a Web server. This server supports the HTTP protocol and usually serves the site home page and processes requests to retrieve static HTML pages and launches the execution of programs (e.g., CGI scripts, servlets). These programs are applications implemented by the application server. Examples of applications include searching for items in a catalog by keyword or retrieving a stock portfolio at an online trader site. In many cases, the application may need data stored in persistent storage (e.g., disks). Database management systems are used to provide efficient access to data in secondary storage. Thus, the application server may need to interact with the database server to obtain the data it needs to execute the requested operation. The result of the execution of an application is usually formatted as an HTML page that is returned by the Web server to the requesting client.

Some of the functions provided by an e-business site require support for authentication and security. For example, an online trading site must be sure that a customer who logs in to the site is providing accurate identification (authentication). Also, when sending a password or credit card information to the site, a customer wants to make sure that this confidential data is protected during transmission. For that matter, data is encrypted. A secure Web server is used to provide a secure exchange of messages between the client and the e-business site. Chapter 5 discusses authentication protocols,

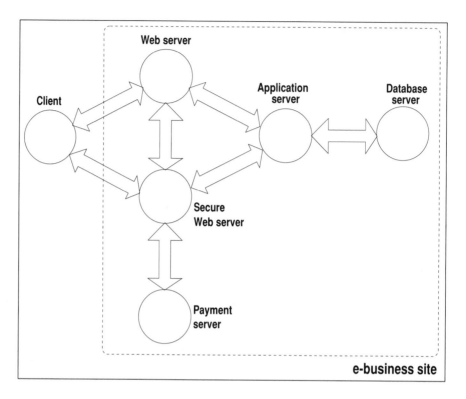

Figure 3.2. Servers of an E-Business Site.

such as the Secure Sockets Layer (SSL) and the Transport Layer Security (TLS) protocol as well as the exchange of messages necessary to establish secure connections between a client and a server.

Another important server for sites that accept payments on line is the payment server. This server implements the payment protocols used to transfer monetary funds from the customer's financial institution to the merchant's financial institution. Chapter 6 discusses payment protocols such as SET.

3.4   The Anatomy of Client/Server Interactions

An e-business function is implemented through client/server interactions. There may be many different interactions associated with the execution of one e-business function as illustrated in Fig. 3.3.

A C/S interaction starts when a client process makes a request to a server process, called primary server, and ends when the client process receives a reply from the primary server. The primary server may need to request assistance from other servers, called secondary servers, to execute the request from the client. In this case, the primary server acts as a client to the secondary servers. An example of a C/S interaction is shown in Fig. 3.4. A client sends a request to a Web server, which sends a request to an application server, which in turn requests data from the database server. The application server receives the data from the database server and builds an HTML page that is returned to the Web server, which replies to the client.

The execution of e-business functions is not deterministic. For example, in the case of Fig. 3.4, a request will only be sent to the database server if the application server does not have the data it needs to process the request. Thus, an e-business function is represented by the various possible

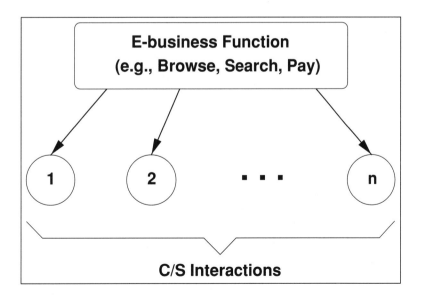

Figure 3.3. E-Business Functions and C/S Interactions.

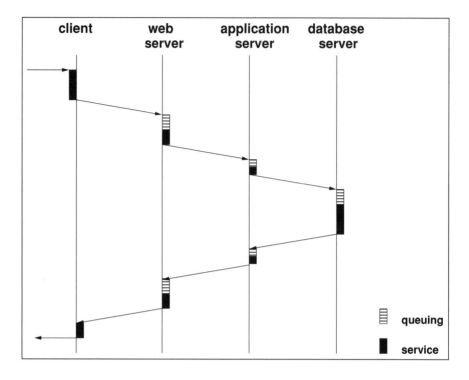

Figure 3.4. Example of a C/S Interaction.

C/S interactions that may occur during the execution of the function (see Fig. 3.3).

A notation is needed to describe the possible interactions between a client and the servers that implement an e-business function. Several notations have been used to describe software architectures and the interaction between software components. Some notable examples include sequence diagrams in the Unified Modeling Language (UML) [2], Message Sequence Charts (MSC) [4], Chemical Abstract Machines (CHAM) [5], the Specification and Description Language (SDL) [8], and communication-processing diagrams [7]. To be useful for performance modeling and capacity planning, these software specification notations have to be annotated with performance related parameters.

3.4.1 C/S Interaction Diagrams (CSIDs)

No standards for performance annotation of software specification languages exist yet. We use our own graphical notation, called *C/S Interaction Diagrams (CSIDs)* (see Fig. 3.5). A CSID must be specified for each e-business function and it represents all possible C/S interactions for that function.

A CSID has nodes (squares and circles) and directed arcs (arrows) connecting these nodes. Nodes of a CSID represent visits to clients and/or servers during the execution of an e-business function. For example, nodes 2, 5, and 9 in Fig. 3.5 indicate visits to the Web server WS at three different points in the execution of the e-business function. Every node is identified by a unique number indicated by the label outside the node. A directed arc $i \rightarrow j$ in a CSID indicates that a message is being sent from node i to node j.

The square nodes, called client nodes, are associated with the client, either at the beginning of a C/S interaction (always node 1) or at the end of the interaction (nodes 3, 6, and 10 in Fig. 3.5). Thus, all C/S interactions in a CSID start with node 1 (called the start node) and end in another client node (called end node).

The circle nodes usually represent servers involved in the implementation of an e-business function. For example, nodes 4 and 8 in Fig. 3.5 are associated with visits to the application server AS. The interior label (e.g.,

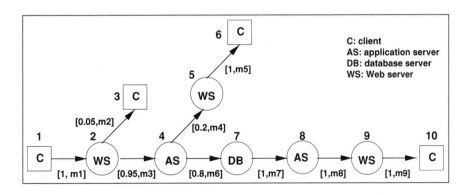

Figure 3.5. Example of a C/S Interaction Diagram (CSID).

WS, AS, DB) of circle nodes indicates the name of the server.

Arcs in a CSID are labeled by pairs of the type $[p, m]$ where p is the probability that the message is sent and m is the message size, in bytes. The resource consumption at the various resources (e.g., CPU or disk) of a client or server represented by a node in the CSID may be different at each visit to the same client or server.

There is only one path from the start node (node 1) to any end node of a CSID. This unique path represents a C/S interaction. For example, the CSID of Fig. 3.5 has three interactions represented in Fig. 3.6.

- Interaction 1: $1 \rightarrow 2 \rightarrow 3$. In this case, the client sends a request to the Web server (node 2). The size of the request is m_1 bytes. With probability 0.05, the Web server refuses a connection and the request fails. The client (represented by node 3) receives a reply message of size m_2 from the Web server. This marks the end of this interaction.

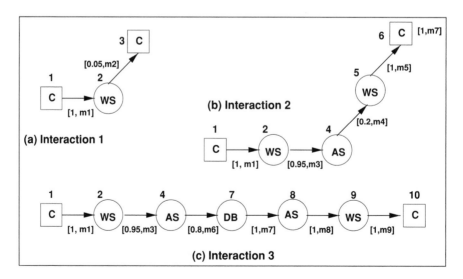

Figure 3.6. C/S Interactions for the CSID of Fig. 3.5: (a) Interaction 1 (b) Interaction 2 (c) Interaction 3.

- Interaction 2: $1 \rightarrow 2 \rightarrow 4 \rightarrow 5 \rightarrow 6$. Here, the Web server accepts the request from the client and sends a request to the application server (node 4) for execution of an application (this happens with probability 0.95). With probability 0.2, an access to the database is not required and the application server returns a dynamically generated page to the Web server (node 5), which replies to the client (node 6).

- Interaction 3: $1 \rightarrow 2 \rightarrow 4 \rightarrow 7 \rightarrow 8 \rightarrow 9 \rightarrow 10$. This interaction is slightly more complex than the previous one. In this case, the application server (node 4) needs to send a request to the database server (node 7). This happens with probability 0.8. The database server sends a reply that is m_7 bytes long to the application server (node 8) and the application server sends a dynamically generated HTML page to the Web server (node 9), which replies back to the client (node 10).

3.4.2 Expanded CSID Notation

Some e-business functions may be very complex and may require a large number of interactions between the various clients and servers. In those cases, it may be more convenient to specify the CSIDs in a hierarchical manner, where arcs represent complex exchange of messages that are further detailed in other CSIDs.

Figure 3.7 shows an example in which the arc $4 \rightarrow 7$ in Fig. 3.5 is refined into a sequence of three arcs. The top part of Fig. 3.7 shows a portion of the CSID of Fig. 3.5. The arc $4 \rightarrow 7$ in the original CSID is labeled "search." This is the name of another CSID, illustrated in the bottom part of Fig. 3.7. This CSID indicates that a search request from the application server to the database server may involve an initial request to the database server in which, for example, the user portfolio is retrieved. Once the DB server responds to the application server, it determines which stocks to trade and sends an update portfolio request to the DB server.

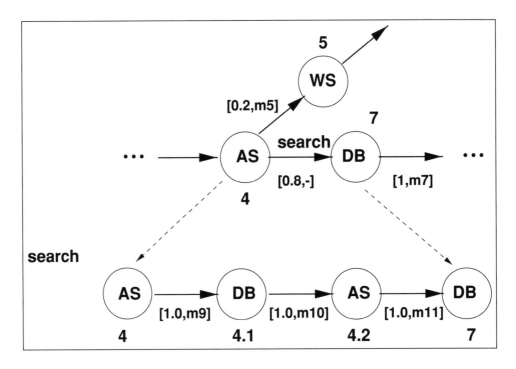

Figure 3.7. Arc refinement for CSIDs.

The label on the arc "search" in the top part of Fig. 3.7 does not show a message size since this arc represents more than one message exchange.

Hierarchical representations of CSIDs are also useful when a sequence of C/S message exchanges is common to the execution of many e-business functions. A good example is authentication, which will be further explained in Chapter 5.

3.4.3   Answering Quantitative Questions with CSIDs

CSIDs are helpful in answering quantitative questions about the execution of e-business functions. We illustrate this by using the CSID of Fig. 3.5 as an example.

Example 3.1

What is the probability that the database server is used during the execution of the e-business function represented by the CSID of Fig. 3.5? What is the average number of times that the application server is activated?

The database server is used only if the sequence $1 \to 2 \to 4 \to 7$ is followed. The probability that this happens is the product of the probabilities along this path, namely $1 \times 0.95 \times 0.8 = 0.76$. The application server appears twice in the CSID: at nodes 4 and 8. If interaction 2 is executed, the application server is used only once (node 4). However, if interaction 3 is executed, the application server is used twice (nodes 4 and 8). The probability that interaction 2 is executed is the product of the probabilities along the path $1 \to 2 \to 4 \to 5 \to 6$, which is $1 \times 0.95 \times 0.2 \times 1 = 0.19$. The probability that interaction 3 is executed is given by the probability of the path $1 \to 2 \to 4 \to 7 \to 8 \to 9 \to 10$, which is 0.76. So, the average number of times that the application server is activated is $1 \times 0.19 + 2 \times 0.76 = 1.71$. ∎

From this example, we learned that the probability that a C/S interaction is executed is the product of the probabilities of all arcs of the CSID associated with the interaction. We also learned that the probability of an execution associated with a node of the CSID is equal to the product of the probabilities along the path from the start node of the CSID to that node.

Example 3.2

Suppose that the Web server, the application server, and the database server run on different machines all connected to the same LAN. What is the average number of bytes that cross the LAN for each execution of the e-business function represented by the CSID of Fig. 3.5?

To answer this question, we look at the three interactions of the CSID and count the total number of bytes crossing the LAN due to each message interchange (represented by the arcs of the CSID). For each interaction, we need to add the message sizes along the path that goes from the start node to the end node of the interaction. This is shown in Table 3.1.

So, the average number of bytes that cross the LAN for the execution of this e-business function is

$$0.05 \times (m_1 + m_2) + 0.19 \times (m_1 + m_3 + m_4 + m_5) +$$
$$0.76 \times (m_1 + m_3 + m_6 + m_7 + m_8 + m_9).$$

Suppose that the message sizes (in bytes) are $m_1 = 200$, $m_2 = 200$, $m_3 = 400$, $m_4 = 2,000$, $m_5 = 2,100$, $m_6 = 500$, $m_7 = 3,000$, $m_8 = 2,000$, and $m_9 = 2,100$. So, the average number of bytes that cross the LAN for every execution of this transaction is

$$0.05 \times 400 + 0.19 \times 4,700 + 0.76 \times 8,200 = 7,145 \text{ bytes.}$$

Suppose that the protocol byte overhead is 10% and that the LAN is a 100 Mbps Ethernet. Assume that the effective bandwidth of the network, after contention due to network traffic is taken into account, is 80 Mbps. What is the maximum number of executions of this e-business function per unit time?

Each transaction transmits, on average, $62,876$ ($= 7,145 \times 8 \times 1.1$) bits once the protocol overhead is considered. Thus, the LAN can support at most $1,272$ ($= 80,000,000/62,876$) transactions per second (tps). Clearly, one would not like to drive the LAN at full capacity because performance would be disastrous. ∎

Table 3.1. Total Message Count for Ex. 3.2.

Interaction	Message Count	Probability
1	$m_1 + m_2$	0.05
2	$m_1 + m_3 + m_4 + m_5$	0.19
3	$m_1 + m_3 + m_6 + m_7 + m_8 + m_9$	0.76

This example shows that the number of bytes generated by the execution of a C/S interaction is equal to the sum of the message sizes of all arcs of the CSID associated with the interaction.

Example 3.3

Consider that the application server requires 50 msec of CPU time during the execution represented by node 4 and 80 msec for the execution represented by node 8 of the CSID. What is the average CPU time at the application server for the e-business function represented by the CSID of Fig. 3.5?

The probability that the execution represented by node 4 takes place is given by the product of the probabilities along the path $1 \rightarrow 2 \rightarrow 4$, which is 0.95. Similarly, the probability that the execution represented by node 8 takes place is given by the product of the probabilities along the path $1 \rightarrow 2 \rightarrow 4 \rightarrow 7 \rightarrow 8$, which is 0.76. Thus, the average CPU time at the application server is $0.95 \times 50 + 0.76 \times 80 = 108.3$ msec, or 0.1083 sec. If the application server has only one CPU, the maximum number of transactions it can handle per second is 9.23 (= 1 / 0.1083) tps. So, even though the network would be able to support 1,272 tps, the e-commerce site is limited to at most 9.23 tps due to the application server CPU. ∎

This example teaches us that the *service demand*, i.e., the total time spent for a request to receive service from a resource (e.g., CPU or disk) at a given server can be obtained by

1. identifying all the nodes in the CSID associated with the server,

2. computing the probabilities associated with each node,

3. obtaining the service demand associated with each node for the resource in question, and

4. adding, for all nodes in question, the products of the probabilities by

the service demand associated with the execution associated with each node.

The notion of service demands and the quantitative procedures described in the previous examples will be formalized in Chapter 8.

Example 3.4

How would the results of Ex. 3.2 change if the Web, application, and database servers run on the same machine? Assume that this machine is connected to the LAN that connects the e-commerce site to the Internet.

If we look at the CSID, we see that the communication represented by arcs $2 \rightarrow 4$, $4 \rightarrow 5$, $4 \rightarrow 7$, $7 \rightarrow 8$, and $8 \rightarrow 9$ is now internal to the machine and does not use the LAN. Therefore, we can recalculate the results of Ex. 3.2 by assuming $m_3 = m_4 = m_6 = m_7 = m_8 = 0$. So, the average number of bytes that traverse the LAN as a result of this transaction is

$$0.05 \times 400 + 0.19 \times 2,300 + 0.76 \times 2,300 = 2,205.$$

Considering the same protocol overhead and bandwidth as in Ex. 3.2, we get that each execution of the e-business function transmits 19,404 ($= 2,205 \times 8 \times 1.1$) bits, on average. Therefore, the LAN can support at most 4,123 ($= 80,000,00 / 19,404$) tps. This is an increase of 3.24 times the network throughput measured in tps when compared with the situation of Ex. 3.2. However, we may need a more powerful machine to support all three servers.   ■

This example illustrates that the mapping of software resources, i.e., servers, to physical resources (e.g., machines and networks) is very useful in determining the performance of an e-commerce site.

Example 3.5

Consider again the CSID of Fig. 3.5. Assume that the Web, application, and database servers are located on different machines and that the Web server is on local area network 1 (LAN 1) and that the application and database servers are on local area network 2 (LAN 2) as illustrated in Fig. 3.8.

We want to compute the average time spent by an execution of the e-business function of Fig. 3.5 in the various networks. For that matter, we make the simplifying assumption that the delay experienced by a message of size MessageSize when traversing a network with round trip time (RTT) NetworkRTT and bandwidth NetworkBandwidth is given by

$$\text{MessageDelay} = 1/2 \ \text{NetworkRTT} + \frac{\text{MessageSize}}{\text{NetworkBandwidth}}. \qquad (3.4.1)$$

The MessageDelay of Eq. (3.4.1) may have to be adjusted to include the CPU time at the sender and receiver ends. As pointed out by Gray [3], high-speed networking has been limited by software overheads. The processing time to send or receive a message can be approximated by the linear relationship $a + b \times$ MessageSize. It has been observed that in traditional message systems, it takes about ten thousand instructions and then ten instructions per byte to send or receive a message [3]. Assume a machine that executes two billion instructions per second. In this case, $a = 10,000/(2 \times 10^9) = 5$ μsec and $b = 10/(2 \times 10^9) = 0.005$ μsec/byte. Thus, it would take 46 ($= 5 + 0.005 \times 8,192$) μsec to send a 8,192-byte message.

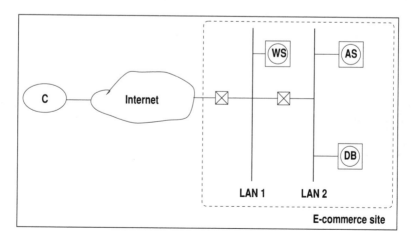

Figure 3.8. Figure for Ex. 3.5

Equation (3.4.1) assumes that all messages fit on a single packet. In this example, we assume the same message sizes as in Ex. 3.2. These values are repeated in Table 3.2.

In order to compute the average communications delay, we need to consider each of the three interactions discussed in Section 3.4.1, namely $1 \to 2 \to 3$, $1 \to 2 \to 4 \to 5 \to 6$, and $1 \to 2 \to 4 \to 7 \to 8 \to 9 \to 10$. The probability of occurrence of each interaction is given in Table 3.1. For each interaction, the total message delay is the sum of the message delays along all arcs of the path. The delay in a single arc is equal to the sum of

Table 3.2. Solution for Ex. 3.5.

		Network		
		Internet	LAN 1	LAN 2
RTT (sec)		0.08	0.001	0.001
Bandwidth (bytes/sec)		16,000	1,100,000	1,100,000
Message	Size (bytes)	Message Delay (sec)		
m_1	200	0.04607	0.00037	-
m_2	200	0.04607	0.00037	-
m_3	400	-	0.00039	0.00039
m_4	2,000		0.00055	0.00055
m_5	2,100	0.06097	0.00056	-
m_6	500	-	-	0.00040
m_7	3,000	-	-	0.00065
m_8	2,000	-	0.00055	0.00055
m_9	2,100	0.06097	0.00056	-
Interaction	Probability (a)	Delay (sec) (b)	(a) × (b)	
1	0.05	0.09288	0.00464	
2	0.19	0.10985	0.02087	
3	0.76	0.11090	0.08428	
			0.10980	

the delays experienced by the message on all networks it traverses.

To make the computation easier, we add a new label to each arc of the CSID. These labels indicate the sequence of networks traversed by the message for a given network topology and location of servers on the networks. This is illustrated in Fig. 3.9 which shows the new labels in parentheses for the CSID of Fig. 3.5.

We show the results of the computations in Table 3.2. The top part of the table shows the bandwidth and round trip times for each of the three networks. The middle part of the table shows the average message delay for each message in each network according to Eq. (3.4.1). Finally, the bottom part of the table shows the delay of each interaction, its probability, and the product of the probability by the delay of each interaction.

We use the notation d (m_i, n) to denote the delay of message m_i on network n. So, d $(m_6, \text{LAN 2})$ stands for the delay of message m_6 on network LAN 2. We now use this notation to indicate the message delays along each of the three interactions.

$$\text{DelayInteraction1} = \text{d } (m_1, \text{Int}) + \text{d } (m_1, \text{LAN 1}) +$$
$$\text{d } (m_2, \text{LAN 1}) + \text{d } (m_2, \text{Int})$$

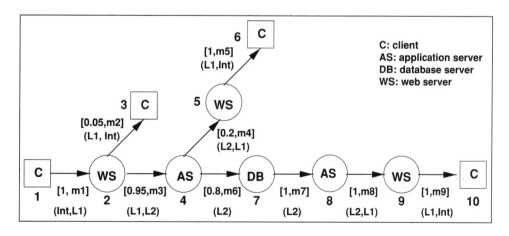

Figure 3.9. CSID of Fig. 3.5 with Network Mapping.

$$\text{DelayInteraction2} = \text{d}(m_1, \text{Int}) + \text{d}(m_1, \text{LAN 1}) + \text{d}(m_3, \text{LAN 1}) +$$
$$\text{d}(m_3, \text{LAN 2}) + \text{d}(m_4, \text{LAN 2}) + \text{d}(m_4, \text{LAN 1}) +$$
$$\text{d}(m_5, \text{LAN 1}) + \text{d}(m_5, \text{Int})$$
$$\text{DelayInteraction3} = \text{d}(m_1, \text{Int}) + \text{d}(m_1, \text{LAN 1}) + \text{d}(m_3, \text{LAN 1}) +$$
$$\text{d}(m_3, \text{LAN 2}) + \text{d}(m_6, \text{LAN 2}) + \text{d}(m_7, \text{LAN 2}) +$$
$$\text{d}(m_8, \text{LAN 2}) + \text{d}(m_8, \text{LAN 1}) + \text{d}(m_9, \text{LAN 1}) +$$
$$\text{d}(m_9, \text{Int}) \tag{3.4.2}$$

The last row of Table 3.2 shows the average communication delay of 0.10980 sec obtained by adding all values in the fourth column, i.e., (a) × (b), in the bottom portion of the table.   ■

We learned from this example that

1. the communication delay of an arc of the CSID is obtained by adding the delay of the message associated with the arc over all networks traversed by that message,

2. the communication delay of an interaction of a CSID is equal to the sum of all the arc delays in the path associated with the interaction, and

3. the average communication delay of a CSID is equal to the weighted sum (the weights are the interaction probabilities) of the interaction delays.

3.5   From CBMGs to CSIDs

The previous sections introduced CSIDs as a way of describing the flow of e-business functions. In this section we discuss the steps to be followed to go from CBMGs to CSIDs.

1. Obtain the static CBMG as described in Chapter 2.

2. From the static CBMG, build a list of all e-business functions.

3. For each e-business function, determine the software servers (e.g., web server, application server, database server, authentication server) involved in its execution. Document the relationship between e-business functions and servers in a matrix as illustrated in Table 3.3.

4. Determine the flow of messages between the client and servers and build a CSID for each e-business function. Figure 3.10 shows the mapping from a CBMG to the CSID for the e-commerce function Pay.

5. Estimate the message sizes for each message arc for all CSIDs.

Table 3.3. E-Business Functions vs. Servers Used.

E-Business Function	Web Server	Trading Server	Authentication Server	Application Server	Database Server
Login	√		√		
Register	√		√		
Search	√			√	√
Select	√			√	√
Browse	√				
Open Account	√	√	√		
Get Quotes	√			√	√
Get Report	√			√	√
View Chart	√			√	√
View Indexes	√			√	√
Trade	√	√	√		√
Create Portfolio	√			√	√
Add to Portfolio	√			√	√
Delete from Portfolio	√			√	√
Asset Planning	√			√	√

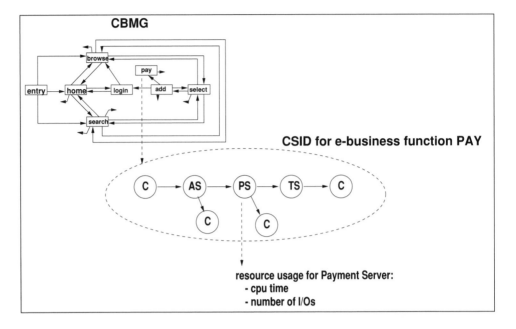

Figure 3.10. From CBMGs to CSIDs.

6. Determine, for each node of each CSID associated with an e-business function, the amount of resources of each type (e.g., processors, storage subsystems) used when the e-business function is executed. This information will be useful later on when we discuss models for performance prediction and capacity planning.

3.6   Summary

We summarize here the important points we learned regarding the use of CSIDs to answer quantitative questions about e-business functions.

- The probability of a C/S interaction is the product of the probabilities of all arcs of the CSID associated with the interaction.

- The probability of an execution associated with a node of the CSID is equal to the product of the probabilities along the path from the root of the CSID to that node.

- The number of bytes generated by the execution of an interaction is equal to the sum of the message sizes of all arcs of the CSID associated with the interaction.

- The total time spent by a transaction receiving service from a resource (e.g., CPU or disk) at a given server can be obtained by

  1. identifying all the nodes in the CSID associated with the server,

  2. computing the probabilities associated with each node,

  3. obtaining the service demand associated with each node for the resource in question, and

  4. adding, for all nodes in question, the products of the probabilities by the service demand associated with the execution associated with each node.

- The mapping of software resources, i.e., servers, to physical resources (e.g., machines and networks) is very useful in determining the performance of an e-commerce transaction.

- The communication delay of an arc of the CSID is obtained by adding the delay of the message associated with the arc over all networks traversed by that message.

- The communication delay of an interaction of a CSID is equal to the sum of all the arc delays in the path associated with the interaction.

- The average communication delay of a CSID is equal to the weighted sum of the interaction delays. The weights are the interaction probabilities.

The next chapter discusses the physical configurations that are typical of e-business sites.

Bibliography

[1] J. Bacon, *Concurrent Systems*, 2nd. ed., Addison-Wesley, Harlow, England, 1998.

[2] G. Booch, J. Rumbaugh, and I. Jacobson, *The Unified Modeling Language User Guide*, Addison Wesley, 1999.

[3] J. Gray and P. Shenoy, "Rules of Thumb in Data Engineering," *Proc. IEEE International Conf. on Data Engineering*, San Diego, CA, April 2000.

[4] International Telecommunications Union, Criteria for the Use and Applicability of Formal Description Techniques, Message Sequence Charts (MSC), 1996.

[5] P. Inverardi and A. L. Wolf, "Analysis of Software Architecture Using the Chemical Abstract Machine Model," *IEEE Tr. Software Engineering*, **21**, no. 4, pp. 373–386, April 1995.

[6] D. A. Menascé and V. A. F. Almeida, "Performance of Client/Server Systems," in *Performance Evaluation - Origins and Directions*, eds. G. Haring, C. Lindemann, and M. Reiser, LNCS Series, Springer-Verlag, 2000.

[7] D. A. Menascé and V. A. F. Almeida, *Capacity Planning for Web Performance: Metrics, Models, and Methods*, Prentice Hall, Upper Saddle River, NJ, 1998.

[8] A. Olsen, O. Faergemand, B. Moeller-Pedersen, R. Reed, and J. R. W. Smith, *Systems Engineering Using SDL-92*, North-Holland, 1994.

[9] R. ORFALI, D. HARKEY, and J. EDWARDS, *Client/Server Survival Guide*, 3rd. ed., John Wiley & Sons, New York, NY, 1999.

Part II
Evaluating E-Business Infrastructure and Services

Chapter 4

Infrastructure for Electronic Business

4.1 Introduction

Here is a central question: how can one plan, manage, and evaluate the infrastructure of an electronic business, such as an auction company or an Internet retailer? Or being more specific, is the infrastructure of a certain e-commerce company sized for peak traffic that occurs in the Thanksgiving to Christmas timeframe or is it planned for average annual traffic and less expensive operational costs? Is the infrastructure scalable to cope with customer surges during a sales promotion? By breaking down the complexity of an electronic business, one can analyze the functionality of each component, evaluate service requirements, and design the systems that will execute the functions required by the services. In other words, the answer to the above question requires the understanding of the system architecture and its infrastructure. Electronic businesses have widely varying scopes, ranging from various types of B2C commerce to a number of B2B models. Several generic services are critical to an electronic business, such as authentication, confidentiality, non-repudiation, payment, and information retrieval services (e.g., search engines, browsing, and publishing tools). In addition to processing commercial transactions, electronic businesses also have other sources of revenue. For instance, popular retailers that attract heavy traffic may sell advertisement space on their pages to third parties. Therefore, an electronic business should be provided with an infrastructure capable of supporting all functions defined by the business. This chapter presents an architectural framework for the infrastructure needed to fulfill the major needs of electronic business services.

4.2   Infrastructure

The infrastructure of an electronic business identifies the functionalities of the hardware and software components, specifies the corresponding service level requirements, and describes the management and operation of the whole system [20]. The infrastructure is usually shared by many applications that rely on the components of the infrastructure and management procedures (e.g., software distribution, backup, recovery, and capacity planning) to provide reliable and efficient services to customers. Commerce servers, transaction servers, database servers, and Web servers are typical software components used by e-business applications. Hardware components include standard pieces such as servers and networks as well as specialized hardware devices such as proxy servers, load balancing systems, firewalls, encryption devices, and interactive voice response units.

4.2.1 Overview

Figure 4.1 illustrates the various models involved in the specification of the infrastructure of an electronic business. The business model consists of several parts that helps one to obtain a detailed characterization of the business system. These parts specify the following business characteristics: situation, purpose, outcome, functions, resources, and location [15]. As discussed in Chapter 1, the business model provides some global data, such as number of customers, orders/day, and average and peak volume of business transactions. The business model is a starting point in the process of specifying the infrastructure requirements.

The functional model specifies the business processes and applications needed to accomplish the services and functions offered to customers. Why is that important for the infrastructure? The answer is straightforward. The process of defining and setting service levels is closely related to the very nature of business processes and applications. Furthermore, business applications are implemented using the infrastructure services.

The architecture of an electronic business is the structure of the system, which comprises the services provided by hardware and software components, the third-party services, and the way services interact. Note that this definition includes important issues, such as the dynamics of the interaction among services, the notion of service providers, and their properties in the context of electronic business, that involve many participants [20]. The architecture of an electronic business consists of two blocks of descriptors: functional and

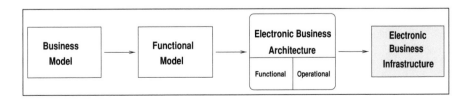

Figure 4.1. Infrastructure Overview.

operational. The first one describes the structure, its components, their interactions, and their interfaces. The latter focuses on the operational view of the system, consisting of the network topology, geographical locations, and the application service levels, expressed by performance, availability, and security requirements. Once a set of functional and operational requirements has been established, one is able to specify the infrastructure that supports the architecture of the system. The choice of optimal designs depends on the metrics that will be used to evaluate the architecture and infrastructure. Given the nature of the electronic business, some quantitative information about the business, the functional model of the applications, and the architecture requirements, one should be able to specify an infrastructure that meets the requirements at minimum cost.

4.2.2   Focus

Information services based on the Internet and the Web are becoming ubiquitous, with everyone using these systems. As the demand on Web services grows, the technological infrastructure of websites and the Internet should have enough capacity to handle changes in demand patterns smoothly. The design of the infrastructure for electronic business and services should focus not only on performance, but also on other key issues that are essential for the quality of information services [9].

4.2.2.1   Performance

In a large Internet retailer store, customers were locked out of the site because of a surge in shoppers during a sales promotion and found the following message when they tried to access the site: "Due to enormous turnout, the check-out lines are currently full. Please try again later" [8]. To avoid losing sales and customers, electronic business sites must be fast and reliable. Performance problems may arise in many points of the World Wide Web. They may occur at the end user because of obsolete system technology or due to the lack of bandwidth of the link to the ISP. Inadequate server and network capacity may cause extra delays at the ISP. Excess of traffic may bring congestion and delays at backbone providers. And finally, performance problems can be found at the e-commerce site.

Although bandwidth and server capacity have improved in recent years, response time continues to challenge system administrators and developers. Complex Web-based commerce applications and the unpredictable nature of traffic stress site performance and can cause response time degradation. The execution of a Web transaction places demands on many site resources (e.g., servers, LANs, databases) and sometimes demands information, such as banners, authorization, and certification, from other sites. All these factors together compound the performance issue in electronic business applications and demand techniques and tools to analyze and understand system behavior.

4.2.2.2 Availability and Maintainability

"We are sorry, but the store is temporarily closed. We expect to be back soon." No customer likes to see this type of message when accessing an electronic store on the Web. It is evident that availability is one of the main service level goals of any electronic business. Low availability can cost an e-business lost revenue, reduced market share, and bad publicity. A natural question that arises is "How can an electronic business achieve high availability?" Certainly, the answer should include infrastructure reliability and software robustness. Geographically separate sites with multiple levels at each site, multiple machines at each level, load balancing mechanisms, and redundant networks is a starting point toward high availability. Permanent system monitoring and measurement procedures can anticipate problems and enhance availability. Before one establishes availability goals for an e-commerce site, answers to the following questions should be reviewed.

- Where are the single points of failure?

- What is the minimum configuration needed to run the site?

- How much self-repairing is the site able to do?

- How much diagnostic and alert information is available to technical and management people?

- What are the emergency procedures?

- What is the historical MTTF (i.e., mean time to failure) and MTTR (i.e., mean time to repair) for the past failures experienced by the site?

Example 4.1

Consider the site of a large portal, visited by millions of people every day. The site is considering several high availability goals, that vary from 99.9% to 99.999%. In determining the proper availability ratio, management is aware that in order to estimate the downtime hours, the following factors should be taken into account: 1) average time to shutdown and boot the computers; 2) time to discover the problems; 3) average time to repair the problems; 4) worst case situation, which represents the longest time to discover the problems; and 5) maintenance hours.

To analyze the feasibility of setting high availability goals, management wants to know what is the maximum number of hours of downtime allowable per year to achieve 99.9%, 99.99% and 99.999% availability. Using the equations of Ex. 1.2 from Chapter 1, we obtain the maximum downtime period per year for each level of availability. These results are shown in Table 4.1. ■

In demanding environments, such as electronic commerce, the cost of maintenance and administration is very high and can vary from two to twelve times the hardware cost [3]. Such maintenance costs associated with corresponding downtime periods are incompatible with the very nature of applications on the Internet, which are used by millions of customers around the world. "The site is under maintenance right now. Please come back later." Such messages are unacceptable for customers of electronic stores. The key

Table 4.1. Availability and Annual Downtime Period.

Availability	Hours of Downtime per Year
99.900%	8.8
99.990%	0.9
99.999%	0.09

concept in maintainability is the ease of replacing or upgrading software and hardware components [9]. In the Web, online companies have to be able to replace and upgrade components of their infrastructure without disrupting customer services.

4.2.2.3 Scalability

Due to the unpredictable behavior of online customers, scalability is a key issue for electronic business systems. Customers expect Web stores to work properly and to be easy to use. They do not accept messages such as the following, which are very common when servers become overloaded. "An error has occurred! Our servers have reached the maximum number of simultaneous users. Please try again later."

The infrastructure of electronic businesses should be designed so that information services scale with demand. For instance, it may be very difficult to access a major newspaper or TV site after some very important breaking news due to site overload. And, as Hennessy points out [9], "those are the most important times to be able to get the service." Therefore, scalability is a critical issue. An electronic business infrastructure is said to be scalable when it provides adequate service levels even when the the workload increases above expected levels. According to Gray [6], sites grow in two different ways, namely *scaling up* and *scaling out*. The former is achieved by replacing servers with larger servers. The latter implies in adding more servers to the site. The following example illustrates the usual way to identify non-scalability in an infrastructure, namely by discovering bottlenecks that limit performance.

Example 4.2

Consider a search site that is powered by a distributed search engine composed of a Web server, which acts as a broker machine and distributes the queries among three data servers. Let us assume that the Web server only uses the processor to redirect the HTTP queries to data servers. Each data server has one large disk. A representation of the architecture of the site is depicted in Fig. 4.2. Because the queries are not evenly distributed among the servers, management is concerned with site performance during possible load spikes. To evaluate how scalable the site is, management needs to know the maximum throughput of the current configuration. During a twenty-five minute period, the following measurements were taken from the distributed search engine:

- observation period: 1,500 sec,

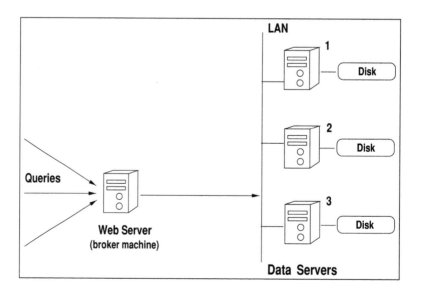

Figure 4.2. Architecture of the Distributed Search Engine.

- total number of completed queries: 23,000,

- completed queries by server 1: 7,000,

- completed queries by server 2: 6,000,

- completed queries by server 3: 10,000.

Processor and disk utilizations were also measured as shown in Table 4.2. From the measurement data, we can compute the average throughput during the observation period as

$$\text{Throughput} = \text{NumberOfCompletedQueries}/\text{ObservationPeriod}$$
$$= 23,000/1,500 = 15.3 \text{ queries/sec.}$$

To calculate the maximum throughput of the search engine in queries/sec, we need to obtain the average service demand, i.e., the average total time spent by a query at the Web server and the data server components (i.e., processor and disk). As will be discussed and formalized in Chapter 8, the service demand at a component i is calculated as the ratio between the utilization of that component and the overall throughput. Thus,

$$\text{ServiceDemand}_i = \frac{\text{Utilization}_i}{\text{Throughput}}. \qquad (4.2.2)$$

For example, the service demand at the CPU of the Web server is 0.0392 sec (= 0.6/15.3). The service demands for all components are shown in

Table 4.2. Utilization of the Components of the Search Engine.

Server	Processor Utilization (%)	Disk Utilization (%)
Web Server	60	-
Data Server 1	40	23
Data Server 2	30	20
Data Server 3	66	33

Table 4.3. The maximum throughput is determined by the component that is the bottleneck, namely the one with the maximum service demand. In this case, the bottleneck is the processor of data server 3 as can be seen in Table 4.3. This component reaches 100% utilization before any of the other components as the load on the system increases. When this happens, the throughput will have achieved its maximum value. From Eq. (4.2.2), we can see that the maximum throughput is the inverse of the maximum service demand because the utilization will be 1 at this point. For our example, the maximum throughput is 23.2 ($= 1/0.0431$) requests/sec.

Figure 4.3 shows three interesting curves as a function of the arrival rate of queries in requests/sec. The throughput increases linearly with the arrival rate until the maximum throughput of 23.2 requests/sec is reached. The response time curve shows that up to around 20 requests/sec, the response time increases very slowly with the arrival rate. As the bottleneck is approached, the response time increases very fast and tends to infinity, i.e., becomes extremely large, as the bottleneck device approaches 100% utilization. ∎

4.2.3   Understanding the E-Business Infrastructure

A key step of any quantitative study of e-business consists of learning what kind of infrastructure is present in the environment or what type of infras-

Table 4.3. Service Demands at the Components of the Search Engine.

Server	Processor Demand (msec)	Disk Demand (msec)
Web server	39.2	-
Data server 1	26.1	15.0
Data server 2	19.6	13.1
Data server 3	43.1	21.6

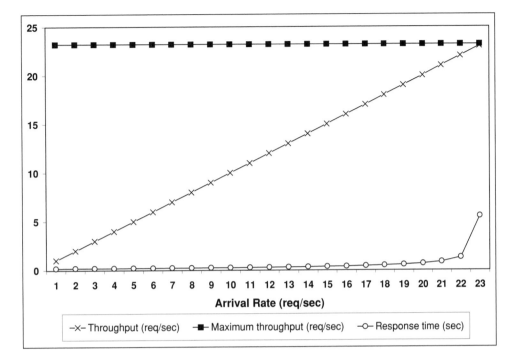

Figure 4.3. Graph of Scalability of the Search Engine.

tructure will be needed to support a new electronic business. The following are some typical questions, whose answers can help explain the infrastructure requirements of an electronic business.

- What is the business model that the site supports? Who are the customers? How much are they willing to pay? What is the expected total market?

- For what category of electronic business is the site specialized: B2C, B2B, or C2C?

- What operating system, Web server, commerce server, database management system, payment system, and proxy servers does the site use?

- What kinds of third-party services are used by the site?

- What are the service level agreements, in terms of availability, performance, and security?

- How scalable is the site infrastructure? What are the scalability constraints?

- What is the aggregate bandwidth at the site location?

- Is there any load balancing scheme in the site?

- What type of redundancy is available at the site (e.g., server redundancy, uninterrupted power service, RAID disks, and multiple Internet backbone providers)?

4.3 Reference Architecture

While the infrastructure describes and characterizes the main components that support an electronic business, a reference architecture covers not only the components, but the way those components are structured and the way they interact with each other. In other words, an infrastructure model provides a static description of resources and services, whereas the architecture includes the dynamics of the system. A reference architecture of a system describes its structure, its components, and their interrelationships. The importance of an architecture is emphasized by the following quotation: "If a project has not achieved a system architecture, including its rationale, the project should not proceed to a full-scale system development. Specifying the architecture as a deliverable enables its use throughout the development and maintenance process" [2]. The architecture of an electronic business system provides a framework for its evolution and for making decisions about the future, such as what technologies to adopt and when to change the system. Thus, the architecture of an electronic business is an essential element in any kind of quantitative study. Figure 4.4 depicts the overall architecture of an electronic business. The architecture is composed of two blocks: one represents the services provided by the site and the other indicates exter-

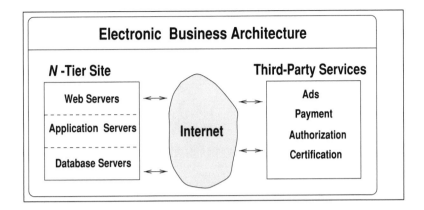

Figure 4.4. Overview of a Typical Electronic Business Architecture.

nal services that may be required by the business. The Internet connects internal services and third party services. An e-business site is usually structured in layers to improve system functionality, performance, scalability, and reliability.

4.3.1   Components

A component is a modular unit of functionality, accessed through defined interfaces. This section discusses the role of the main components of a typical infrastructure for electronic business.

4.3.1.1   Web Server

As shown in Fig. 4.5, a Web server is a combination of a hardware platform, operating system, networking software, and an HTTP server. Web server software, also known as HTTP server or HTTP daemon, are programs that control the flow of incoming and outgoing data on a computer connected to an intranet or to the Internet. The HyperText Transfer Protocol [19] is an application-level protocol layered on top of TCP used in the communication between clients and servers on the Web. HTTP defines a simple request-response interaction, which can be viewed as a Web transaction. In the

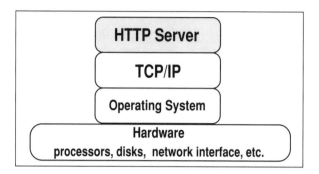

Figure 4.5. Web Server Elements.

original version of the protocol, HTTP 1.0, a new connection is established per request. In the version HTTP 1.1, also called persistent connection, one TCP connection may be used to carry multiple HTTP requests, eliminating the cost of many opens and closes. Basically, Web server software listens for HTTP requests coming from clients over the network. The server program establishes the requested connection between itself and the client, sends the requested file, and returns to its listening function. To speed up the service, HTTP servers handle more than one request at a time. Usually, this is done in three different ways [19]: by forking a copy of the HTTP process for each request, by multithreading the HTTP program, or by spreading the requests among the processes of pool of running processes.

Latency and throughput are the two most important performance metrics for Web servers. The rate at which HTTP requests are serviced represents the connection throughput. It is usually expressed in HTTP operations/sec. Due to the large variability in the size of the requested Web objects, throughput is also measured in terms of megabits per second (Mbps). The time required to complete a request is the latency at the server, which is one component of client response time. The average latency at the server is the average time for handling the requests. Customer response time includes latency at the server plus the time spent communicating over the network plus the processing time on the client machine (e.g., formatting the response).

Thus, customer-perceived performance depends on the server capacity and the network load and bandwidth as well as on the client machine.

4.3.1.2 Application Server

An *application server* is the software that handles all application operations between browser-based customers and a company's back-end databases. For example, an application server in a travel agency Web site translates search requests for flight scripts that access the back-end database. In general, an application server receives client requests, executes the business logic, and interacts with transaction servers and/or database servers. Usually, application servers exhibit the following characteristics: i) host and process application logic written in different programming languages (e.g., Java, C, or C++), ii) manage high volumes of transactions with back-end databases, iii) are compliant with all existing Web standards, including HTTP, HTML, CGI, NSAPI, ISAPI, and Java, and iv) work with most of the popular Web servers, browsers, and databases.

Application servers can be implemented in many different ways, as shown in Figs. 4.6 and 4.7: as CGI scripts, as FastCGIs, server-applications, and server-side scripts. Figure 4.6 (a) shows the CGI approach. In this case, a new process is created to handle each request (see part 2 of the figure). When the request is complete, the process is killed (see part 3 of the figure). The advantage of this approach is that there is complete isolation between the application and the Web server. So, if the application crashes, it will not bring the Web server down. Isolation is also important for security reasons. The drawbacks of using CGI scripts are 1) the overhead involved in creating and killing processes, and 2) the fact that it becomes harder to build persistent applications, i.e., applications that require several interactions with the user. Since the process that implements the CGI script is killed after each interaction, other methods (e.g., cookies) have to be used to pass the application state from one interaction to the next within the

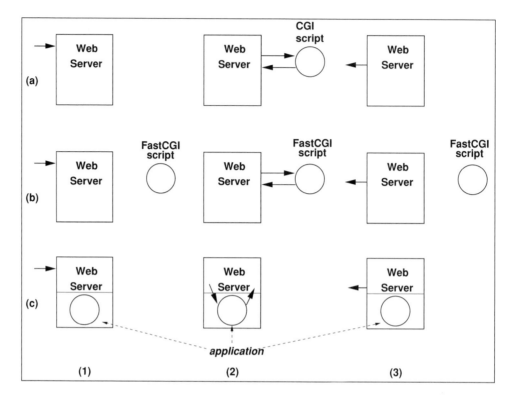

Figure 4.6. (a) CGI scripts (b) FastCGI Scripts (c) Applications within the Server Context.

same transaction.

To overcome some of the problems of CGI scripts, one can use FastCGI scripts (see Fig. 4.6 (b)), which are persistent processes that communicate with the Web server either through TCP or local interprocess communication mechanisms. Fast CGIs provide isolation and persistency as well as better performance than CGI scripts. As shown in Fig. 4.6 (b), the FastCGI script is present throughout the entire life of one or more requests. The communication between the Web server and FastCGI scripts usually involves system calls.

The third approach, shown in Fig. 4.6 (c), is that of applications that run within the context of the Web server. The application is invoked through APIs (Application Programming Interfaces) provided by the Web server software. Examples include ISAPI for Microsoft's IIS Web server and NSAPI for Netscape's Web server. While this approach provides application persistency and exhibits better performance than any of the other methods, it suffers from poor isolation. If an application fails, it can bring down with it the Web server process. Security is also a problem here due to lack of isolation between the application and the Web server.

The last approach is the use of server-side scripting as shown in Fig. 4.7, which shows the sequence of steps that take place when a request for an HTML page arrives. The page, retrieved from the document tree, contains HTML code and a script written in a scripting language. Microsoft's Active Server Pages (ASPs) allow the use of JavaScript and VBscript with ActiveX controls in a page and Netscape's Livewire allow the use of server-side JavaScript. A script interpreter at the Web server interprets the script and dynamically generates an HTML page that is returned to the browser.

The performance tradeoff between CGIs and server-side scripting is illustrated in the following example.

Example 4.3

A Web server is connected to the Internet through a T1 link. Measurements on the server indicate that it takes 5 msec to process the incoming

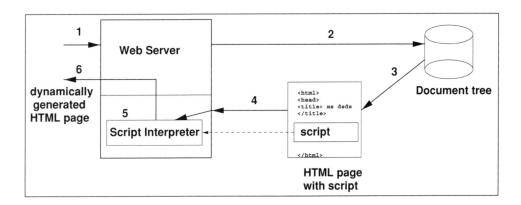

Figure 4.7. Server-Side Scripting.

HTTP request to determine that an application needs to be executed at the server, 20 msec to start and kill a CGI process, 40 msec to execute the CGI script, and 5 msec to reply to the request. The size of an incoming request is 200 bytes and the size of the HTML page returned is 5,000 bytes. How does the Web server throughput vary as a function of the number of concurrent requests in the system for the CGI case and for the case in which the application runs within the Web server context.

The maximum throughput is given by the inverse of the service demand for the bottleneck device (see Chapter 8). In other words, we need to find the device in which a request spends most of its time receiving service. This is the bottleneck. The inverse of the total service time at the bottleneck device is the maximum throughput. The total CPU time, or service demand, for the CGI script case is given by

$$CGICPUServiceDemand = 5 + 20 + 40 + 5 = 70 \text{ msec} = 0.07 \text{ sec.} \quad (4.3.3)$$

The CPU service demand for the case in which the application runs within the Web server does not include the time to start and kill the CGI process. Thus,

$$NoCGICPUServiceDemand = 5 + 40 + 5 = 50 \text{ msec} = 0.05 \text{ sec.} \quad (4.3.4)$$

The service demands at the incoming link and outgoing links are, assuming a 40-byte protocol overhead in the incoming link for the HTTP request and 120-byte protocol overhead in the outgoing link for the HTTP reply,

$$
\begin{aligned}
InLinkServiceDemand &= \frac{(200 + 40) \times 8}{Bandwidth} \\
&= \frac{(200 + 40) \times 8}{1,500,000} = 0.00128 \text{ sec} \\
OutLinkServiceDemand &= \frac{(5,000 + 120) \times 8}{Bandwidth} \\
&= \frac{(5,000 + 120) \times 8}{1,500,000} = 0.0273 \text{ sec}
\end{aligned}
$$

In any of the two cases, CGI or application within the Web server, the CPU is the bottleneck. The maximum throughput for the CGI case is

$$\mathrm{CGIMaxThroughput} = \frac{1}{\mathrm{CGICPUServiceDemand}}$$
$$= 1/0.07 = 14.3 \text{ requests/sec}$$

and the maximum throughput for the non-CGI case is

$$\mathrm{NoCGIMaxThroughput} = \frac{1}{\mathrm{NoCGICPUServiceDemand}}$$
$$= 1/0.05 = 20 \text{ requests/sec.}$$

The overhead incurred by CGI scripts reduces the maximum throughput from 20 to 14.3 requests/sec, a reduction of 28.5%. Figure 4.8 shows the throughput curve for the two cases. This curve was obtained with the models described in Chapters 8 and 9. ■

A *commerce server* is a software platform that combines most of the services required by an e-commerce store, such as an online catalog, transaction processing, payment handling, tax and currency offerings, workflow automation, and online ordering. It also has the capability to integrate with database systems and other corporate applications (e.g., inventory). The following metrics are used to evaluate the performance of application servers: throughput, measured in transactions per second (tps) or transactions per minute (tpm), and response time.

4.3.1.3 Transaction and Database Servers

A transaction processing (TP) monitor [1] [7] comprises three major functions: i) an application programming interface, ii) a set of program development tools, and iii) a system to monitor and control the execution of transaction programs. A TP monitor provides a seamless environment that integrates all the components needed to execute transactions: the database

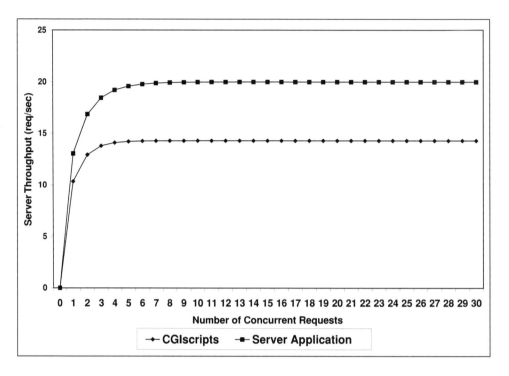

Figure 4.8. Throughput vs. Number of Requests for the CGI and Non-CGI Cases.

system, operating system, and communication system. The growth of e-commerce transactions over the Internet makes TP monitors a key component to guarantee performance, reliability, and scalability.

Like a TP monitor, a database server executes and manages transaction processing applications [1]. It can be a relational database system that supports stored procedures that can issue SQL requests to the database, as shown in Fig. 4.9.

The Transaction Processing Performance Council (TPC) [17] is a non-profit organization that defines transaction processing and database benchmarks. TPC-C, -H and -R are commonly used industry benchmarks that measure throughput and price/performance of online transaction processing (OLTP) environments and decision support systems [7]. TPC-C measures the maximum sustained system performance. It is defined as the number

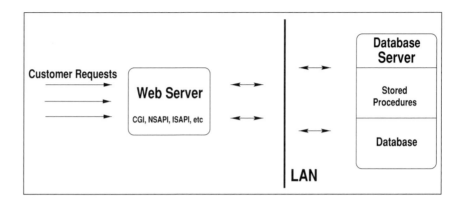

Figure 4.9. Database Server.

of New-Order transactions completed per minute while the system is executing four other transaction types (Payment, Order-Status, Delivery, and Stock-Level). The response time of all transactions should be less than five seconds. The TPC-H (ad hoc, decision support) benchmark represents decision support environments where users do not know which queries will be executed against a database system. TPC-R is similar to TPC-H, but users run a standard set of queries against the database.

4.3.1.4   Mainframe and Legacy Systems

Mainframes and legacy systems are important components of electronic business infrastructure. Very large volumes of business data exists on mainframes [16]. Legacy systems with databases (e.g., IBM's IMS and DB2, Oracle, and Sybase) and online transaction applications (e.g., IBM's CICS) have been used by companies for decades and represent a valuable asset for them. Electronic commerce applications make use of legacy data that reside on back-end mainframes. There exists a number of techniques used to help the integration of Web and mainframes, such as wrapping and back-end scripting. Wrapping refers to hiding the existing legacy applications behind an abstraction layer, representing a programming model [14]. Usually, wrapping is done at the same level as the business logic layer, as discussed in Section 4.3.2. Due to their reliability and capacity, mainframes have been also used as Web servers.

4.3.1.5   Proxies and Caches

Proxy servers and caches are techniques used for improving Web performance, scalability, and security. Caching reduces access time by bringing the data as close to its consumers as possible. Thus, caching improves access speed and cuts down on network traffic, as objects (i.e., pages and documents) often get returned from a nearby cache, rather than from far away servers. Caching also reduces the server load and increases availability in the Web, by replicating objects among many servers. Frequently requested objects are stored at sites close to users, in terms of connectivity. Although caching is a proven technology for static objects (e.g., HTML pages), its use for dynamic objects is still restricted. Dynamic pages, generated by `cgi-bin` scripts, are a very common approach for implementing e-commerce services.

A proxy server is a special type of Web server. It is able to act as both a server and a client. A proxy acts as an agent, representing the server to the client and the client to the server. A proxy accepts requests from clients and forwards them to Web servers. Once a proxy receives responses from remote servers, it passes them to the clients. Originally, proxies were designed to provide access to the Web for users on private networks, who could only access the Internet through a firewall.

Caching has a widespread use in the Web. Basically, it has been used in three ways. On the client-side, browsers maintain small caches of previously-viewed pages on the user's local disk. The second form of use is in the network (i.e., ISPs and backbone providers), where a caching proxy, also known as network caching, is located on a machine on the path from multiple clients to multiple servers. Caching proxy servers can be located near a large community of users, such as on campus or at an intranet server of a company. A different type of proxy is called *reverse proxy*, which is located side-by-side with the servers of a website. Although for browsers and other proxies, the reverse proxy acts as a final server, its main function is to distribute the load among the back-end servers of the site.

Caching effectiveness can be measured by three quantities. *Hit ratio* is defined as the number of requests satisfied by the cache over the total number of requests. Because of the high variability of Web object sizes, it is important to have a metric that includes the size of the object (e.g., HTML document, an MP3 file, and a video file). *The byte hit ratio* is equal to the hit ratio weighted by the object size. The third metric, called *data transferred*, represents the total number of bytes transferred between the cache and the outside world during an observation period. The following example illustrates the use of these metrics.

Example 4.4

The website of an e-retailer receives 3,200,000 requests per month. To postpone a new T1 link to the ISP, the manager of the site is considering using a caching proxy that is available on the ISP. Because caching is useful mainly for static pages, the manager wants to know, a priori, the benefit of a caching proxy for an e-commerce site.

By analyzing the Web server logs, the performance analyst found the following statistics: 65% of the total requests are for GIF files and the rest of the requests are dynamically generated HTML pages. The average size of a GIF file is 7,300 bytes and the HTML pages are 13,500 bytes. If the caching proxy is used to hold GIF pages, what are the cache performance metrics?

The estimated hit ratio is 65%, assuming that the cache stores the GIFs for a long period of time. The saved bandwidth from the e-store site to the ISP is calculated as follows:

$$
\begin{aligned}
\text{SavedBandwidth} &= \text{NoOfRequestsPerPeriod} \times \text{HitRatio} \times \text{AverageSize} \\
&= 3,200,000 \times 0.65 \times 7,300 \\
&= 14,828,125 \text{ KBytes/month} = 45.77 \text{ Kbps.}
\end{aligned}
$$

These results show how caching proxies can contribute to save bandwidth. ■

4.3.1.6 Internet Service Provider (ISP)

Internet service providers (ISPs) have an important contribution to the quality of service offered by electronic business. Physically, customers and merchants connect to an ISP, which in turn connects to one or more backbone network providers. Depending on the ISP installed capacity and traffic, performance problems and delays may occur at that point of the path between customers and business, contributing to an increase in response times.

4.3.2   Multi-Tier Architecture

The architecture of modern information systems consists of three layers, as shown in Fig. 4.10. Web-based applications, such as electronic business, can also be framed in a three-tier architecture. The first layer, also called the presentation layer, embodies the user interface with the Web services. Via interpretation of HTML or XML by a browser, Web users enter data, edit data, and receive information. New interfaces are available for accessing Web services from mobile devices, such as cellular phones and Personal Digital Assistants (PDAs). The business logic layer, also known as application layer, encapsulates a collection of rules to implement the application logic. The separation of the business logic from the presentation layer and the data services gives a new level of autonomy to applications and makes them more robust [12]. In the case of Web-based applications, this middle tier also contains components displayed by the browser, such as Java applets and ActiveX controls. The data service layer consists of persistent data that are managed by mechanisms that guarantee reliability, stability, and availability. Database servers and mainframes are example of components of the data layer.

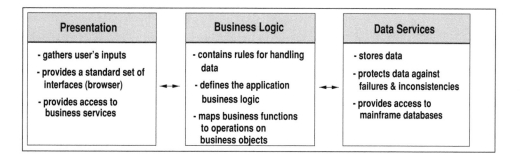

Figure 4.10. Typical Multi-Tier System Architecture.

In distributed systems, middleware is seen as the software that facilitates the integration between clients and servers. Examples of middleware in the Internet are HTTP, SSL, and CORBA.

Web sites basically implement the application and data layers of a system architecture. Figure 4.11 shows a three-tier e-business site, composed of a load balancer, Web servers in layer 1, application servers in layer 2, and data servers in layer 3. These various elements are interconnected through various Local Area Networks (LANs), routers, and firewalls. A firewall is a special type of router that can be configured to block flow of packets from one network to another. This is important to shield important internal servers from external attacks. The flow of a request in Fig. 4.11 would be as follows. Requests arrive at the load balancer through the router that connects the site to the Internet. The load balancer then decides which Web server should receive the request. The next section discusses load balancing in more detail. A firewall (firewall 1) isolates LAN 1 from the internal part of the site. The zone that is accessible to the outside world is called the demilitarized zone (DMZ). Firewall 1 ensures that any of the Web servers in layer 1 only receive requests from the load balancer and not from the outside world. Web servers send requests to application servers. Firewall 2 ensures that application servers are only contacted by Web servers. Finally, if an application server needs data from a database server, the request has to flow through firewall 3.

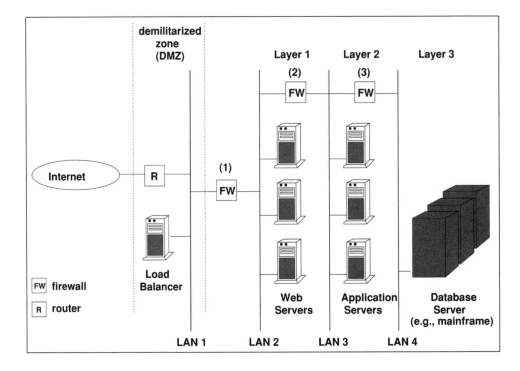

Figure 4.11. Typical Multi-Tier E-Business Site Architecture.

Multi-tier architectures aim at obtaining the following benefits: scalability, availability, security, and integration with legacy data that reside on mainframes. Security can be improved by the use of firewalls that restrict access to application servers and database servers to Web servers only as explained above. Security to users can also be provided by the use of authentication protocols such as SSL and TLS discussed in Chapter 5. Scalability and availability are obtained by using multiple servers at each layer. Also, load balancing mechanisms can be used to improve overall performance.

4.4   Dynamic Load Balancing

With many sites getting millions of hits per day, traffic to a Web server may get too high for one computer to handle it effectively. The obvious solution to servicing a heavy traffic load is to put more servers to work. There are a number of techniques to split the traffic across servers, but three common methods are DNS-based (Domain Name Server), dispatcher-based, and server-based [4].

The latter is a technique by which the server responds to a client with a new server address to which the client will resubmit the request. The redirected URL could be on the same computer as the main server or any one of several back-end mirror computers. The main server redirects the traffic to back-end Web servers according to some load balancing mechanism. Although the technique is transparent to users, it adds an extra connection to the original request and may, in some cases, increase the user response time and network traffic on the Internet or intranets. The DNS service translates a domain name to an IP address. Thus, when the DNS service receives a mapping request, it selects the IP address of one of the servers in the cluster. In round-robin DNS systems, the Web server name is associated with a list of IP addresses. Each IP address on the list maps to a different server, and each server contains a mirrored version of the website or access to a common file system. When a request is received, the Web server name is translated to the next IP address on the list. By translating Web server names to IP addresses in a round-robin fashion, this technique tries to balance the load among the servers. Another technique, called *single-IP-image*, has been used for distributing HTTP requests for a single service to different machines in a cluster. Basically, the technique uses the address of a special TCP router as the single address of the Web cluster. Client requests are addressed to the router that, by its turn, dispatches them to a server, according to some scheduling rules (i.e., server load characteristics). To make the dispatching transparent to users, the selected server returns the response with the router address, rather than its own address.

4.5   Third Party Services

The infrastructure for electronic business includes services provided by many independent institutions and companies. Third parties have widely varying scopes in electronic business, ranging from providing credit card authorization to generating advertisement banners. A special class of third party service providers is defined as

> "A trusted third party is an impartial organization delivering business confidence, through commercial and technical security features, to an electronic transaction. It supplies technically and legally reliable means of carrying out, facilitating, producing independent evidence about and/or arbitrating on an electronic transaction. Its services are provided and underwritten by technical, legal, financial and/or structural means [11]."

Users and businesses demand high availability (i.e., twenty-four hours, 365 days) from information services of trusted third parties. For example, when a credit card authorization system goes offline for a period of time, all the merchants and stores that rely on that party for credit authorization lose customers and revenue. Third party vendors can also be a source of additional delays to website response times. Some retailers adopt the practice of selling ads on their Web storefronts. However, those ads that are generated by external sites may slow down site performance. To minimize the problems caused by external ads, most e-commerce sites establish tight restrictions, such as the maximum size of the advertisement banners or the impossibility of pop-up ads.

Example 4.5

Suppose the Web servers of a portal company are served by a third-party ad server cluster. On average, each page sent out by the portal contains three ad banners. Therefore, a reply to each incoming HTTP request to the portal generates three requests to the ad server. The maximum throughput of the ad server cluster is 1800 ads/sec. What is the maximum number of HTTP requests that can be served by the Web portal?

Every request completed at the portal generates an average of three requests at the ad server. So, the portal throughput cannot exceed one third of the throughput of the ad server. Hence,

$$\text{PortalThroughput} = \text{AdServerThroughput}/\text{NumberOfVisitsToAdServer}$$
$$= 1,800/3 = 600 \text{ requests/sec}.$$

$$(4.5.5)$$

So, the maximum number of HTTP requests that can be served by the Web portal is 600 requests/sec. ■

4.6   Infrastructure Cost

Estimating the cost of e-business infrastructures is a key step toward a quantitative analysis of issues such as ROI (return on investment) and SLAs (service level agreements). The cost of operating a typical e-commerce site can be substantial and includes the cost of site development staff and infrastructure, i.e., hardware, software, and network services. Also, initial costs to set up an e-commerce site must be considered.

Cost models serve several purposes: i) they identify the cost of different types of transactions; ii) they can be used to answer "what-if" questions that come up in capacity planning studies, such as "What is the cost × benefit ratio of installing an additional T3 line in our e-commerce site?" As an example, let us analyze a simple cost model that breaks down the site infrastructure costs into three categories.

- *Capital Equipment.* The costs of equipment that make up the site architecture, i.e., servers, disks, LANs, routers, switches, and firewalls.

- *Network Costs.* The costs of connecting the site to an ISP, comprised of costs due to leased links (eg., T1, T3, or OC-3).

- *Operational Costs.* The costs that stem from the operations needed to keep the site up and running on twenty-four hours a day and seven days a week. It includes personnel, facilities, network operations and maintenance, uninterruptible power service, heating and air conditioning, and building rent.

Example 4.6

Consider an online bookstore that sells books and CDs. Let us assume that total monthly infrastructure cost is around $50,000 and the total number of requests processed by the site during one month was 3,210,102. By analyzing the logs of the Web servers, we found that only 1.5% of all requests (i.e., Search, Browse, Select, Add, and Login) result in purchase. In terms of the infrastructure of the site, what is the average cost of each purchase and the average number of requests per purchase?

Let us first calculate the number of requests per purchase:

$$NumberOfRequestPerPurchase = \frac{TotalNumberOfRequests}{NumberOfPurchases}$$
$$= 3,210,102/(3,210,102 \times 0.015)$$
$$= 66.7 \text{ requests.} \qquad (4.6.6)$$

The average cost per purchase is given by

$$AverageCostPerPurchase = \frac{MonthlyCost}{NumberOfPurchases}$$
$$= \$50,000/(3,210,102 \times 0.015)$$
$$= \$1.04. \qquad (4.6.7)$$

∎

Another cost model for e-business sites could be derived from the cost of using third party companies that provide Web hosting services. In this case, the Web hosting cost should be analyzed together with the service level provided by the third party.

4.7   Summary

As the demand on Web services grows, the infrastructure of websites and the Internet should have enough capacity to handle changes in demand and maintain the quality of service. In this chapter, we analyzed many issues related to the infrastructure to support electronic businesses. A summary of the main issues follows.

- The design of the infrastructure for electronic business and services should focus not only on performance, but also on other key issues that are essential to the quality of information services, such as availability, scalability, and maintainability.

- A series of typical questions, whose answers can help explain the infrastructure requirements of an electronic business, were presented.

- The architecture of an electronic business system provides a framework for its evolution and for making decisions about the future, such as what technologies to adopt and when to change the system.

- The main components of a typical infrastructure for electronic business have strong influence on the quality of service. These components are the Web server, application server, database server, transaction server, mainframe, caching proxy server, and ISP.

- The multi-tier website architecture, composed of Web servers, application servers, and database servers, aim at obtaining the following benefits: scalability, availability, security, and integration with legacy data that reside on mainframes.

- Dynamic load balancing schemes are an obvious solution to split heavy traffic across the multiple servers of an e-business site.

- The infrastructure for electronic business includes services provided by many independent institutions and companies, known as third parties. Performance and availability of third party services are essential for the quality of service perceived by customers.

- Estimating the cost of the e-business infrastructure is a key step toward a quantitative analysis of issues such as ROI (return on investment), SLAs (service level agreements), and cost per transaction.

Bibliography

[1] P. Bernstein and E. Newcomer, *Principles of Transaction Processing*, Morgan Kaufmann Publishers, Inc., San Francisco, 1996.

[2] B. Boehm, "Engineering Context," *First International Workshop on Architecture for Software Systems*, April 1995, Seattle, WA.

[3] A. Brown, D. Oppenheimer, K. Keeton, R. Thomas, J. Kubiatowicz, and D. Patterson, "ISTORE: Introspective Storage for Data-intensive Network Services," *Proc. 7th Workshop on Hot Topics in Operating Systems (HotOS-VII)*, Rio Rico, Arizona, March 1999.

[4] J. Cardellini, M. Colajanni, and P. Yu, "Dynamic Load Balancing on Web-server Systems," *IEEE Internet Computing*, May-June 1999.

[5] L. Camp, M. Harkavy, J. Tygar, and B. Yee, "Anonymous Atomic Transactions," *Proc. Second Usenix Workshop on Electronic Commerce*, 1996.

[6] B. Devlin, J. Gray, B. Laing, and G. Spix, "Scalability Terminology: Farms, Clones, Partitions and Packs: RACS and RAPS," Technical Report MS-TR-99-85, Microsoft Research, Dec. 1999.

[7] J. Gray and A. Reuter, *Transaction Processing: Concepts and Techniques*, Morgan Kaufmann Publishers, Inc., San Francisco, 1992.

[8] CNET, "Net Retailers in Eye of Holiday Storm," November 22, 1999, http://www.cnet.com

[9] J. Hennessy, "The Future of Systems Research," *Computer*, August 1999.

[10] B. Kinicki, D. Finkel, M. Mikhailov, and J. Sommers, "Electronic Commerce Performance Study," *Proc. Euromedia'98 Conference*, DeMonfort University, Leicester, UK, Jan. 1998, pp. 26–34.

[11] D. Lekkas et al, "User Requirements of Trusted Third Parties in Europe," in *User Identification and Privacy Protection: application in public administration and electronic commerce*, IFIP WG 8.5 and WS 9.6, Sweden, June 1999.

[12] S. Lewandowski, "Frameworks for Component-Based Client/Server Computing," *ACM Computing Surveys*, vol. 30, no. 1, 1998.

[13] D. Patterson and J. Hennessy, *Computer Architecture: a Quantitative Approach*, Morgan Kaufmann Publishers, Inc., 1996.

[14] P. Lloyd and G. Galambos, "Technical Reference Architecture, " *IBM Systems J.*, vol. 38, no. 1, 1999.

[15] D. McDavid, "A Standard for Business Architecture Description," *IBM Systems J.*, vol. 38, no. 1, 1999.

[16] C. Peng et al., "Accessing Existing Business Data from the World Wide Web," *IBM Systems J.*, vol. 37, no. 1, 1998.

[17] Transaction Processing Performance Council, www.tpc.org.

[18] G. W. Treese and L. C. Stewart *Designing Systems For Internet Commerce*, Addison Wesley Longman, Inc., Reading 1998.

[19] N. Yeager and R. McGrath, *Web Server Technology*, Morgan Kaufmann Publishers, Inc., San Francisco 1996.

[20] R. Youngs, D. Redmond-Pyle, P. Spaas, and E. Kahan, "A Standard for Architecture Description," *IBM Systems J.*, vol. 38, no. 1, 1999.

Chapter 5

A Quantitative Analysis of Authentication Services

5.1 Introduction

Security is an important attribute of most information systems. E-business is a good example of an application area in which security plays an important role. There are many excellent books that describe in detail how security is implemented in e-commerce [5]. Our focus in this book is to show how the mechanisms and protocols used to support security may impact system performance. It has been reported by many that the throughput of Web servers can be significantly reduced when they have to deal with secure sessions, which require compute-intensive computations [1] [7] [8].

This chapter offers a quantitative analysis of the security mechanisms used in e-business. Many quantitative examples illustrate the tradeoffs between performance and security. In particular, the chapter analyzes how authentication protocols such as the Transport Layer Security protocol, a successor of the Secure Sockets Layer (SSL) protocol, affects performance. To make our presentation self-contained, we present in the next section a crash course on security. Our discussion here rests on security at the network level and not on security at the server level (e.g., operating system and database security or even physical security).

5.2 Security 101

Security can be divided into the following categories: authentication, confidentiality, data integrity, availability (denial of service), and non-repudiation.

5.2.1 Security Categories

Authentication is the process by which two parties involved in a dialogue are given a guarantee that they are indeed interacting with whom they think they are interacting. For example, when you access the website of your favorite online bookstore, you want to make sure that you are indeed interacting with that site and not with an impostor. This is called server authentication. Ghosh describes how impostors can get in the way between a browser and a website [5]. An e-business site may also want to authenticate a business partner to make sure that an order is being placed by someone known and registered with the site. This is called client authentication. Online banking offers a good example of the importance of client authentication [14].

Confidentiality deals with protecting the contents of messages or data transmitted over the Internet from unauthorized people. For example, you want to protect your credit card information when you buy over the Internet.

Data integrity is related to preventing data from being modified by an attacker. Suppose that only your credit card information were protected while being transmitted but the contents of your order (e.g., books ordered and shipping address) were not. Then, an attacker could potentially modify your order while it is being transmitted over the network by adding or deleting books from your order or even changing the delivery address to that of the attacker.

It is also important to guarantee that authentic users of an e-business site are given access to the site when they need it. Suppose that an attacker sets up a program that continuously attempts to be authenticated by a site. Since the attacker is not a valid user, the authentication will fail. However, precious resources would be wasted at the e-commerce site to deny access to the attacker. These resources become unavailable to legitimate users. In an extreme case, such an attack could bring a system to its knees making it unavailable to valid users. This is called a *denial of service* attack and reduces the *availability* of the site.

Non-repudiation is an attribute of secure systems that prevents the sender of a message from denying having sent it. This may be important for e-businesses such as online trading which want to ensure that a customer will not be able to deny having requested to buy or sell securities.

Cryptography can be used to support authentication, confidentiality, data integrity, and non-repudiation. We discuss the basic principles of cryptography in the next subsection.

5.2.2   Cryptography

Cryptography is a technique by which data, called *plaintext*, is scrambled or encrypted in such a way that it becomes extremely difficult, expensive, and time consuming for an unauthorized person to unscramble or decrypt it. The scrambled text is called *ciphertext*. See Shneier [13] for a good discussion on cryptography.

Encryption and decryption comprises the following general steps:

- The sender of a message Msg uses an encryption algorithm Encrypt and an encryption key Key_e to generate the encrypted version $EncryptedMsg$ of Msg. So,

$$EncryptedMsg = \text{Encrypt } (Msg, Key_e). \qquad (5.2.1)$$

- The recipient of an encrypted message $EncryptedMsg$ uses a decryption algorithm Decrypt and a decryption key Key_d to obtain the original message Msg. Thus,

$$Msg = \text{Decrypt } (EncryptedMsg, Key_d). \qquad (5.2.2)$$

There are two classes of cryptographic algorithms: symmetric algorithms and public-key (PK) ones. In symmetric algorithms, the same key is used for encryption and decryption. In other words, $Key_e = Key_d$. This common key is called a secret key and has to be shared between the sender and the receiver of a message. Anyone who discovers the secret key will be able to decrypt any messages encrypted with that key. It is assumed that the encryption and decryption algorithms are known to everyone. Examples of symmetric cryptographic algorithms include the Data Encryption Standard (DES), triple-DES (TDES), IDEA, RC2, RC4, and RC5 [13]. Symmetric cryptography is illustrated in Fig. 5.1.

The PK algorithms use two different keys: a private key (K_{priv}), known only to the receiver of a message, and a public key (K_{pub}) associated to that receiver. The public key is known to everybody and is used for encryption. The receiver uses its private key to decrypt messages sent to it.

We describe, with the help of Fig. 5.2, how public key cryptography works. Suppose that A wants to send a message to B using PK encryption and assume that B's public and private keys are K_{pub}^B and K_{priv}^B, respectively. Then, the steps below are followed:

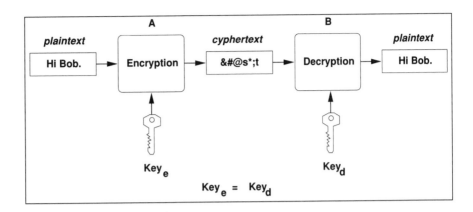

Figure 5.1. Symmetric Encryption and Decryption.

- A encrypts the message Msg using a PK encryption algorithm PKEncrypt and B's public key K_{pub}^B to generate the encrypted message $EncryptedMsg$. Hence,

$$EncryptedMsg = \text{PKEncrypt } (Msg, Key_{\text{pub}}^B). \qquad (5.2.3)$$

- When B receives an encrypted message $EncryptedMsg$, it uses a PK decryption algorithm PKDecrypt and its private key Key_{priv}^B to obtain the original message Msg. So,

$$Msg = \text{PKDecrypt}(EncryptedMsg, Key_{\text{priv}}^B). \qquad (5.2.4)$$

The most common PK algorithm is RSA [12]. An RSA operation, whether encrypting or decrypting, is essentially a modular exponentiation. In general, it is common to choose a small public exponent (e.g., the numbers 17 or 23) for the public key and a large exponent for the private key. This makes encryption faster than decryption [11]. Encryption time is also a function of the size in bits of the modulus, also called key length. It should be noted that longer keys provide significantly increased levels of security.

This behavior of the RSA algorithm was illustrated in measurements [4], which are reproduced in Table 5.1. The table shows the time, in msec,

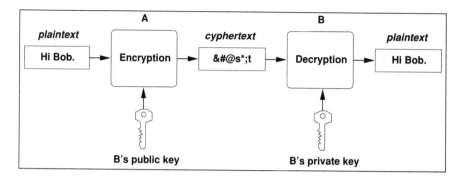

Figure 5.2. Public Key Encryption and Decryption.

required to perform private and public operations on a 128-byte block as a function of the key length used in the operation.

The following conclusions can be drawn from Table 5.1:

- the private key operation time grows with k^3, where k is the key length in bits;

- the public key operation time grows with k^2;

Table 5.1. Timings for PK Operations; Measurements Taken on a Pentium-II 266 MHz Running Linux.

Key Size (bits)	Public Key Operation Time (msec)	Private Key Operation Time (msec)
512	3.5	39.9
768	7.3	112.2
1024	12.8	255.8
1280	19.0	455.5
1536	26.8	771.8
1792	36.2	1214.8
2048	46.8	1796.0

- the public key operation time, even for a small 128-byte block, is of the same order of magnitude of a disk access time; and

- the private key operation time varies from one to two orders of magnitude greater than a disk access time.

The above observations imply that PK encryption cannot be efficiently used for bulk data transfer. As one advantage of PK encryption, it is not necessary to exchange a secret key before two parties can communicate through a secure channel since the key used for encryption is public. Symmetric cryptography, on the other hand, is much faster than PK cryptography but requires the exchange of a secret key. Current software implementations of RSA are a hundred times slower than DES. In hardware, DES is a thousand to ten thousand times faster than RSA [4] [11].

Authentication protocols, as described in Section 5.4, try to used the best properties of both symmetric and PK algorithms: they use PK algorithms to exchange a secret key and symmetric cryptography for bulk secure data transfer.

5.3   Digital Signatures

PK encryption can be used for digitally signing an electronic document in a way that allows for later validation for authenticity [5]. We explain here, with the help of Fig. 5.3, how digital signatures work.

Suppose that A wants to send a message Msg to B. The following steps are followed by A before sending the message.

1. A generates a fixed size string, called the *message digest* (MD), by applying a one-way *hash function* h to the message Msg. So MD = $h\,(Msg)$. For a hash function to be useful for digital signatures, it must have the following properties:

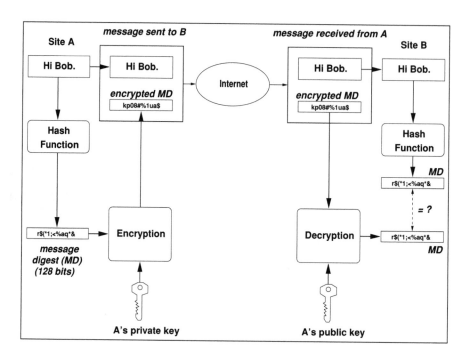

Figure 5.3. Digital Signatures.

- it should be easy to compute $h\ (Msg)$,
- it should be very hard to obtain Msg given $h\ (Msg)$, and
- it should be very hard to find another message Msg' such that $h\ (Msg) = h\ (Msg')$.

Examples of hash functions used to compute message digests are MD4, MD5, SHA, and SHA-1 [13]. The size of the strings generated by these functions are 128, 128, 160, and 160 bits, respectively.

2. The message digest MD is encrypted with A's private key Key^A_{priv}, resulting in an encrypted message digest Encrypt (MD, Key^A_{priv}).

3. At this point, A assembles a message to be sent to B, composed of the original message and the encrypted message digest. Thus, A sends to B the pair $(Msg, \text{Encrypt (MD, } Key^A_{\text{priv}}))$.

4. B receives the pair (Msg, Encrypt (MD, Key^A_{priv})) from A and does the following:

- it computes the message digest MD from the message Msg using the same hash function h used by A.
- it decrypts the encrypted message digest Encrypt (MD, Key^A_{priv}) received from A using A's public key. In other words, B performs the computation Decrypt (Encrypt (MD, Key^A_{priv}), Key^A_{pub}). The result should be the original message digest MD if a) the message was not tampered with during transmission and b) the message was indeed sent by A. If the message was not sent by A, then using A's public key would not produce the same message digest. If the message was corrupted during transmission, a different message digest would have been computed by B.

Steps 1-3 above are the steps needed to sign a message and step 4 is the verification step. A message is signed with the private key of the signer and verified with the public key of the signing party. Thus, for the reasons explained in Section 5.2.2, message verification is much faster than message signing.

So, as we can see, digital signatures can be used to verify the authenticity of the sender of the message and to verify data integrity. If we wanted to ensure confidentiality as well, the message contents should also be encrypted.

We are now ready to explain in the next section how authentication protocols work.

5.4 Authentication Protocols

Secure Sockets Layer (SSL), a protocol developed by Netscape, offers authentication, confidentiality, and non-repudiation of Web servers and end-users. SSL is a session layer protocol that runs on top of TCP and was superseded by the Transport Layer Security (TLS) protocol [3]. TLS is now an IETF RFC and contains minor changes with respect to SSL version 3.0. We will be referring to TLS in the rest of our discussion. However, most of what we say here is also applicable to SSL.

Figure 5.4 depicts the protocol stack showing an application protocol such as HTTP running on top of TLS. TLS allows the server to authenticate itself to the client by presenting to it a verifiable certificate containing a public key (more on this later) and by demonstrating that it can decrypt a message encrypted with that public key (this demonstrates to the client that the server has the corresponding private key). The client may optionally authenticate itself to the server.

TLS itself is decomposed into two protocols: the TLS Handshake Protocol and the TLS Record Protocol. The TLS Record Protocol compresses data, applies MAC (Message Authentication Code) to the messages, and encrypts data using symmetric encryption.

The Handshake Protocol is responsible for the selection of

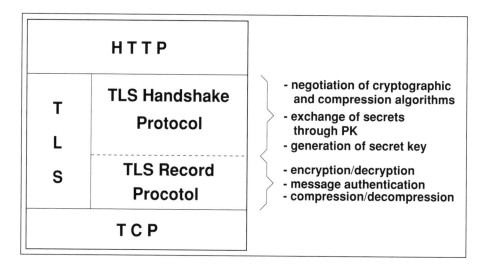

Figure 5.4. Protocol Stack Including HTTP, TLS, and TCP.

- the PK algorithm (e.g., RSA) and key used for the transmission of a shared secret,

- the bulk encryption algorithm (e.g., DES) and secret keys to be used during the session by the Record Protocol,

- the MAC (e.g., MD5) used by the Record Protocol for message authentication, and

- the compression algorithms to be used by the Record Protocol.

During the handshake phase of the protocol, the server authenticates itself to the client and the client optionally authenticates itself to the server. The authentication is accomplished with a combination of certificates issued by trusted Certificate Authorities (CAs), signature and verification using message digests and PK encryption as explained in the following section.

5.4.1 Authentication with Certificates

We describe in this subsection how servers authenticate themselves to clients. The reverse is quite similar. When a server wants to authenticate itself to a client, the server must present to the client a certificate signed by a trusted Certificate Authority (CA). Such authorities endorse the identity of the sites registered with them.

The process of generating a certificate is illustrated in Fig. 5.5.

The server information (e.g., name, issuer CA, serial number, and validity) and its public key are part of the certificate along with a digest of the server information encrypted with the CA's private key. This combination forms a standard X.509 certificate [2].

Most browsers have a list of trusted CAs. This list includes the public key for each CA. When a browser receives a server certificate, it checks for the issuing CA on its list and retrieves the CA's public key. This key is used to decrypt the message digest in the certificate (see Fig. 5.6). The browser

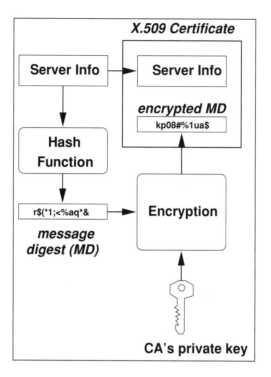

Figure 5.5. Generation of a Server Certificate.

uses the same hash function used to create the message digest in the first place and recreates the message digest from the server information. If the recreated digest matches the decrypted digest, the certificate was signed by the CA and the server is authenticated.

5.4.2   Description of TLS

TLS is a client server algorithm. We describe next the exchange of messages that takes place when a client wants to establish a secure connection with a server. Figure 5.7 shows the CSID that represents the authentication protocol. The figure shows two interactions: $1 \rightarrow 2 \rightarrow 3 \rightarrow 4$ and $1 \rightarrow 2 \rightarrow 5 \rightarrow 6 \rightarrow 7$. The former represents the case in which a secure TLS connection has to be established from scratch (full handshake) and the latter

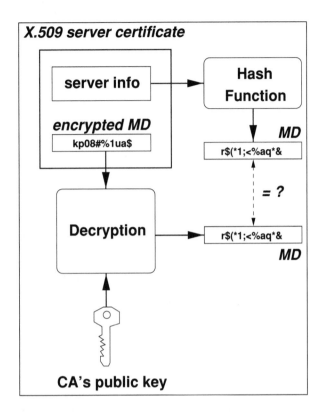

Figure 5.6. Verification of a Server Certificate.

represents the case in which a TLS session is setup by using the session state cached at the server from a recent session between the same client and the server. By allowing session states to be cached, TLS allows for faster session establishment as illustrated below.

We describe below the steps followed during the establishment of a secure connection in the case of a full handshake.

1. The client sends a "Client Hello" message to the server to indicate that it wants to start the handshake process. This message contains a random number generated by the client (28 bytes), the time measured at the client (4 bytes), a session ID (from 0 to 32 bytes), the set of cryp-

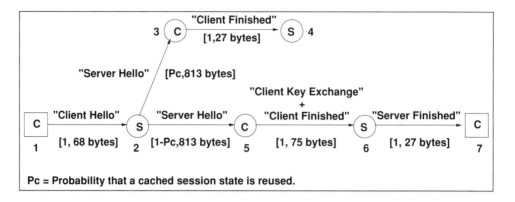

Figure 5.7. CSID for the Connection Establishment Phase of TLS.

tographic algorithms (cipher suites)(2 bytes) supported by the client for key exchange, for bulk encryption, and for message authentication, the compression method to be used (1 byte), and the protocol version (1 byte).

2. The server receives the "Client Hello" message and sends a "Server Hello" message to the client. This message contains a X.509 server certificate (750 bytes), a server random number (28 bytes), a server session ID (0 to 32 bytes) different from the client session ID, the cipher suites supported by the server (2 bytes), and the compression method supported by the server (1 byte).

3. The client receives the "Server Hello Message" and authenticates the server using its certificate, generates a premaster secret (48 bytes), which is encrypted with the server's public key and sent to the server in a "Client Key Exchange Message." The client then generates the key to be used for bulk encryption from the premaster secret and the client and server random numbers.

4. The client sends a twenty-seven-byte "Client Finished" message to the server to indicate that it is done with the handshake.

5. The server receives the "Client Key Exchange Message" and decrypts the premaster secret using its private key. The server then generates the key used for bulk data transmission from the premaster secret, the client and server random numbers.

6. For verification purposes, the server encrypts a digest of all messages previously received from the client with the key for bulk encryption and sends it to the server in a twenty-seven-byte "Server Finished" message. This marks the end of the handshake process.

If the client establishes a new session while its session state is cached at the server, TLS can skip the authentication and secret negotiation steps. To establish a TLS session using cached state, the client sends the session ID of the session it wants to reuse. If the state of that session is still cached at the server, it replies with a "Server Hello" message with a session ID equal to the client session ID sent in the "Client Hello" message and new server random numbers. The client and server generate new session keys from the cached state and the new random numbers. Session caching eliminates the use of PK during session establishment and cuts down the number of messages from four to three (see Fig. 5.7).

An analysis of the CSID for TLS (see Fig. 5.7) reveals the following.

- A full handshake adds two round trip times (RTTs) between the client and server to the network delay involved in fulfilling an HTTP request. The round trip latency for a slow Internet is on the order of 161 msec and for a fast Internet is on the order of 89 msec [9]. This implies that authentication with TLS adds from 178 to 322 msec to the response time perceived by a user during the authentication phase.

- The byte overhead of a TLS connection, in the case of a full handshake, is 983 bytes (assuming thirty-two bytes for client and server IDs). The average size of a page returned by an HTTP request is about 4 Kbytes.

So, the overhead is almost 25%. If the client is coming over a slow modem connection, one can expect effective transmission rates on the order of 4 Kbytes/sec. Thus, the byte overhead of TLS' Handshake Protocol, incurs an additional 240 (= 983/4096) msec to the latency mentioned above.

The description of TLS presented in this section was simplified to abstract the main features of the protocol. Dierks and Allen [3] provide a complete description of the protocol.

This section discusses, through several examples, how authentication protocols such as TLS affect the performance of e-business sites.

In the examples discussed in this section, we use the timings for client and server operations [1] displayed in Tables 5.2 and 5.3.

We also assume in the examples the following setting. Several clients are connected to the server through a high-speed LAN. Clients continuously request files that are 16,384 bytes long. The average CPU time involved in accessing a file at the server is 0.002 sec when no processing is involved for establishing secure connections, and the average disk time to retrieve a file at the server is 0.010 sec.

The encryption/decryption rates as well as the message digest generation/verification rates are given in Table 5.4 for 1024-byte blocks and for three encryption/decryption algorithms (RC4, DES, and 3DES) and for

Table 5.2. Timings in (msec) for Client Operations During TLS Handshake.

Key Size (bits)	Verification of Server Certificate	Encryption of Master Secret w/Public Key	Key Generation from Master Secret	Total Time
512	2.40	1.31	0.10	3.81
768	3.61	2.16	0.10	5.87
1024	7.09	5.20	0.10	12.39

Table 5.3. Timings in (msec) for Server Operations During TLS Handshake.

Key Size (bits)	Decryption of Master Secret with Private Key	Generation of Keys from Master Secret	Total
512	10.13	0.10	10.23
768	23.66	0.10	23.76
1024	47.93	0.10	48.03

three MD generation/verification algorithms (MD5, SHA, and SHA1). It should be noted that performance decreases as one goes from the first to the last row in the table and security increases in the same direction.

Example 5.1

We consider in this example the impact on server throughput, measured in requests/sec, due to the use of TLS. We assume here that all requests involve a full handshake, i.e., no session reuse is assumed. It is assumed that RC4 is used as the algorithm for data encryption and that MD5 is used for message authentication by TLS' Record Protocol. The results of this example consider four cases: i) insecure connections, and secure connections using TLS for key sizes of ii) 512, iii) 768, and iv) 1024 bits for the PK cryptography used in the Handshake Protocol.

Table 5.4. Encryption/Decryption and Message Digest Generation/Verification Rates (in Mbps).

Encryption/Decryption		MD Generation/Verification	
RC4	140	MD5	180
DES	40	SHA	130
3DES	15	SHA1	130

We evaluated the server throughput as a function of the load, measured by the number of clients actively sending requests to the server. The first step in evaluating the server throughput is computing the service demands, i.e., total time spent by a request at the client, network, server CPU, and server disk.

The time spent at the client is the sum of the time spent during the handshake phase (see Table 5.2) plus the time spent in decryption and verification during the file retrieval phase. The time spent at this phase is computed by dividing the file size by the proper rates given in Table 5.4. For example, in the case of a 1024-bit key for the PK algorithm used in the handshake phase and for RC4 and MD5 as the algorithms used by the Record Protocol, the service demand at the client can be computed as

$$0.01239 + \frac{16,384 \times 8}{140,000,000} + \frac{16,384 \times 8}{180,000,000} = 0.01405 \text{ sec.} \tag{5.4.5}$$

The first term in Eq. (5.4.5) is the time spent during the handshake part of the session. The second and third parts of the equation represent the times spent decrypting and verifying a file that is 16,384 bytes long.

The server CPU computation is similar. We must now use the values in Table 5.3 for the time spent during the handshake at the server and the values in Table 5.4 to compute the time spent in the file transfer phase. For example, the service demand at the server CPU assuming 1024-bit keys is given by

$$0.002 + 0.04803 + \frac{16,384 \times 8}{140,000,000} + \frac{16,384 \times 8}{180,000,000} = 0.05169 \text{ sec.} \tag{5.4.6}$$

The first term in Eq. (5.4.6) is the CPU time at the server excluding TLS-related processing. The second term is the handshake part, and the third and fourth account for time spent during the file tranfer phase in TLS-related processing. Table 5.5 shows the service demands for all resources and the three key sizes.

The throughput curves, shown in Fig. 5.8, were obtained with the help of queuing network models such as the ones discussed in Chapters 8 and 9. The

Table 5.5. Service Demands (in msec) for RC4 and MD5.

Resource	Key Size (bits)		
	512	768	1024
Client	5.474	7.534	14.054
Network	1.737	1.737	1.737
Server CPU	13.894	27.424	51.694
Server disk	10.000	10.000	10.000

purpose of this chapter is not to discuss the models themselves but rather to illustrate the tradeoffs between security and performance. At any rate, the curious reader may want to know that we used a closed queuing network model to solve the examples in this section. The MS Excel workbook called `ch05-examples.xls` and used in this and other examples in this chapter, can be downloaded from the site associated with the book (see the preface) by following the link called **Chapter 5**.

Figure 5.8 shows that in all four cases, the throughput increases almost linearly at the beginning as the load increases and saturates at its maximum value. The maximum throughput is limited by the bottleneck resource, i.e., the one with the largest service demand. The bottleneck for the insecure connection case is the disk at the server, which has the largest service demand. However, when secure connections are used, the bottleneck shifts to the CPU.

The maximum throughput is the inverse of the maximum service demand (see Chapter 8) [9]. So, the maximum throughput in the case of insecure connections is $1/0.01 = 100$ requests/sec. For key sizes of 512, 768, and 1024 bits, the upper bound on the throughput falls to 72.0 ($= 1/13.894$) requests/sec, 36.4 ($= 1/27.424$) requests/sec, and 19.3 ($= 1/51.654$) requests/sec, respectively. Thus, the maximum throughput for 1024-bit keys, recommended for US domestic use, is 20% of the throughput one obtains

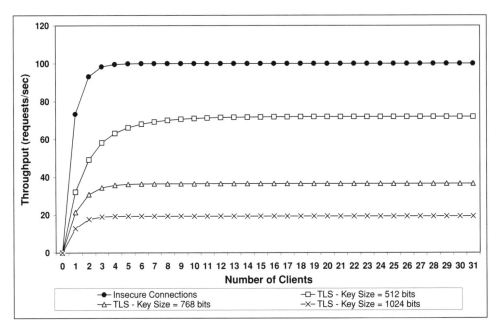

Figure 5.8. Throughput (in requests/sec) vs. Number of Clients for Insecure Connections and TLS for Various Key Sizes (RC4 Is Used for Encryption and MD5 for Message Authentication During Data Transfer).

without the use of cryptography.

The response time vs. throughput curve for the same case is given in Fig. 5.9. As it can be seen for each of the four cases, as the server approaches saturation, the response time goes to infinity very quickly. ∎

This example showed us that the service demand posed at the client and server processors due to the use of authentication protocols is the sum of the time spent during the handshake phase plus the time spent during the data transfer phase on encryption/decryption and message digest generation and verification.

Example 5.2

Consider the previous example, but assume now that 40% of the requests are for insecure documents and the remaining 60% for secure documents.

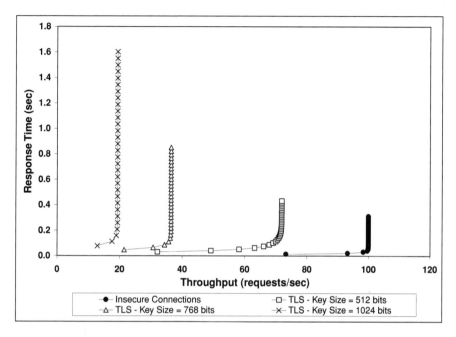

Figure 5.9. Response Time vs. Throughput (in requests/sec) Insecure Connections and TLS for Various Key Sizes (RC4 Is Used for Encryption and MD5 for Message Authentication During Data Transfer).

What is the maximum server throughput assuming 1024-bit keys and RC4 and MD5 for the data transfer phase?

We have to recompute the service demand for the server CPU by averaging the cases of secure and non-secure requests. So, the new CPU demand at the server becomes

$$0.4 \times 0.002 + 0.6 \times 0.051694 = 0.0318 \text{ sec}, \qquad (5.4.7)$$

which is higher than the 0.010 sec at the disk. So, the CPU is still the bottleneck, but the maximum throughput is 31.43 (= 1/0.0318) requests/sec, 62% higher than the maximum throughput for the case when all requests require the establishment of a TLS session. We can generalize this analysis for any value F_s of the fraction of secure connections. The upper bound on the throughput X is given by

$$X \leq \frac{1}{\max\left[0.010, (1 - F_s) \times 0.002 + F_s \times 0.051694\right]}. \tag{5.4.8}$$

The relationship between the maximum throughput and the fraction of secure connections is illustrated in Fig. 5.10. As seen for low values of F_s, the bottleneck is the disk and the throughput is bounded at 100 requests/sec. As more requests use the TLS protocol, the bottleneck moves to the CPU and the maximum throughput drops in a nonlinear way with the fraction of secure connections. ∎

Example 5.3

Consider now that management wants to evaluate the impact of using stronger algorithms for the data transfer phase. Instead of using RC4 and

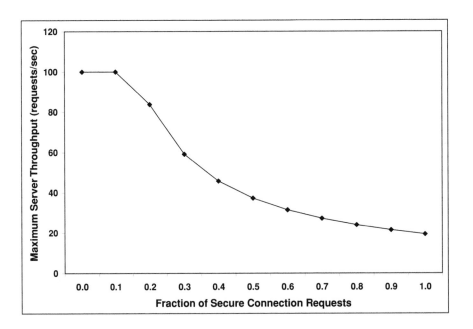

Figure 5.10. Maximum Throughput (in requests/sec) vs. Fraction of Secure Connections.

MD5, management wants to know how the server maximum throughput is going to be impacted if 3DES and SHA1 were used instead.

To answer this question, we use the rates given in Table 5.4 and redo the computations shown in Eqs. (5.4.5) and (5.4.6) to compute the service demands. From the service demands, we compute the upper bound on the throughput as the inverse of the maximum service demand. The results of this computation are shown in Fig. 5.11. The picture shows the price to be paid for increased security. For example, the use of 3DES and SHA-1 for 512-bit keys yields a maximum throughput of 45.4 requests/sec as opposed to 100 requests/sec for insecure connections and 71.9 requests/sec for the RC4/MD5 combination. ∎

The most computationally intensive part of PK cryptography is performing integer modular exponentiation on large numbers. Several manufactur-

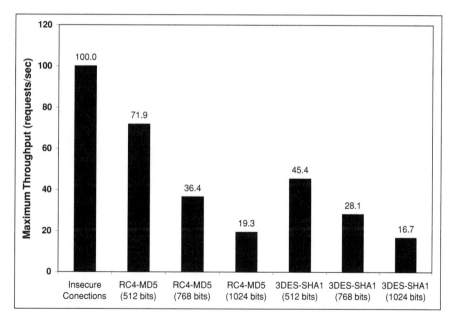

Figure 5.11. Maximum Throughput (in requests/sec) for Insecure Connections and TLS for Various Key Sizes (Combinations of Data Transfer Encryption/Message Authentication Algorithms Are RC4/MD5 and 3DES/SHA-1.)

ers have designed PK math processors that can be used to offload the most time-consuming aspects of PK encryption to special purpose machines called *cryptographic accelerator cards*. These cards implement several modular exponentiation functions including RSA and others as well as random number generation for secure key generation. A 1024-bit private key operation takes on the order of 5 msec in these accelerator cards, a fifty-fold speed increase when compared to performing this operation on a Pentium-II 266 MHz machine (see Table 5.1) The following example illustrates the impact of using cryptographic accelerators.

Example 5.4

Assume that a cryptographic accelerator is used to reduce the PK operation times during the handshake protocol of TLS by a factor of fifty. What are the new bounds on the server throughput?

To answer this question, we need to recompute the service demand at the CPU for the handshake PK operations. In the case of a 1024-bit key for the PK algorithm used in the handshake phase and for RC4 and MD5 as the algorithms used by the Record Protocol, the service demand at the client becomes

$$\frac{0.01239}{50} + \frac{16,384 \times 8}{140,000,000} + \frac{16,384 \times 8}{180,000,000} = 0.001912 \text{ sec} \qquad (5.4.9)$$

and the server CPU demand becomes

$$0.002 + \frac{0.04803}{50} + \frac{16,384 \times 8}{140,000,000} + \frac{16,384 \times 8}{180,000,000} = 0.004625 \text{ sec.} \quad (5.4.10)$$

Equations (5.4.9) and (5.4.10) show where the factor of fifty is applied in reducing the service demand. Table 5.6 shows the new service demands for all resources and the three key sizes. As it can be seen from the table, the largest value of the service demand is for the disk for all three values of the key size. Therefore, the maximum throughput is 100 (= 1/0.010)) requests/sec. ■

Table 5.6. Service Demands (in msec) for RC4 and MD5.

Resource	Key Size (bits)		
	512	768	1024
Client	1.741	1.782	1.912
Network	1.737	1.737	1.737
Server CPU	3.869	4.140	4.625
Server disk	10.000	10.000	10.000

Example 5.5

Suppose that in the case of Ex. 5.1, 60% of the TLS sessions use previously cached state. What are the new values of the CPU service demands at the server? What is the maximum server throughput in this case?

In the case of cached sessions, the server only needs to generate keys from the cached master secret and the newly generated random numbers. So, using the values of Table 5.3, the service demand at the server for 1024-bit keys becomes

$$0.002 + 0.00010 + \frac{16,384 \times 8}{140,000,000} + \frac{16,384 \times 8}{180,000,000} = 0.00376 \text{ sec.} \quad (5.4.11)$$

The second term in Eq. (5.4.11) is the time to generate the keys from the master secret (see Table 5.3) and this term replaces the value of 0.04803 of Eq. (5.4.6).

So, the average service demand at the server CPU, considering the cached and non-cached cases is

$$0.6 \times 0.00376 + 0.4 \times 0.05169 = 0.0229 \text{ sec.} \quad (5.4.12)$$

In the case of 100% non-cached session establishments, the maximum throughput for 1024-bit keys is 19.3 requests/sec (see Ex. 5.1). In this case, the maximum throughput is 43.67 ($= 1/0.0229$) requests/sec, a 2.26-fold increase in throughput as compared with the case of 100% non-cached connections. ∎

5.5   Summary

Security is an important element in the design of e-business sites. However, as most things in life, it isn't free. Performance is the price to be paid for providing authentication, confidentiality, integrity, and non-repudiation to transactions carried out over the Web. This chapter covered the basic principles of security, symmetric and public key encryption, digital signatures, and certificates.

A description of the Transport Layer Security (TLS) protocol was provided along with several numerical examples that illustrated the tradeoffs between performance and security. This tradeoff is becoming more and more important as the demand for secure transactions increases at a very fast rate. The scalability of various distributed authentication protocols such as PKCROSS and PKDA is presented by Harbitter and Menascé [6].

The following points summarize the lessons learned from this chapter.

- Private key (PK) cryptography is orders of magnitude faster than public key cryptography but requires that the communicating parties share a secret key.

- It is much faster to encrypt a message with the public key than to decrypt it with the recipient's private key.

- PK algorithms and one-way hash functions can be used to generate digital signatures. The message is signed with the sender's private key and verified with the sender's public key. Therefore, it is much faster to verify than to sign messages.

- The TLS protocol uses PK encryption during its handshake phase to exchange secrets between the client and the server. These secrets are used to generate private keys used during the data transfer phase.

- The use of authentication protocols such as TLS can decrease server performance by a significant factor.

- Clients in a TLS protocol can reuse session states, and therefore avoid going through the expensive PK operations, if the server still keeps the state of an existing or previous session with that client in its session cache. This can significantly improve performance.

- Cryptographic accelerator cards can substantially reduce the time spent in the most expensive cryptographic operations so that server performance is increased. Since cards are costly, they are typically used on a limited number of front-end Web servers [10].

- TLS is a stateful protocol because state has to be maintained throughout an entire TLS session. This property of the protocol constraint front-end load balancers to route all requests of the same connection to the same Web server. This is called *session stickiness* and may reduce the effectiveness of a load balancer [10].

The next chapter examines the impact of payment protocols such as SET on performance.

Bibliography

[1] G. Apostolopoulos, V. Peris, and D. Saha, "Transport Layer Security: How Much Does It Really Cost?," *Proc. IEEE Infocom*, March 1999.

[2] CCITT, Recommendation X.509: The Directory Authentication Framework, 1988.

[3] T. Dierks and C. Allen, "The TLS Protocol," Version 1.0, *The Internet Engineering Task Force (IETF)*, RFC 2246, January 1999.

[4] W. Freeman and E. Miller, "An Experimental Analysis of Cryptographic Overhead in Performance-Critical Systems," *Proc. Seventh Int. Symp. Modeling, Analysis and Simulation of Computer and Telecommunication Systems (MASCOTS'99)*, Oct. 24-28, 1999, College Park, MD, pp. 348–357.

[5] A. K. Ghosh, *E-Commerce Security: Weak Links Best Defenses*, John Wiley & Sons, New York, NY, 1998.

[6] A. Harbitter and D. A. Menascé, "Performance Issues in Large Distributed System Security," *Proc. 1999 Computer Measurement Group Conference*, Anaheim, CA, Dec. 6-11, 1998, pp. 456–467.

[7] B. Kinicki, D. Finkel, M. Mikhailov, and J. Sommers, "Electronic Commerce Performance Study," *Proc. Euromedia'98 Conference*, DeMonfort University, Leicester, UK, Jan. 1998, pp. 26–34.

[8] A. Lightman, "E-Commerce: the Ins and Outs of Web Site Outages," *Red Herring*, September 1999.

[9] D. A. Menascé, and V. A. F. Almeida, *Capacity Planning for Web Performance: Metrics, Models, and Methods*, Prentice Hall, Upper Saddle River, NJ, 1998.

[10] Microsoft Corp., "A Blueprint for Building Web Sites Using the Microsoft Windows DNA Platform," Jan. 2000, http://msdn.microsoft.com/library/techart/dnablueprint.htm.

[11] RSA Laboratories, "How fast is RSA?," RSA frequently asked questions, http://www.rsasecurity.com/rsalabs/faq/3-1-2.html.

[12] RSA Laboratories, "PKCS #1: RSA Cryptography Specifications," Version 2.0, September 1998.

[13] B. Schneier, *Applied Cryptography*, John Wiley & Sons, New York, NY, 1996.

[14] P. Wing and B. O'Higgins, "Using Public-Key Infrastructures for Security and Risk Management," *IEEE Comm. Magazine*, Sept. 1999, pp. 71–73.

Chapter 6

A Quantitative Analysis of Payment Services

6.1 Introduction

The use of authentication protocols, such as TLS and SSL, to support payments over the Web takes care of mutual authentication between customer and merchant and guarantees that both order and payment information (e.g., credit card number) will be protected when transmitted over the Internet. However, authentication protocols do not guarantee that payment information will be protected while stored in the merchant's computer systems. Also, authentication protocols do not protect customers from misuse of their credit card information by merchants. Merchants are not sure whether customers are legitimate holders of the credit card and customers are not sure if merchants are authorized to receive payments with specified credit cards.

Payment protocols, such as Secure Electronic Transactions (SET), aim at solving these problems. In this chapter, we first provide an overview of what happens when one uses a credit card for payment in the physical world. Then, we discuss how SET allows for credit card payments to take place over the Internet. This chapter is not intended to be a thorough description of SET, but it describes SET at a high enough level of detail to provide the reader with an overall picture of the protocol as well as its performance implications. SET provides a much higher level of security than SSL or TLS. There is, however, a performance penalty as we discuss in this chapter. It should be pointed out that SET is a very complex protocol. Interested readers are referred to Merkow [5], Sherif [8], and SET [7] for more detailed information on SET and to Lu [4] for a formal verification of SET properties. We discuss in this chapter the cryptographic processes used by SET as well as the flow of messages involved in SET transactions. The performance of SET transactions is then discussed through various numerical examples. The chapter concludes with a brief discussion of other payment services.

6.2   Payment Methods

What happens when you go to your favorite brick-and-mortar bookstore GreatBooks and use your credit card to pay for the books you want to buy? We illustrate the process with the help of Fig. 6.1. Suppose you want to use your Visa credit card issued by MyCityBank (the issuer bank). You go to the register, remove your plastic credit card from your leather wallet, and give it to the cashier. She swipes the card through the card reader at the POS (Point-of-Sale) terminal and enters the amount of the transaction (say $52.00) and hits ENTER. This starts an *authorization* request which is sent to the Card Processing Center. The authorization request includes the

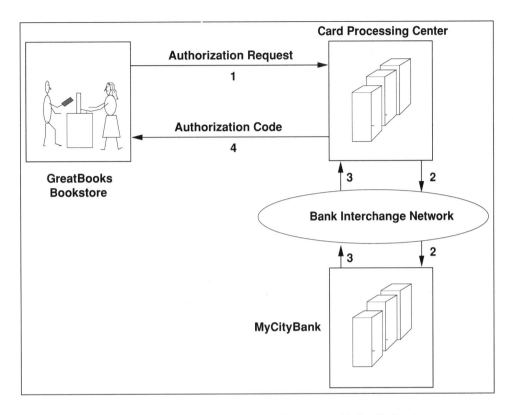

Figure 6.1. Authorization Process for Payments with Credit Cards.

issuer bank ID, the credit card number, and the transaction amount. The Card Processing Center contacts MyCitybank through the Bank Interchange Network and sends the authorization request. MyCitiBank checks your open-to-buy availability, i.e., the amount of money you are currently authorized to spend on your credit card. If this amount is at least equal to the $52.00 required for you to buy the books, the open-to-buy amount is reduced by $52.00 and an authorization code is sent back to the Card Processing Center, which sends it back to GreatBooks bookstore. This debit from your account is temporary and becomes permanent when *settlement*, as described next, takes place.

The POS terminal generates a record, called a *capture record*, for every authorization. The merchant collects several capture records and places them in a *batch settlement file*. Capture records in a batch settlement file contain transactions that may be associated with many different issuer banks for that credit card brand. GreatBooks bookstore sends batch files to the Credit Card Processing Service (see Fig. 6.2). The Credit Card Processing Service sorts the batch settlement file by bank identification number and sends a portion of the batch to each of the issuer banks. Let us take a look at what happens at MyCityBank for example. MyCityBank will transform the temporary debit into a permanent one that will appear in the credit card statement for all transactions that you and others generated in that settlement file for MyCityBank. In the process of doing this, it will compute the total amount of these transactions (say $1,500.00) and generate a wire transfer to the bank that GreatBooks selected to be its *acquirer bank* for Visa (MyStoreBank in the example of Fig. 6.2).

Next section discusses how payments with credit cards can be securely carried out over the Internet using the Secure Electronic Transaction (SET) protocol. Section 6.5 discusses other payment service options for e-business.

6.3   SET - Secure Electronic Transactions

SET (Secure Electronic Transaction) was developed by the SET Consortium, which includes organizations such as Visa, MasterCard, GTE, IBM, Microsoft, VeriSign, SAIC, RSA Data Security, and others [5]. SET provides confidentiality of payment and order information. Payment information cannot be viewed by the merchant; only by the payment authorization and processing entities. Order information can only be seen by the merchant and not by the payment processing entities. Through SET, merchants are authenticated to guarantee they can accept payment card transactions and cardholders are authenticated as legitimate users of a credit card.

Instead of using a plastic credit card, customers use an *electronic wallet*

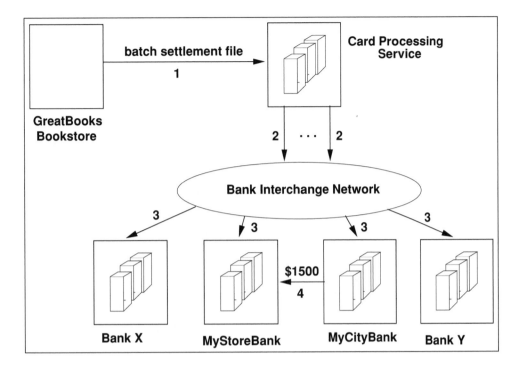

Figure 6.2. Settlement Process for Payments with Credit Cards.

(e-wallet). This is a helper application or a plug-in to the browser and is used to store all the information about the credit cards the customer possesses as well as SET digital certificates for each of these cards. A digital certificate (see Section 5.4.1) serves the purpose of the signature and a picture ID on credit card transactions carried out in the physical world. Cardholders, merchants, and payment gateways have SET digital certicates used for mutual authentication during a SET transaction.

The three main entities involved in a SET purchase transaction are the customer's e-wallet, the merchant's POS software, and the payment gateway. The *payment gateway*, also called the acquirer payment gateway, is the interface between the acquirer bank and the banking network that supports authorizations and settlement [5]. The payment gateway serves the same purposes as the Card Processing Service described before.

6.3.1   Use of Cryptography in SET

The main cryptographic processes used by SET to carry out its transactions are authentication through digital certificates, digital signatures, digital envelopes, double signatures, and simple encapsulation with signature and baggage. Chapter 5 explained how digital certificates can be used to authenticate two parties involved in a message exchange. As we saw, digital certificates are used to carry the public key of the certicate owner. Digital certificates are issued by trusted Certificate Authorities (CAs), which sign the certificates with their private keys. In SET, CAs are organized in a hierarchical fashion. From the top down, the hierarchy consists of a root CA, a brand (e.g., Visa or MasterCard) CA, a geopolitical (e.g., Brazil) CA, and a cardholder CA. Each CA in the chain signs the certificates it issues. SET requires that all certificates in the chain be verified.

Digital signatures in SET work as described in Chapter 5. The thing to keep in mind is that digital signatures in SET use the Secure Hashing Algorithm (SHA-1) to generate message digests and 1,024-bit RSA for encrypting the message digest with the sender's private key. It should also be noted that when SET uses symmetric encryption, it uses the Data Encryption Standard (DES) as explained in the following subsections.

6.3.1.1   Digital Envelopes

A *digital envelope* is basically a DES-encrypted message along with the RSA-encrypted key used in DES encryption. The process of creating and opening a digital envelope is illustrated in Fig. 6.3. To create a digital envelope, the sender randomly generates a key to be used in DES encryption (step 1). This key is used to encrypt the message using DES (step 2). The DES key is encrypted with RSA using the receiver's public key (step 2). The digital envelope is then formed by concatenating the DES-encrypted message with the RSA-encrypted DES key. This envelope is transmitted to the receiver (step 3).

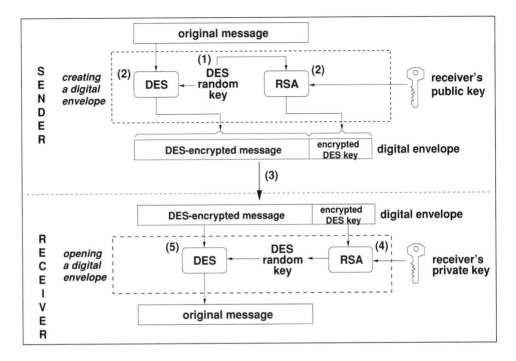

Figure 6.3. Creating and Opening a Digital Envelope.

Only the intended receiver will be able to open the digital envelope because the receiver's private key is necessary to decrypt, using RSA, the DES key (step 4). The DES key is then used to decrypt the DES-encrypted message to obtain the original message (step 5).

So, creating a digital envelope requires one DES encryption and one RSA public operation. Opening a digital envelope requires one DES decryption and one RSA private key operation.

6.3.1.2 Double Signatures

When SET sends an authorization request from the e-wallet to the merchant's POS software, it sends both order information and payment information. However, as we mentioned at the beginning of this section, SET shields the payment information from the merchant but allows it to pass to the payment gateway as we will see in Section 6.3.2. For that purpose, SET uses a doubly signed message. We illustrate the creation of a doubly signed message with the help of Fig. 6.4.

Imagine that the e-wallet (EW) wants to send a two-part message to the merchant's POS software. Part one of the message is intended to the merchant and part two to the payment gateway. The e-wallet software creates a digital envelope for the message intended to the merchant using the merchant's public key and a digital envelope for the message intended to the payment gateway (PG) using the payment gateway's public key (step 1). At the same time, a message digest is created for both messages using SHA-1 as a hashing algorithm (step 2). Both message digests are concatenated (step 3). A message digest of the concatenated message digest is generated using SHA-1 (step 4) and is encrypted using RSA with the e-wallet private

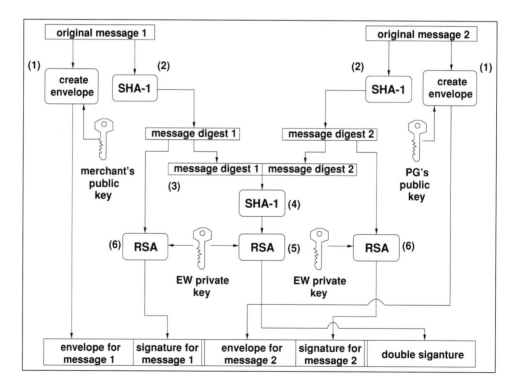

Figure 6.4. Double Signature in SET.

key (step 5). This is the double signature for the message. Each of the message digests generated in step 2 are encrypted using RSA with the e-wallet's private key (step 6). This creates a digital signature (see Chapter 5) for each of the messages. The doubly signed message is then composed of the concatenation of the envelope for message 1, the signature for message 1, the envelope for message 2, the signature for message 2, and the double signature.

When the merchant receives the doubly signed message, it cannot open the digital envelope addressed to the payment gateway (message 2 in Fig. 6.4). It can however open the digital envelope for the message addressed to the merchant (message 1) and verify the signatures as shown in Fig. 6.5. In step 1, the merchant opens the envelope for the message addressed to it using RSA and the merchant's private key. This recovers the original message. Using SHA-1, a digest of this message is created (step 2). The message digest for message 2 is recovered by using RSA and the e-wallet's public key (step 3). Both message digests are then concatenated and a digest of the concatenated digest is generated using SHA-1 (step 4). In step 5, the double signature is decrypted using RSA and the e-wallet's public key. The result of this operation should be identical to the digest of the concatenated message digests if i) the doubly signed message came from the customer's e-wallet, ii) message 1 was addressed to the merchant and signed by the customer, and iii) message 2 was signed by the customer.

Double signing (see Fig. 6.4) involves the following cryptographic operations: two create digital envelope operations (each requires one DES operation and one RSA public key operation); three SHA-1 operations; and three RSA private key operations. Processing a doubly signed message (see Fig. 6.5) requires one open envelope operation (one DES and one RSA private key operation), two SHA-1 operations, and two RSA public key operations.

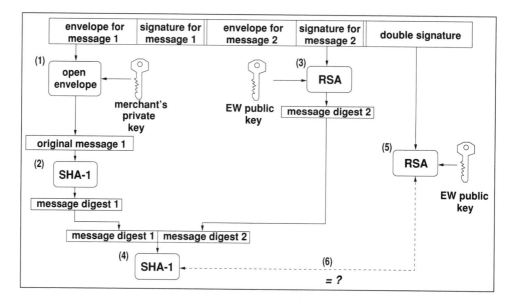

Figure 6.5. Merchant Opening a Doubly Signed Message.

6.3.1.3 Simple Encapsulation with Signature and Baggage

There are some instances in SET where additional levels of security and protection are needed when sending messages. These messages carry an extra piece of information, called a *baggage*, that may be used in a reply message as will become clear when we describe the message flows in Section 6.3.2. A baggage is a mechanism by which encrypted data is appended to a message in such a way that the message and baggage are linked to one another [5].

Figure 6.6 describes how a message and its baggage are signed and encapsulated. We will refer to this process as EncB. A digest of the baggage is created using SHA-1 (step 1). The original message and the digest of the baggage are concatenated (step 2). The result of this step is signed with the sender's private key (step 3). The results of steps 2 and 3 are concatenated (step 4). A digital envelope for the concatenation obtained in step 4 is created (step 5). Finally, the result of step 5 is concatenated with the baggage (step 6) resulting in an encapsulated signed message with baggage.

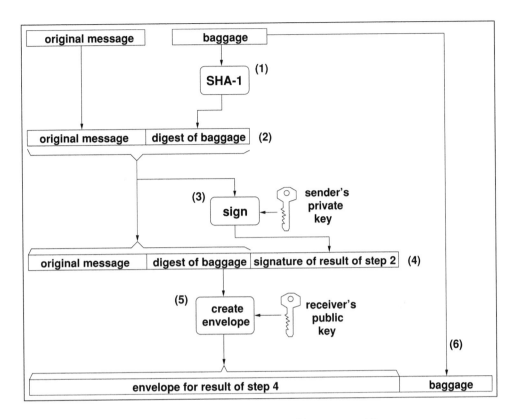

Figure 6.6. Simple Encapsulation with Signature and Baggage.

The receiver of an EncB message will be able to open the envelope with its private key and verify the signature of step 4 using the sender's public key. Once the envelope is opened, the receiver can retrieve the digest of the baggage and regenerate it from the baggage to further verify the integrity of the baggage.

Generating an EncB message requires one SHA-1 operation, one sign operation (one private RSA and one SHA-1 operation), and one create envelope operation (one public RSA and and one DES operation). Receiving an EncB message requires one open envelope operation (one private RSA and one DES operation), one signature verification (one public RSA and one SHA-1 operation), and an additional SHA-1 operation for checking the integrity of the baggage.

6.3.2 SET Message Flow

SET is only invoked when the customer is ready to make a payment. At this point, the customer has already sent an order to the e-business site and is probably looking at a screen that describes the order with all the items to be purchased as well as the total price to be paid. The customer then selects the credit card to be used and SET starts its operation.

With the help of the CSID of Fig. 6.7, we describe next the flow of messages between the entities involved in a a SET payment transaction. We use EW, M, and PG to denote the customer's e-wallet, the merchant's POS software, and the payment gateway, respectively.

We concentrate on the payment and authorization transactions only since capture processing can be carried out out-of-band in SET and because SET servers may be dedicated to authorization only; capture and settlement may be highly batched reducing the transaction volume significantly [5].

1. {PInitReq: EW → M} The e-wallet sends a Purchase Initiate Request (PInitReq) message to the merchant server. This message contains, among other things, the following information: credit card brand name (e.g., Visa or MasterCard), bank identification number, a cardholder challenge string used by the merchant in its response to the e-wallet, and a list of digital certificates stored in the customer's e-wallet. These

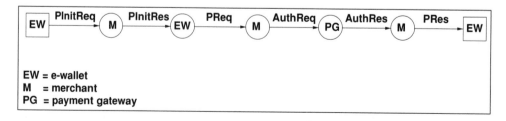

Figure 6.7. CSID for SET Payment Transaction.

certificates comprise the chain of certificates from the root CA to the cardholder CA and are used to authenticate the cardholder as a valid holder of a credit card. These certificates contain the public key that should be used to send messages to the cardholder.

2. {PInitRes: M → EW} The merchant's POS software replies to the e-wallet's PInitReq message with a Purchase Initiate Response (PInitRes) message. This message is signed using the merchant's private key. The PInitRes message includes, among others, the following fields: unique transaction id, e-wallet generated challenge string, and the chain of digital certificates for the payment gateway.

3. {PReq: EW → M} The e-wallet is now ready to send a Purchase Request (PReq) message to the merchant's POS software. This message is doubly signed and is composed of two parts: an order instructions part and a payment instructions part. The order instructions part (e.g., goods ordered, quantity, price, shipping address) can only be decrypted by the merchant. The payment information (e.g., credit card number, amount of transaction) is sent by the merchant to the payment gateway in the AuthReq message (see next). Since this part of the message was encrypted with the payment gateway's public key, it can only be opened with its private key. Remember that the e-wallet obtained the payment gateway's public key in the message PInitRes sent to it by the merchant.

4. {AuthReq: M → PG} As with payments with physical credit cards, the merchant's POS software needs to obtain an authorization for the transaction from the payment gateway by sending an Authorization Request (AuthReq) message. This message is sent as an encapsulated signed message (EncB), with the baggage being the payment information encrypted with the payment gateway's public key.

5. {AuthRes: PG → M} The payment gateway checks the open-to-buy

availability with the card issuer bank and returns an authorization code to the merchant in an Authorization Response (AuthRes) message. This message is also sent as an EncB message, and the baggage is information needed at capture time as well as information to be sent by the merchant to the e-wallet (e.g., an explanation regarding the outcome of the transaction). This latter part is encrypted with the customers' public key so that it can only be decrypted by the e-wallet.

6. {PRes: M → EW} The final message in the sequence, the Purchase Response (PRes) is sent by the merchant to the e-wallet after the merchant receives the AuthRes message. The PRes message is signed by the merchant and contains among, other things, a completion code indicating the result of the transaction as well as data sent by the payment gateway to be seen by the e-wallet only.

6.4   SET Performance

The performance of servers that implement the SET protocol is largely determined by the number of cryptographic operations used to implement the message flow described in the previous subsection.

Table 6.1 shows a summary of the number of basic cryptographic operations, i.e., public and private RSA, SHA-1, and DES operations, needed to execute the encryption operations used by SET. The number 4 in the verify certificate line comes from the number of certificates to be verified in the four-level CA hierarchy.

Table 6.2 shows the number of SET cryptographic operations executed by the e-wallet, the merchant's POS software, and the payment gateway to execute the flow of messages for payment authorization described in Section 6.3.2. If we combine Tables 6.1 and 6.2, we obtain the number of basic cryptographic operations for the three SET participants:

Table 6.1. Number of Basic Cryptographic Operations per SET Cryptographic Operation.

SET Operation	RSA private	RSA public	SHA-1	DES
Sign	1	-	1	-
Verify signature	-	1	1	-
Verify certificate	-	4	4	-
Create envelope	-	1	-	1
Open envelope	1	-	-	1
Double sign	3	2	3	2
Process double signature	1	2	2	1
Generate an Encb message	1	1	2	1
Receive an EncB message	1	1	2	1

- *e-wallet*: four public and four private RSA operations, six SHA-1 operations, and two DES operations,

- *merchant's POS software*: five public and five private RSA operations, nine SHA-1 operations, and three DES operations,

- *payment gateway*: two public and two private RSA operations, four SHA-1 operations, and two DES operations.

The following numerical examples illustrate the performance impacts of using SET in e-business.

Example 6.1

An e-tailer, aware that SET could offer more security than TLS to its customers, decided to determine the performance impact of SET on its server. The IT manager decided to compare the implementation of TLS with SET in terms of performance and asked the analysts to conduct an experiment. The merchant's POS software would run on the same machine as the Web

Table 6.2. Number of SET Cryptographic Operations for E-Wallets, Merchants, and Payment Gateways for Payment Transactions Operation.

	SET Participant		
SET Operation	E-Wallet	Merchant	Payment Gateway
Sign	1	2	-
Verify signature	2	1	-
Double sign	1	-	-
Process double signature		1	-
Generate an Encb message	-	1	1
Receive an EncB message	-	1	1

server. Clients would send requests from a high-speed LAN to the server. The client, network, server CPU, and server disk service demands for the TLS case are assumed to be the same as in the last column of Table 5.5 of Chapter 5. These values are reproduced in Table 6.3.

The SET service demand parameters are essentially the same except for the server CPU. As in Ex. 5.1, we assume that the CPU time per request for non-SET-related processing is 2 msec. The timings for 1,024-bit public and private key encryption and SHA-1 and DES operations are compatible with those of Ex. 5.1: 47.93 msec per private key RSA operation, 5.2 msec per RSA public key operation, 0.00788 msec per SHA-1 operation, and 0.2048 msec per DES operation. We can now compute the service demand at the server CPU using the number of basic cryptographic operations for the merchant as described:

$$2 + 5 \times 47.93 + 5 \times 5.2 + 9 \times 0.00788 + 3 \times 0.2048 = 268.3 \text{ msec} = 0.2683 \text{ sec.}$$
$$(6.4.1)$$

The service demand at the e-wallet can be obtained in a similar way. The difference lies in the number of cryptographic operations.

$$4 \times 47.93 + 4 \times 5.2 + 6 \times 0.00788 + 2 \times 0.2048 = 213 \text{ msec} = 0.213 \text{ sec.} \quad (6.4.2)$$

Table 6.3. Service Demands (in msec) for Ex. 6.1.

Resource	TLS	SET
E-Wallet	14.054	213.0
Network	1.737	1.737
Server CPU	51.694	268.3
Server Disk	10.000	10.000
Payment Gateway	-	106.7
Financial Network	-	80.0

Finally, the service demand at the payment gateway is obtained as

$$2 \times 47.93 + 2 \times 5.2 + 4 \times 0.00788 + 2 \times 0.2048 = 106.7 \text{ msec} = 0.1067 \text{ sec.} \quad (6.4.3)$$

Table 6.3 shows the service demands for the TLS case and for the SET case. The network resource in the table refers to the LAN connecting the clients to the server. The last row in the table represents the time spent by the request at the financial network including the acquirer bank. In this example, we are assuming that when TLS is used, payment authorization is not done in real time.

As we can see from Table 6.3, the bottleneck in both cases is the CPU at the merchant server. As we saw in previous chapters, the maximum throughput can be obtained as the inverse of the service demand at the bottleneck device. Thus,

$$\text{MaxThroughputTLS} = 1/\text{TLSCPUDemand} = 1/0.051694$$
$$= 19.345 \text{ requests/sec} \quad (6.4.4)$$

and

$$\text{MaxThroughputSET} = 1/\text{SETCPUDemand} = 1/0.2683$$
$$= 3.727 \text{ requests/sec.} \quad (6.4.5)$$

Therefore, the SET throughput is less than one-fifth of TLS throughput. Similar results were obtained through experiments, as reported in [9]. Figure 6.8 shows how the throughput varies with the number of clients.

Figure 6.9 shows the variation of the response time versus the throughput. As seen in the figure, as the throughput starts to approach the maximum throughput, the response time grows very fast and approaches infinity.

The curves shown in this example were obtained with the help of queuing network models such as the ones discussed in Chapter 9. The MS Excel workbook called `ch06-examples.xls`, used in this and other examples in this chapter, can be downloaded from the website associated with the book (see the preface) by following the link called `Chapter 6`.   ■

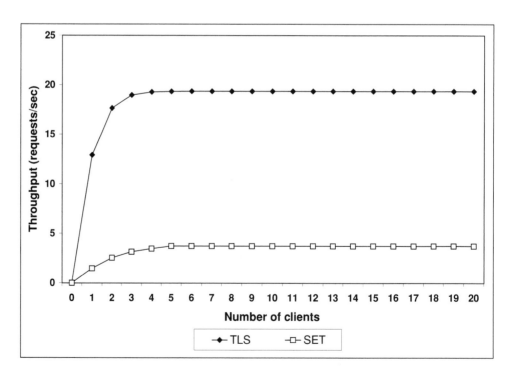

Figure 6.8. Throughput for SET and TLS vs. Number of Clients.

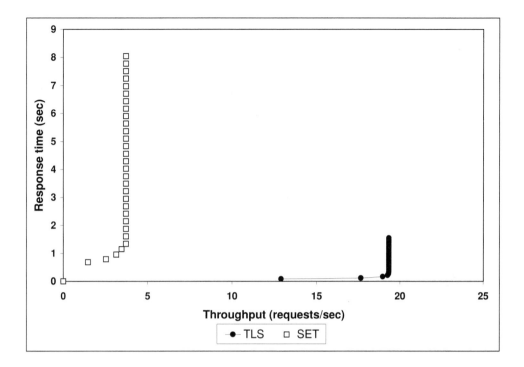

Figure 6.9. Response Time vs. Throughput for SET and TLS.

Example 6.2

The manager of Ex. 6.1 was not happy with the results and wanted to know how a cryptographic accelerator could help to increase the throughput of the e-business site under SET.

Assume that the cryptographic accelerator can speed up cryptographic operations by a factor of fifty. The new values of the service demands for the SET case when the server uses a cryptographic accelerator are shown in Table 6.4. Note that only the SET-related operations of the server CPU are reduced by a factor of fifty. The throughput is now limited by SET-related processing at the e-wallet since this becomes the bottleneck. The maximum throughput is now 4.69 (= 1/0.213) requests/sec, not quite near a fifty-fold improvement as the IT manager expected. Why is that?

Well, when the number of clients is fixed, as in the experiment considered

Table 6.4. Service Demands (in msec) for Ex. 6.2.

Resource	SET
E-Wallet	213.0
Network	1.737
Server CPU	2 + 266.3 / 50 = 7.33
Server Disk	10.0
Payment Gateway	106.7
Financial Network	80.0

above in which a number of clients are coming from a local area network, the server throughput can be limited by how fast clients are able to submit requests to the server. However, when the number of clients is very large as is the case with public websites, the number of clients is not the limiting factor. In this case, we should look at the system composed by the server, the payment gateway, and the financial network. In this case, the bottleneck is the payment gateway with a service demand of 106.7 msec. The maximum throughput then is 9.37 (=1/0.1067) requests/sec, a 2.5 (=9.37/3.727) times increase in throughput. If the payment gateway also uses a cryptographic accelerator, its service demand becomes 2.134 (= 106.7/50) msec. The bottleneck now moves to the financial network with its service demand of 80 msec. So, the maximum throughput becomes 12.5 (1/0.080) requests/sec, a 3.35-fold increase in throughput when compared with the case in which neither the merchant server nor the payment gateway uses a cryptographic accelerator. ∎

Example 6.2 showed clearly that as one bottleneck is removed, another is created. Because of this, one may not be able to reap the full benefits of reducing the service demand at the bottleneck device.

Much of the criticism of SET as a solution to highly secure e-business is based on poor performance, especially in early implementations [2]. However, many factors are already contributing to change this scenario [2]. The first is due to the steady increase in computing power. According to Moore's law [6], computers become faster by a factor of 1.6 annually, or roughly twice as fast every eighteen months. The second factor is the development of faster cryptographic algorithms, such as the ones based on *elliptic curve cryptography (ECC)* [3], which may represent speed improvements of four to ten times when compared to RSA algorithms.

In the following examples, we explore SET performance considerations by looking four years ahead using assumptions based on the increase of computational power due to Moore's law and using assumptions regarding the growth in the volume of secure transactions during the peak period [2]. These assumptions are summarized in Table 6.5. Processing speed improvements will be referred to as speedup in the following examples.

Since we are only interested in SET performance, we will ignore the time spent by transactions in the financial network. We will only consider the merchant server and the payment gateway.

Example 6.3

Consider that the SET service demands shown in Table 6.3 are for the current year for a specific hardware used by the merchant server and the

Table 6.5. Processing Speedup and Transaction Growth Assumptions.

Year	Processing Speedup	Volume of Secure Transactions (tps)
1	1.00	14
2	1.60	19
3	2.56	23
4	4.01	26
5	6.41	29

payment gateway. Assume the processing speedups of Table 6.5. How will these demands vary over the next five years?

The CPU demand at year n is given by

$$\text{CPUDemandAtYear\_n} = \frac{\text{CPUDemandAtYear\_1}}{\text{SpeedupAtYear\_n}}. \quad (6.4.6)$$

So, for example, the CPU demand at the merchant server on year 5 will be 41.9 (= 268.3/6.41) msec assuming no improvements in cryptographic algorithms. Table 6.6 shows the CPU demands for the merchant and gateway CPU. The fourth and fifth columns assume an improvement of 500% in cryptographic performance due to the use of new algorithms, such as ECC at the beginning of year 3. The service demands reported on Table 6.6 display the service demands at the end of each year. At the end of year 3, the CPU demand at the merchant would be 26% of the demand at year 1 if ECC is used. ∎

Example 6.4

Consider the same CPU service demands as in Table 6.6 and the forecast number of SET transactions per year shown in Table 6.5. We want to compute the CPU utilization in each year at the merchant and payment gateway with and without ECC. Assume that the CPU utilization at the merchant for non-SET transactions is 70%.

Table 6.6. CPU Service Demands (in msec) Over a Five-Year Period.

Year	Merchant (no ECC)	PG (no ECC)	Merchant (ECC at YR 3)	PG (ECC at YR 3)
1	268.3	106.7	268.3	106.7
2	167.7	66.7	167.7	66.7
3	104.8	41.7	69.9	27.8
4	66.9	26.6	44.6	17.7
5	41.9	16.6	27.9	11.1

The CPU utilization can be computed as

$$CPUUtilization = CPUServiceDemand \times TransactionVolume \qquad (6.4.7)$$

as described in more detail in Chapter 8. For example, the CPU utilization at the merchant in the case of no use of ECC in year 5 would be computed as

$$0.70 + 0.0419 \times 29 = 1.91 \qquad (6.4.8)$$

or 191%! This says that we either need faster CPUs or more CPUs. Table 6.7 shows the CPU utilization for the given transactions volumes and service demands. ∎

Example 6.5

As Table 6.7 shows, in many cases the resulting utilization exceeds 100%, i.e., 1. This fact is better illustrated in Fig. 6.10. What is the required number of CPUs to reduce the CPU utilization to an average of 60% over all CPUs?

We start with the relationship

$$0.60 = \frac{TotalCPUUtilization}{NumberOfCPUs}. \qquad (6.4.9)$$

Table 6.7. CPU Utilizations Over a Five-Year Period.

Year	Merchant (no ECC)	PG (no ECC)	Merchant (ECC at YR 3)	PG (ECC at YR 3)
1	4.456	4.456	1.4938	1.4938
2	3.886	3.886	1.26706	1.26706
3	3.111	2.307	0.95863	0.63909
4	2.440	1.860	0.69182	0.46121
5	1.914	1.509	0.48273	0.32182

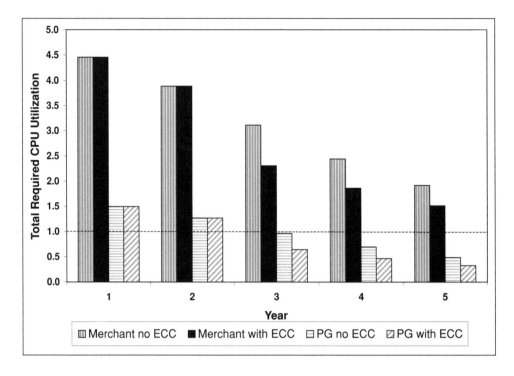

Figure 6.10. Total CPU Utilization for Ex. 6.4.

Given the total CPU utilization shown in Table 6.7, the required number of CPUs to achieve an average of 60% utilization per processor is given by

$$\text{NumberOfCPUs} = \left\lceil \frac{\text{TotalCPUUtilization}}{0.60} \right\rceil. \qquad (6.4.10)$$

Table 6.8 shows the number of required CPUs for each case.   ∎

6.5   Other Payment Services on the Internet

Besides SET, there are other payment protocols being discussed, implemented, and tested. Among these, we briefly discuss the following: electronic checking, digital cash, and W3C's common markup for micropayment per-fee-links.

An *electronic check* is similar to a paper check but safer. As in SET, a customer needs a e-wallet to store information on the browser about the

Table 6.8. Required Number of CPUs Over a Five-Year Period.

Year	Merchant (no ECC)	PG (no ECC)	Merchant (ECC)	PG (ECC)
1	8	8	3	3
2	7	7	3	3
3	6	4	2	2
4	5	4	2	1
5	4	3	1	1

checking account. When the customer is ready to make a payment, an encrypted message is sent to the merchant's site. This message is encrypted with the merchant's public key and has the account number of the checking account encrypted with the customer's bank public key for added protection. The merchant verifies that the information in the electronic check (i.e., the amount) is correct and sends the electronic check to the bank to obtain funds. The e-wallet at the customer side keeps a log of all checks issued, similar to a checkbook register in the physical world.

Digital cash, or *e-cash*, is aimed at transactions that deal with small amounts of money, such as in providing access to publications or real-time information (e.g., stock quotes). In digital cash systems, users can store e-cash in their e-wallets. E-cash is generated by a bank and digitally stamped by it. The amount of e-cash is withdrawn from the customer account and sent to the customer e-wallet to be stored. To make a payment with e-cash, customers send the the right amount of e-cash to the merchant software, which sends it to the bank for verification and redemption [1].

The World Wide Web Consortium (W3C) has specified, as part of its electronic commerce activities, a system for micropayments [10]. The idea is that one may have to pay a fee to traverse certain links. W3C's specification has produced an extensible way to embed in a Web page all the information needed to initialize a micropayment. At the browser side, multiple e-wallets and payment systems may coexist and interact with the per-fee link handler.

6.6   Concluding Remarks

Payment is one of the important aspects of an e-business transaction. As in the physical world, payment can be made through credit cards, electronic checks, or digital cash. In e-business, the parties involved in a transaction need to have all sorts of guarantees that are much easier to obtain in the physical world. For example, merchants need to know they are dealing with a legitimate holder of a credit card, cardholders need to know they are dealing with a legitimate merchant and not with an impostor, merchants need to know that the customer has the funds to pay for the purchase, and customers need to know that their order and payment information will not be disclosed while being transmitted over the network and that merchants will not misuse their credit card information.

The Secure Electronic Transaction (SET) protocol provides these guarantees. In this chapter, we provided a high level description of SET and of the various cryptographic processes it uses. The performance impacts of SET were discussed through several numerical examples. The use of cryptographic accelerators, more and faster processors, and the use of faster cryptographic algorithms, such as ECC, will allow SET implementations to scale for high volumes of transactions.

Bibliography

[1] D. Kosiur, *Understanding Electronic Commerce*, Microsoft Press, Redmond, Washington, 1997.

[2] C. LeTocq and S. YOUNG, "Set Comparative Performance Analysis," GartnerGroup, San Jose, CA, Nov. 2, 1998.

[3] P. Lambert, "Elliptic Curve Cryptography Delivers High Performance and Security for E-Commerce," *Comp. Security J.*, vol. XIV, no. 4, 1999, pp. 23–29.

[4] S. Lu and S. A. Smolka, "Model Checking the Secure Electronic Transaction (SET) Protocol," *Proc. Seventh Intl. Symp. Modeling, Analysis and Simulation of Computer and Telecommunication Systems*, College Park, MD, Oct. 24-28, pp. 358–365.

[5] M. S. Merkow, J. Breithaupt, and K. L. Wheeler, *Building SET Applications for Secure Transactions*, John Wiley & Sons, New York, NY, 1998.

[6] G. Moore, "Nanometers and Gigabucks - Moore on Moore's Law," University Video Corporation Distinguished Lecture, 1996, www.uvc.com.

[7] SET, "The SET Standard Technical Specification," www.setco.org/download.html.

[8] M. H. Sherif, *Protocols for Secure Electronic Commerce*, CRC Press, Boca Raton, FL, 2000.

[9] N. V. Someren, *The Need for Cryptographic Accelerators in Electronic Commerce*, nCipher Inc., Santa Clara, CA, April 30, 1977.

[10] World Wide Web Consortium (W3C), *Common Markup for Micropayment Per-Fee Links*, www.w3c.org/ECommerce/Activity.html.

Part III
Capacity Planning
for E-Business

Chapter 7

A Capacity Planning Methodology for E-Business

7.1 Introduction

In the previous chapters, we saw many typical examples of capacity planning situations. In this chapter, we discuss in detail a methodology for carrying out capacity planning studies in the context of e-business. This methodology is different from the ones used in Web server or client server environments [6] [7] because it includes the business level and customer behavior levels.

We start by defining adequate capacity and then present an example of a capacity planning situation. The capacity planning methodology is then presented and the various steps of the methodology are presented in light of the example. Some of the steps of the methodology are covered in much greater detail in other chapters of this book.

7.2 Capacity Planning and Adequate Capacity

Capacity planning is the process of *predicting* when future load levels will saturate the system and of determining the most cost-effective way of delaying system saturation as much as possible [6] [7]. Future load levels are generally a function of a combination of three factors: natural evolution of existing workloads, deployment of new applications and services, and changes in customer behavior. This last factor includes traffic surges due to new situations (e.g., breaking news, TV ad campaigns, or the release of a new product) as well as changes in customer navigational patterns due to the availability of new business functions. Prediction is key to capacity planning because one needs to be able to determine how an e-business site will react when changes in load levels and customer behavior occur or when new business models are developed. This determination requires predictive models and not experimentation.

One important question when planning the capacity of a site is, "How much capacity is adequate to support the operation of the site?" Figure 7.1 shows the elements that define adequate capacity.

The picture shows that the notion of adequate capacity for an e-business site is a function of the three following elements.

1. *Service level agreements (SLAs).* These are upper or lower bounds on performance (e.g., response time and throughput) and availability metrics. Examples of SLAs include "server-side response time ≤ 2 sec," "site availability $> 99.5\%$," and "session throughput $\geq 30{,}000$ sessions/day." SLAs are determined by the management of the e-

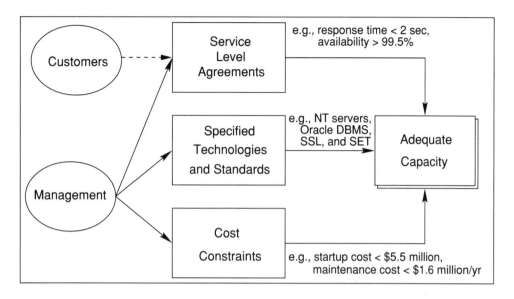

Figure 7.1. Definition of Adequate Capacity.

business site with an indirect input from customers (see dashed line in Fig. 7.1). The input from customers is indirect because, while they do not have a say on what the SLAs should be, they implicitly expect a certain quality of service. If these expectations are not met, customers typically become impatient and take their business elsewhere after approximately eight seconds of waiting for a page to download. This practice has been known in the industry as the *eight-second rule* and it relates to the end-to-end response time, which includes the server-side response time plus all the network time. Experimental evidence has shown that a mere increase of one second above the eight-second threshold may increase the click-out rate from 8% to 30%. Bad performance may scare prospective buyers during a single visit or may lead them to avoid a site altogether.

2. *Specified technologies and standards.* Many different technologies and standards may be selected when designing an e-commerce site. For example, management may decide that NT servers should be used,

that Oracle software be used to support database management tasks, and that SSL and SET be used to support authentication and payment services. These choices place constraints on how adequate capacity is provided.

3. *Cost constraints.* If we had all the money in the world to spend, it would be quite easy to build an e-commerce site with the best possible performance. However, any organization has budgets and constraints on how much it can spend to launch and operate a site. These constraints dictate how much capacity can be made available.

We then say that an e-commerce site has adequate capacity if the service level agreements are continuously met for a specified technology and for specified standards and if the services are provided within cost constraints.

7.3 A Capacity Planning Situation

An online auto-buying service just launched its site and is seeing the number of requests to the site grow at a very fast rate. While this is good news, management is concerned that pretty soon performance may degrade and customers may move to other sites. In particular, management is considering several new initiatives, described below, and they want to know how these initiatives will impact the IT infrastructure. Answers to questions such as "Will the IT infrastructure support an increase in traffic?" "What kind of changes should be done in the IT infrastructure to support new services and new business models?" "Will there be very large delays?" "Will there be a need to upgrade the configuration?" "How? By adding more servers? Increasing the bandwidth?" need to be obtained.

- A very expensive marketing campaign is about to be released. It will consist of TV ads as well as ads in the Sunday edition of the major newspapers around the country. The marketing department, based on conversations with its advertisement agency, has three estimates on the number of people reached by these ads: a pessimistic, a realistic, and an optimistic estimate.

- Currently, the online dealer has four thousand affiliated dealers, less than one-fifth of the auto dealers in the US. Management wants to launch an aggressive plan to sign up ten thousand new dealers in the next year.

- The dotcom auto dealer is considering changing the way it does business. Currently, customers only have access to vehicles available at one of their affiliated car dealers. If a sale takes place through the online service, the dealer pays a fee to the online service. The new model under consideration is an auction-based one. Customers would be able to configure the vehicle they want by selecting make, model, year, mileage range, options, color, and price range according to the Kelley Blue Book, a publication that keeps track of prices for new and used vehicles. Any of the affiliated dealers would then be able to bid on the request.

- The board is also considering a proposal to extend the scope of the site to that of a portal for vehicle-related issues. New services would include brokering car insurance and car financing services, and providing links to car trade magazines and allowing customers to search for articles on cars by keywords as well as providing access to several types of vehicle rating and evaluation services.

- Another proposal calls for extending the site's multimedia capabilities for luxury vehicles. Customers would be allowed to see video clips showing details of the car's interior, trunk, and engine compartment as well as a virtual test drive in different road conditions.

The various initiatives described above require that a capacity planning methodology for e-business be strictly followed. In the next section, we present an outline of the methodology and provide details of each step in the subsequent sections. We use the online auto-buying service example to illustrate how the various steps are carried out.

7.4 The Methodology

Following the reference model for electronic business discussed in Chapter 1, we defined a capacity planning methodology that covers the business level, the customer behavior level, and the resource level. A high level view of the methodology is illustrated in Fig. 7.2. It shows that capacity planning for e-business is composed of three main planning processes: business and functional planning, customer behavior planning, and IT resource planning. These planning processes are explained in detail in the following sections.

The business and functional planning processes are influenced by business evolution plans and function evolution plans. Evolution in customer behavior affects the customer behavior planning process and plans to evolve the infrastructure affect the IT resource planning process as indicated in Fig. 7.2.

The outcome of the planning process is a set of plans for modification and evolution of the site in terms of business model, e-commerce functions offered, customer behavior models, and IT infrastructure.

7.5 Business Level

Business and functional planning involves characterizing the business and analyzing the functions to be provided by the e-commerce site as depicted in Fig. 7.3.

7.5.1 Business Characterization

The goal of the business characterization step is to generate a *business model*, as described in Chapter 1, comprised of the following elements.

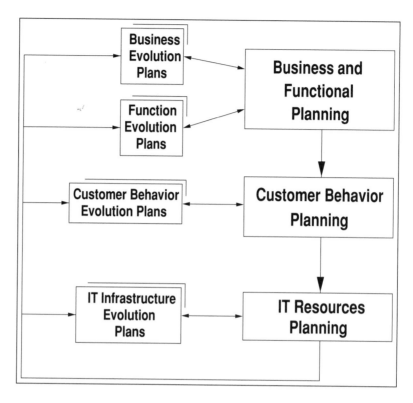

Figure 7.2. High-Level View of a Capacity Planning Methodology for E-Business.

7.5.1.1   Type of Business

This describes the type of business conducted over the Web. Some examples of types of businesses include B2C e-tailer, B2C service, C2C auction, B2C auction, and B2B purchasing. B2C e-tailers include e-businesses that sell goods, such as books, toys, CDs, and computers, to customers. In the case of B2C service e-businesses, customers do not buy goods but buy services such as brokerage of security trading or home loan financing. In C2C auctions, the e-commerce site implements the mechanisms that allow customers to auction goods and bid on goods being auctioned by others. A B2C auction allows customers to advertise what they want so that businesses can bid on their requests. For example, a B2C travel site may allow customers to indicate their hotel needs for a given city, time period, room type, and price

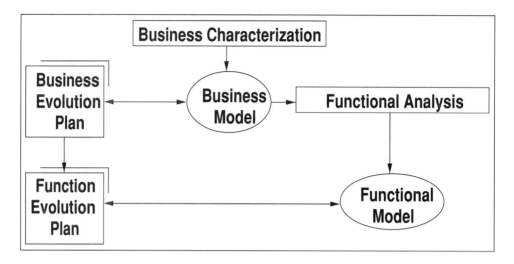

Figure 7.3. Business Level Aspect of a Capacity Planning Methodology for E-Business.

range and receive quotes from hotels that have rooms available. Finally, B2B purchasing can be illustrated by the case in which companies buy parts from other companies. Clearly, many e-businesses combine more than one of the types of businesses illustrated above.

7.5.1.2 Type of Delivery

This element describes what type of delivery, if any, is associated with the business model. Examples include physical delivery of goods (e.g., books and toys), real-time digital delivery over the Internet (e.g., newspaper article, technical report, or digitized music), subscription-based digital delivery over the Internet (e.g., software upgrade downloads), and no delivery as in the case of online brokerage.

7.5.1.3 Use of Third-Party Services

This element describes what third-party services, such as advertisement and payment gateways, are used to support the e-business.

7.5.1.4   Business Quantitative Descriptors

The nature of these descriptors varies significantly depending on the type of e-business. The purpose of these descriptors is to provide business-related attributes that are important for capacity planning purposes. For example, consider the following quantitative descriptors associated with an online bookstore:

- Total number of books stored in the online catalog;

- Number of users registered in the site: A customer profile, payment, and shipping information is kept for each customer, and e-mail notifications based on customer reading preferences are sent periodically;

- Buying pattern: A frequency distribution of the number of books bought in a month per registered customer (see Fig. 7.4 for an example) shows that most customers bought one book per month and the average is around 1.88 books bought per month per registered customer;

- Book price range: The price range distribution per book category (e.g., technical and non-technical as shown in Fig. 7.5) shows that technical books tend to be more expensive than non-technical books and that the average price of a non-technical book is $27.70 while the average cost of a technical book is $43.90;

- Catalog quantitative descriptors: For each book in the catalog, the price and number of copies sold per month since publishing should be kept.

Business quantitative descriptors are useful in forecasting the number of transactions of each type that the system has to be able to process in order for desired revenue goals to be reached.

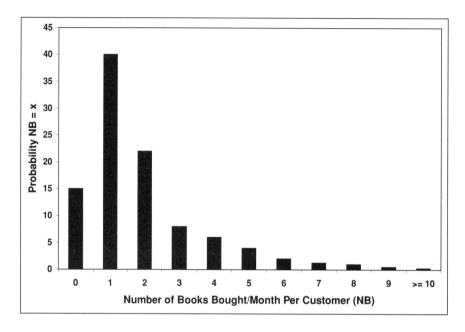

Figure 7.4. Example of Buying Pattern for Online Bookstore Example.

7.5.1.5   Market Composition

This element describes the composition of the market. For example, the market for an online bookstore located in the US could be global but with a higher concentration of customers coming from the US. An online bookstore specializing in Brazilian and French books, located in the US, is more likely to get the majority of its requests originating from areas of the US and Canada with large Portuguese and French-speaking communities. Some online businesses may even restrict their market to specific countries due to legal constraints.

7.5.1.6   Hours of Operation

This element of the business model establishes the hours of operation for the e-business. Most e-businesses have a requirement to be operational twenty-four hours a day, seven days a week. However, some e-businesses, by the very nature of their business, see the bulk of their activities during specific times

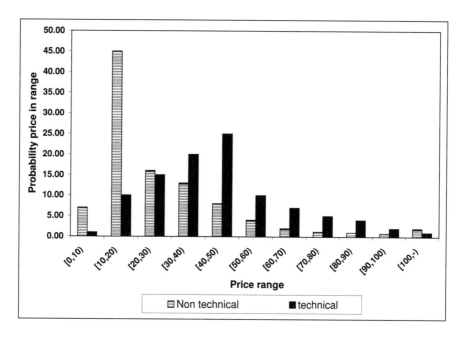

Figure 7.5. Example of Price Range for Online Bookstore Example.

in the day. For example, online trading sites see the bulk of their activities when the markets are open.

Example 7.1

The business model for our online auto-buying service example could be described as follows.

- Type of Business: B2C service.

- Type of Delivery: none. The online service in our case only provides the name, address, and telephone number of the dealer that has agreed to sell the vehicle at the price and under the conditions agreed upon by the customer. The customer must arrange with the dealer to take delivery of the vehicle and make the payment.

- Use of Third-Party Services: the site uses an ad rotation service to display banners on its home page.

- Quantitative Descriptors:

  - Number of affiliated dealers: 4,000.
  - Statistics on the number of vehicles sold per month by each dealer.
  - Statistics on the number of vehicles sold per month per vehicle category (e.g., sport, passenger, luxury, SUVs, pickups, and trucks).
  - A database containing all the vehicles in the inventory of each dealer with their price.
  - Number of different car makes, models, and body styles from which to select.
  - Number of new cars added daily to the inventory per dealer.

- Market Composition: 85% US and 15% Canada.

- Hours of Operation: twenty-four hours a day and seven days a week.

This example illustrates the type of information that comprises the business model.   ∎

7.5.2   Functional Analysis

The purpose of the functional analysis step is to produce a *functional model* (see Fig. 7.3). This model describes the functions provided by the e-business site. The functional analysis can be carried out by examining the site and making an inventory of the functions offered by the site. One of the purposes of the functional model is to support a capacity planning effort, which is quantitative in nature. Thus, one needs to add relevant quantitative and performance-related information to the description of each function. This type of information includes the following.

- *Interaction Model.* This describes how a user interacts with the e-business site to execute the function. An example could be that two consecutive HTML forms are needed to implement the function.

- *Web Technology Used.* Different technologies may be used to implement an e-business function. Some examples include HTML forms, Java applets, ActiveX controls, CGI scripts, and servlets.

- *Use of Authentication.* This information specifies if an authentication protocol such as SSL or TLS is used to implement the e-business function.

The information associated with the functions described by the functional model are useful for building CSIDs for each e-business function. We illustrate the functional analysis step using our online auto-buying example.

Example 7.2

The functional model for the online auto-buying service includes the following functions.

- Car Selection Function: Customers select a vehicle by choosing their state, the vehicle's make, model, body style, and year. The interaction model is three consecutive HTML forms, and the Web technology used is HTML forms and CGI scripts. There is no use of authentication.

- Option Selection: Once a car is selected, the customer can select options (e.g., rear seat impact air bag, power glass moonroof, parking distance control, neon lights, and onboard navigation system). The price displayed changes as options are selected or deselected. The interaction model is one HTML form, and the Web technology used is Java applet to present available options and recompute price as a function of selected option. There is no use of authentication.

- Color Selection: Once a car and options are selected, the customer can select exterior and interior colors. The interaction model is one HTML form, and the Web technology used is HTML forms and CGI scripts. Authentication is not used.

- Selection of Extended Service Contract: The customer is now given the option of choosing an extended service contract for the new vehicle. The interaction model is one HTML form, and the Web technology used is Java applet to present available extended service contracts and recompute price as a function of selected option. Authentication is not used.

- Entry of Personal Data: A form is presented to the customer to obtain personal data for contact. The interaction model is one HTML form, and the Web technology is HTML forms and CGI. Authentication is used via SSL.

- Financing Application: Customers can apply for financing of their vehicles through the site. The interaction model is one HTML form, and the Web technology is HTML forms and CGI. Authentication occurs with SSL.

- Entry of Delivery Information: Through this function, the customer enters the address to which the vehicle should be delivered as well as the desired delivery date. The interaction model is one HTML form, and the Web technology is HTML forms and CGI. Authentication occurs with SSL.

- Hold Car: A selected vehicle can be held by making a credit card deposit. The interaction model involves one HTML form, and the Web technology involves HTML forms and CGI. Authentication is used via SSL.

- View Status of Previous Order: Customers are allowed to view the status of a previous request. The interaction model is one HTML form, and the Web technology is HTML forms and CGI. There is no use of authentication.

- Cancel Order: Orders can be cancelled for full refund of credit card deposit through this function. The interaction model is one HTML form, and the Web technology is HTML forms and CGI. Authentication occurs with SSL.

■

7.5.3 Business Evolution Analysis

Plans for evolving the business may have considerable impact on the required capacity to run the e-business. We illustrate this by going back to our online auto-buying e-business.

Example 7.3

Going back to the capacity planning situations described in Section 7.3, identify the planned business evolutions and describe how they could affect the site's performance and required capacity.

- *Marketing Campaign.* If the marketing campaign is successful, it will attract many customers to the site, which should be prepared to handle the surge in demand without site outages and with acceptable performance. Otherwise, the money spent in the advertising campaign will be wasted and could even have a negative effect. The capacity planner must work with the three estimates provided by the advertisement agency (i.e., optimistic, realistic, and pessimistic) and predict how the site will be able to cope with the additional workload intensity, especially for the optimistic estimate.

- *Signing Up More Dealers.* As more dealers sign up, the size of the database that holds the inventory of cars increases. Searches in the database will tend to become slower if proper actions are not taken (e.g., replicating the database into more than one database server and increasing the I/O bandwidth of the database server). Also, the rate at which the database is updated increases since more vehicles will be added and deleted from the database per unit time.

- *Adopting a Bidding Scheme.* In this case, a new database holding all the entries in the Kelley Blue Book has to be built. A new application has to be deployed that allows users to configure their cars from the online version of the Blue Book. New workloads have to be added to the site. One workload allows the dealers to interact with the site to receive customer requests by e-mail. Another new workload allows dealers to bid on requests while another application ranks the bids and notifies customers by email. They can now visit the site, view the bids, and complete the purchase if they like any of the options. The capacity planner has to estimate the service demands and workload intensities of these new applications to properly size the site for this new business model.

- *Creating Portal.* This new business model may generate an increase in workload intensity since the site will become more attractive because a wide array of services will be offered. Also, several new applications will have to be supported. New partners (e.g., insurance companies, financing companies) will come into play. Applications to interact with them will pose additional load on the site. If not properly planned, the increased workload intensity and increased service demand on the various servers and I/O devices can severely impact the site's performance.

- *Adding More Multimedia Capability.* The added multimedia features may put a strain on the bandwidth of the link that connects the site to the ISP. Internal networks and I/O devices may also be affected. The performance analyst needs to analyze the impact of these new workloads to plan the capacity of the site under this new scenario.

7.5.4   Function Evolution Analysis

This step analyzes how the functions offered by an e-business site will evolve over time. This evolution may be influenced by business evolution plans as indicated in Fig 7.3. Consider our online auto-buying example again.

Example 7.4

Let us examine how the functional model would change under the various scenarios described in Section 7.3.

- *Marketing Campaign.* No changes to the functional model occur here.

- *Signing Up More Dealers.* The functional model does not change.

- *Adopting a Bidding Scheme.* In this case, the functions Car Selection, Option Selection, Color Selection, Selection of Extended Service Contract, Hold Car, View Status of Previous Order, and Cancel Order, described in Ex. 7.2, are deleted and the following new functions are added.

  - Car Configuration: The customer configures a car according to the Kelley Blue Book entries by selecting the vehicle's make, model, body style, year, mileage range, and condition. The interaction model is four HTML forms, and the Web technology used is HTML forms and CGI scripts. There is no use of authentication.

  - View Bids: The customer can view the bids on his request and select one for purchase. The interaction model is two HTML forms, and the Web technology is HTML forms and CGI. There is no use of authentication.

  - Cancel Request: Requests can be cancelled through this function. The interaction model is one HTML form, and the Web technology is HTML forms and CGI. Authentication occurs via SSL.

- *Creating a Portal.* The following new functions are added.

  - Browse: The Customer selects various links on issues of interest to potential car buyers and car aficionados. The interaction model is one HTTP request, and the Web technology is HTTP. There is no use of authentication.

  - Apply for Insurance: The customer enters additional data and submits an application for car insurance. The interaction model is one HTML form, and the Web technology is HTML forms and CGI. Authentication occurs via SSL.

  - Search: This function provides access to a search engine that looks for articles about vehicles in several trade magazines and consumer reporting magazines. The interaction model is one HTML form, and the Web technology is HTML forms and CGI. There is no use of authentication.

- *Adding More Multimedia Capability.* The following new function is added.

  - Virtual Test Drive: This function allows the customer to get a better feel of a vehicle through multimedia-rich technologies. The interaction model is one HTML interaction, and the Web technology is Quicktime. There is no use of authentication.

■

7.6 Customer Behavior Level

Chapter 2 presented in detail the notions of the customer behavior model and described two types of models: the customer behavior model graph (CBMG) and the customer visit model (CVM).

Figure 7.6 depicts the customer behavior level of the capacity planning methodology. The main steps in this level are customer behavior characterization and customer behavior evolution plan. The former generates a customer behavior model that can be in the form of a CBMG or a CVM. The latter provides plans for evolution of the customer behavior. These plans may result from planned modifications to the site layout, which may change the possible navigational patterns. The customer behavior characterization step uses as input the functional model as seen in Section 7.6.1.

7.6.1   Customer Behavior Characterization

We illustrate here, through our dotcom car selling company example, the customer behavior characterization level.

Example 7.5

Build the static portion of the CBMG for the online auto-buying service according to the functional model of Ex. 7.2.

This CBMG is shown in Fig. 7.7. Note that the transition probabilities and think times are not shown in the static CBMG. The figure shows that customers can go back to the Select a Car state as many times as they want while they have not selected all the options, color, and service contract of the car. Once everything is chosen, customers go through a sequence of steps

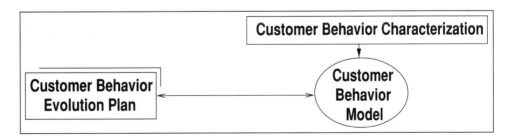

Figure 7.6. Customer Behavior Level Aspect of a Capacity Planning Methodology for E-Business.

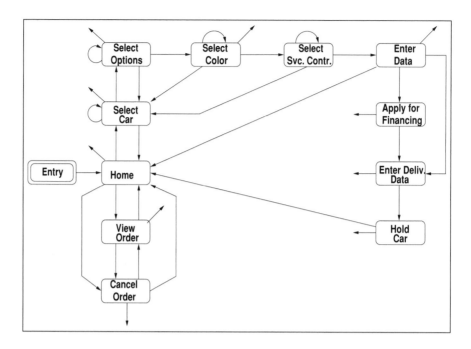

Figure 7.7. Customer Behavior Model Graph for the Online Auto-Buying Service.

that lead them to the Hold Car state. Note that this CBMG does not have a Pay state since, according to the business model, customers pay directly to the dealership that finds their selected car. In the Hold Car state, customers only pay a fee to hold the car. The dangling arrows from all states represent exits from the site. ■

Chapter 11 discusses the methods for obtaining the static and dynamic aspects of a CBMG. This includes obtaining transition probabilities and think times from HTTP logs. It also shows how to generate clusters of CBMGs that represent customers with similar behavior.

7.6.2 Customer Behavior Evolution Analysis

Changes in business models or new services added to the e-business site may cause changes to the customer behavior model as illustrated below.

Example 7.6

Figure 7.8 shows how the CBMG of Fig. 7.7 would be modified to reflect the situation of adding the virtual test drive feature to the site. The figure shows that from the Select Options state, customers may go to the Virtual Test Drive state or proceed directly to the Select Colors state.   ■

7.7   Resource Level

At this point, we have a good characterization of the e-business, the functions it offers, and the way customers behave, as captured in the business, function, and customer behavior models. The next level in the capacity plan-

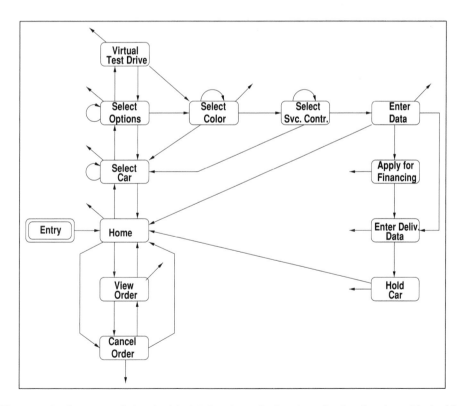

Figure 7.8. Customer Behavior Model Graph for Online Auto-Buying Service with the Virtual Test Drive Feature.

ning methodology, IT resource planning, deals with the IT resources used to support the e-business. Figure 7.9 shows the main steps involved at this level: IT environment characterization, workload characterization, workload forecasting, performance modeling, calibration and validation, and what-if analysis. The resource level part of the methodology is based on three models, the workload, performance, and cost models, and two descriptions, the IT infrastructure and workload descriptions. The following subsections describe each of these steps in more detail.

7.7.1   Characterizing the IT Environment

This step generates a *description of the IT infrastructure* as well as a *workload description*. The description of the IT infrastructure includes the type of hardware (e.g., server machines, disk farms, routers, load balancers, fire-

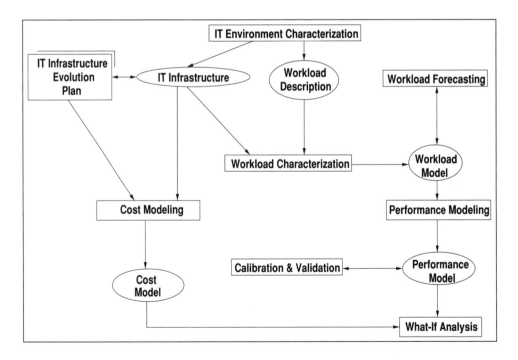

Figure 7.9. Resource Level Aspect of a Capacity Planning Methodology for E-Business.

wall), servers (e.g., Web servers, application servers, database servers, domain names servers), software (e.g, operating systems, middleware, database management systems), network connectivity, network protocols, and payment services.

Example 7.7

Going back to our example, the IT infrastructure could be represented by Fig. 7.10. It is composed of one Web server, one application server, and one database server. A T3 link connects the site to the Internet via a router, which is connected to a 100 Mbps Ethernet network (LAN 1). The web server is on LAN 1 and the other servers are on LAN 2, which is connected to LAN 1 by a firewall. All three servers run MS Windows NT Server as the operating system. The Web server stores all static pages and runs MS IIS as the HTTP server. The application server runs MS Site Server Commerce Edition, which provides management of customer profile information and site personalization, store front operations, such as catalog management and shopping cart functions, and tools to analyze customer behavior. The database server uses MS SQL Server to manage the various databases that support the site functionality.

The site supports SSL besides the other obvious protocols such as TCP/IP and HTTP. ■

The workload description comprises all the transactions and/or requests that support the e-business functions included in the functional model as well as any other auxiliary programs. This description also includes the identification of peak usage periods and service-level agreements at the level of transactions and batch programs (e.g., programs that send e-mail to customers about promotions).

Example 7.8

Table 7.1 shows an example of the transactions that would correspond to two of the e-business functions shown in Ex. 7.2. The third column in the

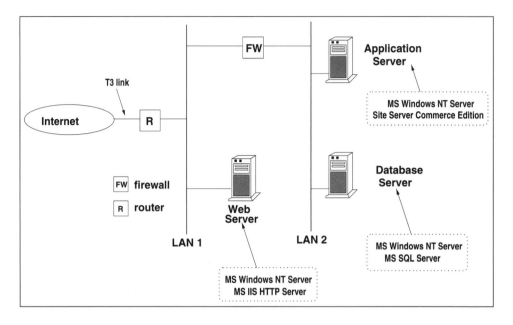

Figure 7.10. IT Infrastructure for the Online Car-Buying Service.

table shows where the transaction is executed. For instance, the Web server receives a request, called LaunchShowCarModels in the table, to start the execution of a transaction to select the models of a given make. This transaction is executed at the application server and is called DisplayCarModels. This application invokes a database stored procedure called SearchCarModels, which executes in the DB server. The application server builds the page with the reply and sends it to the Web server, which sends the page, using the HTTP protocol, back to the client. This execution of the Web server corresponds to the transaction SendReply.   ∎

7.7.2   Workload Characterization

Workload characterization is the process of precisely describing, in a qualitative and quantitative manner, the global workload of an e-business site. The process starts with the qualitative workload description obtained in the IT Environment Characterization step. This step mapped the e-business func-

Table 7.1. Example of Part of the Workload Description for the Online Car-Buying Example (WS = Web Server; AS = Application Server; DB = Database Server).

E-Business Function	Transaction	Server
Car Selection	LaunchShowCarModels	WS
	DisplayCarModels	AS
	SearchCarModels	DB
	LaunchShowCars	WS
	DisplayCarsByMake	AS
	SearchCarsByMake	DB
	SendReply	WS
Option Selection	LaunchShowOptions	WS
	DisplayCarOptions	AS
	SearchCarOptions	DB
	SendReply	WS

tions into transactions and batch programs (see Table 7.1 for an example). The transactions associated with each e-business function are called *basic components*. We now build Client/Server Interaction Diagrams (CSIDs) for each e-business function (represented by a state of the CBMG) and assign transaction names for each of the non-client nodes in the CSID. Figure 7.11 shows an example of the CSID for the Option Selection function. It shows the transaction names associated with nodes of the CSID and the size of the messages exchanged between the various servers and the networks involved.

The basic components are then characterized by workload intensity (e.g., transaction arrival rates) and service demand parameters at each resource. The parameters for a basic component may be directly obtained from measurements, using performance monitors and accounting systems, or they may be derived from other parameters that are measured directly. Measurements must be made during peak workload periods and for an appropriate moni-

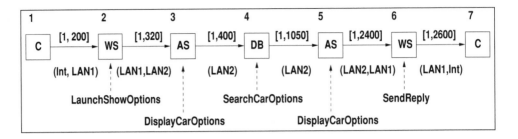

Figure 7.11. CSID for the Option Selection E-Business Function.

toring interval (e.g., one hour).

7.7.2.1 Breaking Down the Global Workload

When the workload intensity is high, large collections of workload measures can be obtained. Dealing with such collections is seldom practical, especially if workload characterization results are to be used for performance prediction through analytic models [6]. One should substitute the collection of measured values of all basic components by a more compact representation—one per basic component. This representation is called a *workload model*—the end product of the workload characterization step. See the following example for an illustration of this point.

Example 7.9

Consider that the database server of our online car-buying service was monitored during a peak period of thirty minutes. During this period, the CPU time and the number of I/Os for each of the ten thousand transactions executed in that period were recorded. Some transactions are fairly simple and use very little CPU and I/O, whereas other more complex ones may require more CPU and substantially more I/O. Figure 7.12 shows an example of a graph depicting points of the type (number of I/Os, CPU time) for the transactions executed in the measurement interval. The picture shows three natural groupings of the points in the two-dimensional space shown in the graph. Each group is called a *cluster*—the larger circles in the figure— and

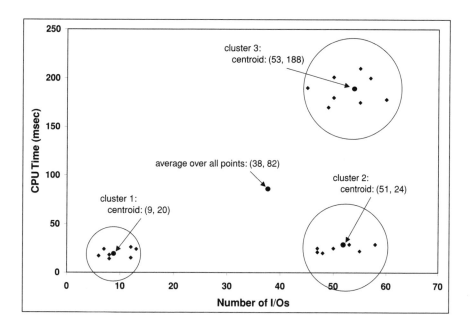

Figure 7.12. Graph for Workload Characterization Example (no. of I/Os, CPU time).

has a *centroid* defined as the point whose coordinates are the average among all points in the cluster. The "distance" between any point and the centroid of its cluster is the shortest distance between the point and the centroid of all clusters. The coordinates of the centroids of clusters 1, 2, and 3 are (9, 20), (51, 24), and (53, 188), respectively. Thus, instead of dealing with CPU and I/O demands for all ten thousand transactions, a workload model composed of the coordinates of the three clusters provides a more compact representation of the resource consumption of the workload. For instance, transactions of class 1 perform an average of nine I/Os and use an average of 20 msec of CPU time.

The graph in Fig. 7.12 also shows the point whose coordinates, (38, 82), represent the average number of I/Os and the average CPU time over all points. It is clear that if we were to represent all the points by this single point—the single cluster case—we would obtain a much less meaningful representation of the global workload than the one provided by the three clusters. Thus, the number of clusters chosen to represent the workload impacts the accuracy of the workload model. ■

Clustering algorithms [2] [3] [4] [6] [7] can be used to find groupings or patterns in large volumes of data. Each group, called a cluster, represents a typical basic component of the workload. The parameters that describe a basic component are derived from the coordinates of the centroid associated with that component.

7.7.2.2   Data Collection Issues

The parameters of the basic components are either obtained directly from measurements or derived by combining several measured values. Performance monitoring and accounting tools are used for that purpose. In an e-commerce site environment, one needs to use measurements obtained from the operating system, from the application server, and from the database server. The challenge is to correlate independent measurements taken at the various layers of an e-commerce site (e.g., Web server layer, application layer, and database layer) and allocate them to the execution of the same e-business function (see Ex. 7.10).

Example 7.10

Consider the online auto-buying service and the e-business functions described in Ex. 7.2 and the IT infrastructure described in Ex. 7.7. Assume that various types of monitors were used to take measurements on processor, I/O, and network activity during a period of one hour. From these measurements, service demands were calculated for the Web server, application server, database server, LANs 1 and 2, and the link that connects that site to the Internet. Remember that the service demand is the total service time spent in executing a function and does not include any time waiting to use any of the site's resources.

Table 7.2 shows an example of these service demands. For the three servers, both processing (P) and I/O (I) service demands are shown. Also,

Table 7.2. Service Demands (in msec) for Ex. 7.10. WS = Web server; AS = application server; DB = database server; P = processing; I = I/O.

E-Business Function	Server			LAN 1	LAN 2	Link
	WS	AS	DB			
Car Selection	P: 5.2	P: 25.0	P: 20.0	0.492	0.532	16.4
(20,000 requests)	I: 9.5	I: 15.0	I: 40.0			
Option Selection	P: 4.8	P: 18.0	P: 13.0	0.328	0.352	12.0
(18,900 requests)	I: 8.5	I: 14.0	I: 20.0			
Color Selection	P: 4.9	P: 13.0	P: 13.0	0.287	0.328	12.0
(14,120 requests)	I: 8.2	I: 12.0	I: 20.0			
Extended Services	P: 5.1	P: 12.0	P: 13.0	0.295	0.492	11.5
(8,020 requests)	I: 8.4	I: 10.0	I: 20.0			
Entry of Personal Data	P: 32.0	P: 16.0	P: 0.0	0.655	0.000	32.8
(892 requests)	I: 15.0	I: 30.0	I: 0.0			
Financing Application	P: 35.0	P: 15.0	P: 0.0	0.778	0.000	21.8
(230 requests)	I: 14.0	I: 25.0	I: 0.0			
Entry of Delivery Info	P: 32.0	P: 18.0	P: 0.0	0.410	0.000	19.1
(670 requests)	I: 14.0	I: 24.0	I: 0.0			
Hold Car	P: 31.0	P: 35.0	P: 30.0	0.819	0.901	43.7
(584 requests)	I: 15.0	I: 90.0	I: 80.0			
View Previous Order	P: 4.8	P: 12.0	P: 11.0	0.205	0.229	27.3
(89 requests)	I: 6.7	I: 0.0	I: 15.0			
Cancel Order	P: 5.2	P: 13.0	P: 18.0	0.246	0.262	30.0
(33 requests)	I: 7.1	I: 0.0	I: 30.0			

for each e-business function, the total number of executions of the function is shown. From the table, one can compute workload intensity parameters such as the rate at which e-business functions are executed. For instance, the rate at which the Car Selection function is executed is 5.55 (=20,000 /3,600) executions/sec and the rate at which the Hold Car function is executed is 0.162 (=584 / 3,600) executions/sec. The ratio of customers who hold a car to the number of customers who execute a car selection operation is 2.92% (=584 / 20,000).

The table also gives us useful information regarding the performance of the site. For example, for each e-business function we can compute the minimum time needed to execute the function by adding all the service demands for that function. If we take Hold Car as an example, we have that the minimum time spent at the server (including the link that connects the site to the Internet) is 31.0 + 15.0 + 35.0+ 90.0 + 30.0 + 80.0 + 0.819 + 0.901 + 43.7 = 326.4 msec = 0.326 sec. Since many requests are in execution concurrently, there will be waiting times at the various resources and the time spent at the e-business site will actually be higher than this minimum value. Chapters 8 and 9 discuss performance models that can be used to compute these waiting times.   ■

A description of the design and implementation of a tool for measuring the performance of e-commerce sites is described by Paixão et al [8]. The tool, called PROFIT, logs measurements from the Web server, commerce server, and database server for each request. A unique identifier is assigned to each request to allow the logs to be coalesced and results integrated for easy visualization. This tool provides *internal monitoring* capabilities only. Other tools provide *remote monitoring* of a site for purposes of measuring response time and availability as perceived by customers from various geographical regions. In this case, the server is seen as a black box.

Readers interested in tools for performance measurement can find an analysis of the various roles and challenges for building measurement tools in a paper by Buzen [1].

7.7.3 Workload Forecasting

Workload forecasting is the process of predicting how system workloads will vary in the future. Through this process one can answer important questions. "How will the number of customers visiting the site vary over the next six months?" "How will the number of customers buying computer books from an online bookstore vary over time?" Answering such questions involves evaluating workload trends if historical data are available and/or analyzing the business or strategic plans of the organization and then mapping these business plans to changes in business processes.

During workload forecasting, basic workload components are associated to business processes so that changes in the workload intensity of these components can be derived from the business process and strategic plans.

Example 7.11

Our online auto-buying service is watching traffic grow very fast. They decided to plot the number of weekly sessions to try to forecast the increase in traffic to the site in the future.

Figure 7.13 shows how the number of weekly sessions varied over the past ten weeks (solid line). Using the regression techniques available in Microsoft's Excel, we added a trend line to the graph (dashed line). A very good fit (R^2 is almost equal to one) to the curve is the exponential fit

$$\text{NumberWeeklySessions} = 224,885 \; e^{0.1977 \times \text{Week}}. \qquad (7.7.1)$$

Using this equation, we can predict that the number of sessions on week eleven will be

$$224,885 \; e^{0.1977 \times 11} = 1,978,886 \text{ sessions.} \qquad (7.7.2)$$

■

Chapter 12 discusses workload forecasting techniques for e-business in more detail.

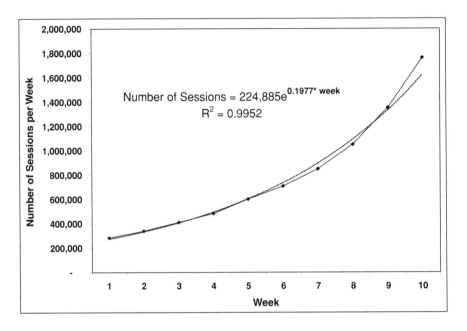

Figure 7.13. Number of Weekly Sessions for Ex. 7.11.

7.7.4 Performance Modeling

An important aspect of capacity planning involves predicting whether a system will deliver performance metrics (e.g., response time and throughput) that meet desired or acceptable service-levels. Performance prediction is the process of estimating performance measures of a computer system for a given set of parameters. Typical performance measures include response time, throughput, resource utilization, and resource queue length. Examples of performance measures for the online car-buying service include server-side response time for submitting a financing application, client-side response time for executing a Hold Car function, the utilization of LANs 1 and 2, and the throughput and average number of requests queued at the Web server.

Performance parameters are divided into the following categories.

- *System Parameters*: Characteristics of an e-commerce site that affect performance include, for example, load-balancing disciplines at the load balancer, maximum number of TCP connections in progress (i.e, size of the TCP listen queue), maximum number of threads supported by the database management system, and network protocols used.

- *Resource Parameters*: Intrinsic features of a resource that affect performance include, for example, disk seek times, latency and transfer rates, network bandwidth, router latency, and CPU speed ratings.

- *Workload Parameters*: These parameters are derived from workload characterization and divided into two subcategories.

  - *Workload Intensity Parameters* provide a measure of the load placed on the system, indicated by the number of units of work that contend for system resources. Examples include the number of sessions started per day, number of hits/day to the Web proxy server, number of pay operations requiring secure connections/sec, and number of database transactions of each type executed per unit time.

  - *Workload Service Demand Parameters* specify the total amount of service time required by each basic component at each resource. Examples include the CPU time of transactions at the application server, the total transmission time of replies from the Web server back to the customer, and the total I/O time at the database server for the Select Car function. These numbers are 25 msec, 16.4 msec, and 40 msec, according to Table 7.2.

Performance prediction requires the use of models. Two types of models may be used: simulation models and analytical models. Both types of models have to consider contention for resources and the queues that arise at each system resource—CPUs, disks, routers, firewalls, load balancers, and communication lines. Queues also arise for software resources—HTTP threads, database locks, and protocol ports.

The various queues that represent an e-commerce site are interconnected, giving rise to a network of queues, called a queuing network (QN). Chapters 8 and 9 discuss, in detail, techniques used to build and solve performance models of e-commerce sites.

7.7.5 Calibration and Validation

A performance model is said to be valid if the performance metrics (e.g., response time, resource utilizations, and throughputs) calculated by the model match the measurements of the actual system within a certain acceptable margin of error. Accuracies from 10 to 30% are acceptable in capacity planning [6].

During workload characterization, measurements are taken for service demands and workload intensity and for performance metrics such as response time, throughput, and device utilization. The same measures are computed by means of the performance model. If the computed values do not match the measured values within an acceptable level, the model must be calibrated [7]. Otherwise, the model is deemed valid and can be used for performance prediction. A detailed discussion of performance model calibration techniques is given in a previous publication [6].

7.7.6 Cost Modeling

Based on the plans to evolve the IT infrastructure and based on the existing IT platform, one should develop *cost models* that allow us to forecast the cost of changes in the infrastructure. Chapter 4 referred to the various elements of a cost model for an IT infrastructure. When different scenarios are evaluated, one needs to predict how much additional disk storage, processing capacity, main memory, and network bandwidth will be neeed for each scenario and how much these elements cost now and in the future.

While obtaining current costs is straightforward, cost prediction may not be immediate. We can use however some *rules of thumb (ROT)* to obtain first cut approximations to cost predictions. We provide below some ROTs discussed by Gray [5]. ROTs one through four assume that the increase in performance occurs with no cost increase.

1. Memories get four times larger every three years (from Moore's Law).

2. Processors get four times faster every three years (from Moore's Law).

3. Secondary storage capacities are increasing one hundred times per decade.

4. Link bandwidth increases by a factor of four every three years (from Gilder's Law).

5. The ratio between the number of MB of RAM needed by a system and its MIPS rating is rising from one to four. This ratio is called α and is known as Amdahl's Memory Law.

7.7.7 What-If Analysis

Once the performance model is built and solved, various analyses can be made regarding cost-performance trade-offs. The performance model along with cost models for the various configuration alternatives can be used to assess various scenarios and configurations. "Should we mirror the Web server to balance the load, cut down on network traffic, and improve performance?" "Should we replace the existing Web server with a faster one?" "Should we replicate the database and distribute it into more than one database server?" For each scenario, we can predict the performance of each basic component of the global workload and assign a dollar value.

The comparison of the various scenarios yields inputs to the plans to evolve the IT infrastructure, the way customers interact with the site, the business model, and the business processes. This feedback is illustrated in

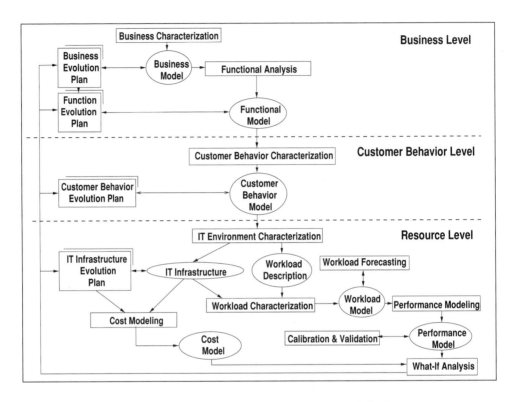

Figure 7.14. A Capacity Planning Methodology for E-Business.

Fig. 7.14, which shows the complete methodology discussed in this chapter.

7.8 Concluding Remarks

In this chapter, we learned the concepts of capacity planning and adequate capacity. We saw that capacity planning relies on predictive performance models. These models will be treated in detail in Chapters 8 and 9.

A methodology for capacity planning for e-business sites was presented and illustrated through various examples. For e-business, capacity planning entails three planning activities: business and functional planning, customer behavior planning, and IT resource planning.

Business and functional planning involves characterizing the business and analyzing the functions to be provided by the e-commerce site. Customer behavior planning includes the activities related with understanding how customers interact with the site and building customer behavior models. Finally, IT resource planning deals with the IT resources used to support the e-business and the models used to characterize the workload and predict the performance of the various transactions derived from the execution of e-business functions.

The capacity planning process involves various models. The business model describes the type of business (e.g., B2C e-tailer, C2C auction, and B2C service), the type of product or service delivery (e.g., physical goods, real time digital delivery over the Internet, and digitized music), use of third-party services, market composition, and hours of operation. The business model also includes several quantitative business descriptors (e.g., number of customers, number of items in the catalog, and number of catalog items sold per month per category). These descriptors provide business-related attributes that are important for capacity planning purposes. The functional model describes the functions provided by the e-business site. The customer behavior model describes how users navigate through the site as they use the various e-business functions. The workload model provides a synthetic description of the various transactions that implement the e-business functions. This description includes workload intensity parameters and service demand parameters. Finally, the performance model is a representation of the e-business site that can be used to predict the performance of the site under the workload described by the workload model as well as to answer various what-if questions.

Bibliography

[1] J. P. Buzen, "Perspectives on Performance Measurement," *Proc. Computer Measurement Group Conference*, Reno, NV, Dec. 5-10, 1999, pp. 583–592.

[2] M. Calzarossa and G. Serazzi, "Workload Characterization: a Survey,"

Proc. IEEE, vol. 81, no. 8, Aug. 1993, pp. 1136–1150.

[3] B. Everitt, *Cluster Analysis*, Halsted Press, New York, 1980.

[4] D. Ferrari, G. Serazzi, and A. Zeigner, *Measurement and Tuning of Computer Systems*, Prentice Hall, Upper Saddle River, NJ, 1983.

[5] J. Gray and P. Shenoy, "Rules of Thumb in Data Engineering," *Proc. IEEE International Conf. on Data Engineering*, San Diego, CA, April 2000.

[6] D. A. Menascé, V. Almeida, and L. W. Dowdy, *Capacity Planning and Performance Modeling: From Mainframes to Client-Server Systems*, Prentice Hall, Upper Saddle River, NJ, 1994.

[7] D. A. Menascé and V. Almeida, *Capacity Planning for Web Performance: Metrics, Models and Methods*, Prentice Hall, Upper Saddle River, NJ, 1998.

[8] G. T. Paixão, W. Meira Jr., V. A. F. Almeida, D. A. Menascé, and A. Pereira, "Design and Implementation of a Tool for Measuring the Performance of Complex E-commerce Sites," *Proc. 11th International Conf. Modelling Tools and Techniques for Computer and Communication System Performance Evaluation (Tools 2000)*, Schaumburg, IL, March 27-31, 2000.

Chapter 8

Performance Modeling Concepts

8.1 Introduction

The goal of this chapter is to provide insight and intuition regarding how performance models can be constructed, solved, and used in the context of electronic business environments. The emphasis here is on the development of a complete understanding of simple performance models. The chapter begins by analyzing some fundamental questions. What is a performance model? Why do we need models? What is the basic information required by performance models? The fundamentals of performance models are then introduced. These include concepts such as service time, service demand, waiting time, response time, throughput, and performance laws. A first cut scalability analysis technique is also introduced with the study of performance bounds. Bounds on performance measures can be obtained through the use of simple models that can be solved by "back of the envelope" calculations. Performance bounding is a handy technique for scalability analysis, a key issue for electronic business.

Instead of relying on ad hoc procedures and rules of thumb, this chapter provides a uniform way of quantitatively analyzing e-commerce applications. The simple performance models are based on a variant of queuing theory [10] called "operational analysis" [7] [14]. Delays in electronic business transactions have two components: service time and waiting time. Service time is defined as the time spent using resources, such as Web servers, commerce servers, authentication servers, payment servers, databases, processors, disks, and communication links. Waiting times arise when several requests from customers contend for the use of a finite-capacity resource. Let us consider the case of a burst of customers that arrive at an e-commerce site due to a new TV ad campaign. If the website capacity is inadequate, customers may experience long waiting times to get access to the site's resources.

Performance models can be developed at different levels of detail. This chapter explains how to develop simple performance models that help the reader understand why some systems work well whereas others are so slow. The next chapter discusses more detailed models and their solution techniques.

8.2   Performance of a Simple E-Business Server

Consider a small online toy store. The configuration of its website consists of two servers connected by a 100 Mbps LAN. One server works as the storefront, providing the home page with its business functions and the other holds the database. A performance model can be developed at different levels of detail. In this example, we look at performance from the server-level point of view. A server-level approach considers the server being modeled as a "black box." In this case, the internal details of the box (e.g., processor, disks, and network interface) are not modeled explicitly. Figure 8.1 depicts the toy store website architecture. The store offers several business functions, such as Add to Cart, Search, Browse, Welcome, Register, and Pay. For the sake of simplicity, let us assume that customers have only one navigational pattern: they visit the home page and then do a number of catalog searches for their favorite toys.

Management wants to increase the customer base and decides to launch an ad campaign on some popular family-oriented magazines. To provide management with information regarding the system usage, the Webmaster monitored the site during the peak hour and collected the measurements displayed in Table 8.1.

The company managers are concerned with the increase of visitors during the peak hour. So, they posed the following general questions about the performance of the site. What is the online store performance if the number of customer sessions double during the peak hour? What is the LAN utilization if the size of the catalog pages increases by 200%, due to new pictures that have higher resolution? What is the impact on performance if customers change their navigational pattern and the number of catalog

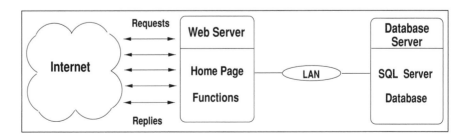

Figure 8.1. Small Online Toy Store Site Architecture.

Table 8.1. Input Data for the Simple Problem.

Type of Data	Value
Number of completed customer sessions	35,000
Web server total busy period	1,200 sec
DB server total busy period	2,100 sec
Measurement interval	3,600 sec

searches increases by 50%? Posing questions is an important step toward performance modeling. Actually, the questions help define the approach to be taken to develop a model. Because these questions do not ask for response time, we will concentrate on the development of models that provide measures such as throughput and resource utilization.

Throughout the chapter, we will see how to develop simple models to answer those general questions posed by management. The next chapter shows how to deal with more powerful performance models that are capable of providing answers to questions that refer to the internal components of the servers. For instance, what is the percentage of response time reduction if the speed of the disk subsystem of the DB server is upgraded by 20%?

8.3   What Is a Performance Model?

A model is a representation of a system. It could be a physical, logical, or functional one. While a model represents a system, it should be as simple as possible and it should be capable of capturing the most relevant characteristics of the system under study. Often, a model of a system helps one understand some fundamental characteristics of the system. Let us take Zipf's Law [16] as an example. It was originally applied to the relationship between a word's popularity in terms of rank and its frequency of use. Zipf observed that the distribution of word frequencies in English, if the words are ordered according to their ranks, is an inverse power law with the exponent close to one. Thus, Zipf's Law states that if one ranks the popularity of words in a given text (denoted by ρ) by their frequency of use (denoted by f), then

$$f \sim \frac{1}{\rho}. \tag{8.3.1}$$

Zipf's Law indicates that a few elements score very high and a very large number of elements score very low. In the middle, there are a medium number of elements. For example, a few words in the English language are very popular (e.g., and, the, here) while there is a huge number of words whose probability of use is almost zero (e.g., façade, Zipf).

Analysis of experimental data suggests that many phenomena in the Web can be modeled by Zipf's Law [2] [3] [5]. The highly uneven popularity of various Web documents is a well-documented phenomenon. Popularity measures the distribution of Web requests on a per-file basis.

Several empirical measurements indicate that Zipf's Law applies quite strongly to documents served by Web servers [1] [3] [6], yielding the relationship

$$P = \frac{k}{r}, \tag{8.3.2}$$

where P is the number of references to a document whose rank is r and k is some positive constant. Equation (8.3.2) is a model that represents well the distribution of references among documents in a Web server. This means that the nth most popular document is exactly twice as likely to be accessed as the $2n^{th}$ most popular document. In other words, some documents are very popular while most documents receive just a few references.

Zipf's Law helps us understand certain asymptotic properties of Web caching performance. From Zipf's Law, we notice that there exists a concentration of Web accesses to "hot documents," which contributes to improve cache performance. The lower in the rank (i.e., small values of r), the higher the number of references. The results obtained from Zipf's model can be used to characterize WWW workloads, analyze document dissemination and replication strategies, and model the behavior of caching and mirroring systems.

There are many types of models. For instance, in electronic business, graph-based models are used to represent the customer behavior, such as the Customer Behavior Model Graph (CBMG), described in Chapter 2. This type of model provides insight into the way customers interact with an e-commerce site. From the model, one can derive quantitative information such as how many times a business function (e.g., Pay, Login, Search, and Browse) is invoked per visit to the site or the average number of functions requested by a customer during his/her visit to the site. In Chapter 3, we presented C/S Interaction Diagrams (CSIDs), which are useful for representing all possible interactions between customers and a site for a business function.

A *resource model* represents the structure and the various components of an electronic business site. *Performance models* represent the way system's resources are used by the workload and capture the main factors determining system performance. These models use information provided by resource and workload (e.g., CSIDs) models. Performance models are used to compute both traditional performance metrics such as response time, throughput, utilization, and mean queue length as well as innovative business-oriented performance metrics, such as revenue throughput or lost-revenue throughput. Basically, performance models can be grouped into two categories: analytic and simulation models.

Analytical models specify the interaction between the various components of a system via formulas. For instance, let us analyze the minimum possible HTTP transaction time [8]. The following expression is a model for the minimum possible request response time, $RT_{\min}$.

$$RT_{\min} = \text{RTT} + \text{request}_{\min} + \text{SiteProcessingTime} + \text{reply}_{\min}, \qquad (8.3.3)$$

where RTT is the round trip delay inherent in network communication, $\text{request}_{\min} = \text{RequestSize/Bandwidth}$ is the minimum time needed to send the request to the e-commerce site, SiteProcessingTime is the time spent processing the request at the e-commerce site, and $\text{reply}_{\min}$ = ReplySize / Bandwidth is the minimum time needed to send the reply back from the e-commerce site to the client.

Equation (8.3.3) is a simple example of an analytic model. It describes the relationship between performance metrics (i.e., $RT_{\min}$) and the parameters of the system (i.e., Bandwidth and RTT) and its workload parameters (i.e., RequestSize and ReplySize).

Simulation models mimic the behavior of the actual system by running a simulation program. The structure of a simulation program is based on the states of the simulated system and events that change the system state. A simulation program mimics the transitions among the system states according to the occurrence of events in the simulated system. Simulation programs measure performance by counting events and the duration of relevant conditions of the system. The main advantage of simulation is its great generality. On the other hand, simulation programs may be expensive to develop and to run. For instance, let us consider that the average service time to search an item in the catalog of an electronic retailer is 0.5 sec. When a search request arrives, the simulation program switches to a state that represents the searching activity. The program may randomly pick a number between 0.1 and 2.0, play as if the database were busy for that amount of time searching for the item, advance the simulation clock by that amount, compute that as part of the database busy period and continue, executing other events that represent the requests processed by the store [9] [13]. A discussion on modeling contention for software resources in e-business applications is found in Chapter 10.

8.3.1   Why Do We Need Models?

Performance models help us understand the quantitative behavior of complex systems, such as electronic commerce applications and entertainment.

Commerce is naturally a transaction-based system, where response time is critical. Entertainment is based on streaming technology, which also has critical performance requirements. In addition to that, models have been used for multiple purposes in systems.

- In the infrastructure design of e-business and Web-based applications, various issues call for the use of models to evaluate system alternatives. For example, a distributed Web server system is any architecture consisting of multiple Web server hosts distributed on a LAN, with some sort of mechanism to distribute incoming requests among the servers. So, for a specific type of workload, what is the most effective scheme for load balancing in a certain distributed Web server system? Models are also useful for analyzing document replacement policies in caching proxies and bandwidth capacity of certain network links. In summary, performance models are an essential tool for studying resource allocation problems in the context of e-commerce.

- Most e-commerce applications operate in multi-tiered environments. As discussed in Chapter 3, e-commerce applications are usually composed of different processes that may run on different hosts. Applications are rarely designed with network costs in mind. Therefore, models can be used to analyze performance of distributed applications and evaluate networking impact.

- Performance tuning of complex applications is a huge territory. When an e-commerce application presents performance problems, a mandatory step to solve them is to tune the underlying system. This means to measure the system and try to identify the sources of performance problems: application design, lack of capacity, excess of load, or problems in the infrastructure (i.e., network, servers, ISP). Performance models can help find performance problems by answering what-if questions as opposed to making changes in the production environment.

- As discussed in the previous chapters, doing business on the Internet means dealing with unpredictable traffic volumes. At the same time, customers demand that e-business companies offer good quality of service, in terms of response time, availability, and reliability. With so much at stake, capacity planning is a critical technology for e-business. The heart of a capacity planning process is its ability to predict the performance of a given site configuration executing a given workload generated by the site's customers. Performance models can be used for predictive purposes. They can answer what-if questions regarding performance impacts due to changes in components, elements, and workload of an e-commerce site. Performance models can help analyze trade-offs among future scenarios.

8.3.2 A Modeling Paradigm

Modeling paradigms can be viewed from different perspectives. One such perspective, called modeling/prediction paradigm, is illustrated in Fig. 8.2. It consists of three different phases: 1) modeling the system, 2) validating the model, and 3) using the model to predict future system performance. The initial step of the modeling phase consists of building an adequate performance model of the e-business. Although it could be of any type, this chapter focuses on analytical models. Once a suitable model has been developed, the necessary input parameters must be obtained and some assumptions must be stated. This constitutes the second step of the modeling phase. After building the model and obtaining its parameters, one has to solve the model, using analytic or simulation techniques. In other words, one has to compute the results of the model, i.e., the performance metrics. Simple techniques to solve performance models are introduced later in this chapter. Complex models are solved by efficient techniques discussed in Chapter 9.

After calculating the results, a question naturally arises: "How accurate are the results?" This means that the model results must be compared

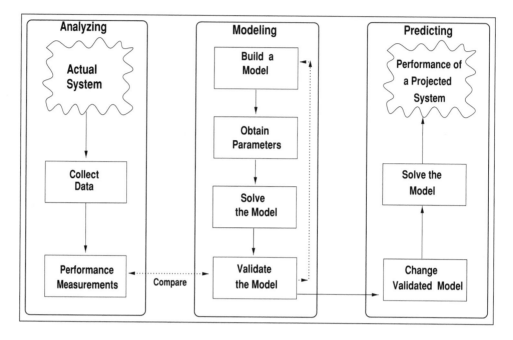

Figure 8.2. Modeling/Prediction Paradigm.

against measurement data obtained from the actual system, as indicated by the leftmost block of Fig. 8.2. For instance, the response time of e-commerce transactions computed by the model should be compared against the response time measured in the actual e-commerce environment. This comparison check is analyzed and deemed "acceptable" or "unacceptable" by the performance team. As a rule of thumb, resource utilization within 10%, system throughput within 10%, and response time within 20% are considered acceptable [11] [13]. So, the reader must be asking, "What should I do if the comparison is unacceptable?" The starting point is to review all the steps of the modeling and characterization process to determine the sources of errors, which may exist in the measurement process or in the modeling phase. Several examples throughout the book will show how to construct models and how to measure and extract model parameters from actual systems.

Once the model has been validated, it can be used to predict the performance of new system scenarios, as shown by the rightmost block of Fig. 8.2. In this case, changes are made to the validated model. For instance, what will be the site's response time for the Browse transaction if the traffic becomes ten times greater than the current average traffic? To answer this type of what-if question, one has to change the model parameters to reflect the new traffic intensity and solve the response time model again, to obtain the performance measures of the projected environment.

8.3.3 Revisiting the Simple Problem

The framework provided by the reference model discussed in Chapter 1 is our starting point for developing a model to answer the questions posed in Section 8.2. The reference model in Fig. 8.3 consists of four layers grouped into two main blocks. The upper block focuses on the nature of the business and the processes that provide the services offered by the electronic business site. The lower block concentrates on the way customers interact with the site and the demand they place upon the resources of the site infrastructure. In other words, the lower part represents the models that are capable of answering our questions. Thus, we will concentrate on the lower part of the reference model, as indicated by the dashed rectangle in Fig. 8.3.

In this simple example, the Customer Behavior Model Graphs (CBMG) exhibited in Fig 8.4 is very straightforward. Solving the CBMG (as explained in Chapters 2 and 11), we obtain the visit ratios to each state: for each visit to the home page, a customer performs 2.5 catalog searches on the average.

In our simple example, the only business function used is the Search transaction. To understand this business function, we examine the the Client/Server Interaction Diagram (CSID) derived from the CBMG. From the server logs, we calculate the fraction of refused connections. Figure 8.5 displays the CSID. As specified by the problem statement, every customer

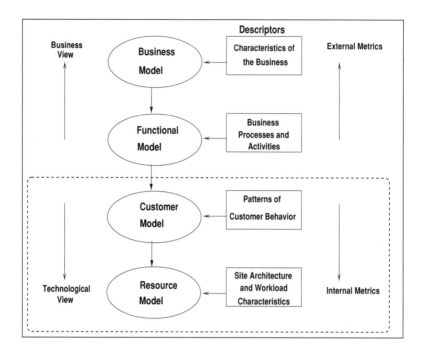

Figure 8.3. Reference Models for Electronic Business.

that gets into the store home page performs a number of catalog search operations. In Fig. 8.5, the interaction $1 \rightarrow 2 \rightarrow 4 \rightarrow 5 \rightarrow 6$ specifies the Search function. In this case, the client sends a requests to the e-commerce Web server, represented by node 2. The size of the request is m_1 bytes. With probability 0.95, the Web server (WS) accepts the connection and sends a message of size m_3 to the database server. The database server replies to the WS with a message of size m_4. Finally, the Web server replies to the client with a message of size m_5. With probability 0.05, as indicated by the

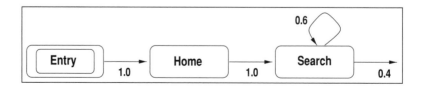

Figure 8.4. CBMG for the Customer of the Online Toy Store.

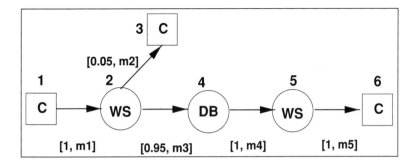

Figure 8.5. CSID for Search Function of the Online Toy Store.

interaction $1 \rightarrow 2 \rightarrow 3$, the server is overloaded and refuses the connection. The server sends a message of size m_2, which closes the interaction.

Now we are able to understand how the WS and database servers are used during the execution of a Search function. The database server is used only if sequence $1 \rightarrow 2 \rightarrow 4 \rightarrow 5 \rightarrow 6$ is followed. The probability that this happens is 0.95. The Web server appears twice in the same sequence and once in the sequence $1 \rightarrow 2 \rightarrow 3$, which happens with probability 0.05. So, the average number of times the Web server is activated is $2 \times 0.95 + 1 \times 0.05 = 1.95$, and the average number of times the database server is activated during the execution of a search function is $1 \times 0.95 = 0.95$.

So, what have we learned from the two models (i.e., CMBG and CSID) developed in this step? First of all, we now know that each customer that visits the online toy store performs 2.5 catalog search operations on the average. Furthermore, we learned that on average, the execution of a Search function activates the Web and database servers 1.95 and 0.95 times, respectively. In summary, we know the number of times the business functions are invoked during a customer session and how many times the e-commerce site resources are demanded by the business function. The bottom part of Table 8.2 reflects the quantitative information added to the problem by the models developed in this step.

Table 8.2. Input Data for the Simple Problem.

Type of Data	Value
Number of completed customer sessions	35,000
Web server busy period (sec)	1,200
DB server busy period (sec)	2,100
Measurement interval (sec)	3,600
Number of searches per customer session	2.5
Number of visits to the Web server per search	1.95
Number of visits to the database server per search	0.95

8.4   Service Time and Service Demand

An e-commerce transaction has been defined as a request from a customer to execute one of the functions provided by the e-business site. Consider any resource i used by an e-commerce transaction. There are different levels of resources. We may be looking at high-level resources such as payment and authentication servers. Or we may be interested in low-level resources, such as the processor and the disks of a server or a LAN segment, or even a router. A transaction may need to visit resource i several times before it completes. For example, a Browse transaction may need to perform several I/O operations at certain disks, use the CPU at the database server several times, and use various networks to carry the request and reply involved in the transaction. In this chapter, we look at the transaction execution path from a server perspective. The server-level performance model views the server being modeled as a "black box." Thus, the execution path of a *pay* transaction may involve several visits to the Web server, DB server, authentication server, and payment server. Let V_i be the average number of visits made by a transaction to resource i and let S_i be the average service time per visit at the resource. The average service demand, D_i, at resource i is defined as the total service time of a transaction at resource i and can be computed as the product of the average number of visits to the resource by the average time spent per visit at the resource. Thus,

$$D_i = V_i \times S_i. \qquad (8.4.4)$$

The next sections explore in detail how service times can be computed for various categories of resources found in e-commerce systems.

Example 8.1

Consider a site that provides business-to-business services to the pharmaceutical distribution industry. The Web server has interfaces with a legacy mainframe system. The site processes twenty thousand orders per day. Ninety percent of the orders have an average of six line items and 10% have twenty-eight line items. The processing of the twenty thousand orders per day involves the legacy system in real time. Each line item takes 0.5 sec to be processed by the mainframe. Viewing the mainframe as a "black box," what is the service demand at the mainframe per order processed?

From the definition of service demand, we know that

$$D_{\mathrm{mainframe}} = V_{\mathrm{mainframe}} \times S_{\mathrm{mainframe}}$$

and $V_{\mathrm{mainframe}} = 1$. To calculate $S_{\mathrm{mainframe}}$, we need to compute the average service time, as follows:

$$S_{\mathrm{mainframe}} = 0.10 \times (28 \times 0.5) + 0.90 \times (6 \times 0.5) = 4.1 \text{ sec.}$$

Thus, $D_{\mathrm{mainframe}} = V_{\mathrm{mainframe}} \times S_{\mathrm{mainframe}} = 1 \times 4.1$ sec.   ∎

8.4.1   Service Times at a Server

Simply stated, a server is a combination of a hardware platform, operating system, server software, and content. Usually, the hardware platform consists of processors, memory, I/O subsystems (i.e., disks), network interface units, and special device controllers (e.g., audio and video units). The calculation of service time at any resource of a system can be computed according to its definition.

By definition, the service demand of a transaction at resource i specifies the total amount of service time required by the transaction during its execution at the resource. It is worth repeating that service demand refers only to the time a request spends actually receiving service. It does not include waiting times. Recall that V_i denotes the average number of visits that a request makes to queue i and S_i represents the mean service time per visit to resource i. Thus, service time of a transaction at resource i is given by $S_i = D_i/V_i$.

8.4.2   Service Times in Communication Networks

A message from a client to a server or from a server to another server has to go through several protocol layers and may have to be transmitted through one or more networks as depicted by Fig. 8.6. In this figure, a message from a Web server to the database server has to cross a 10 Mbps Ethernet and a 100 Mbps backbone FDDI. Messages generated by an application have to go through a protocol stack that involves, at least, a transport layer protocol (e.g., TCP or UDP), an internet protocol (e.g., IP or IPX), and a network protocol (e.g., Ethernet or Token Ring). Protocol entities at each layer communicate with each other by exchanging Protocol Data Units (PDUs) composed of a header and a data area. PDUs receive different names for different protocols and usually have a maximum size for the data area. At the network layer, the maximum size of the data area is called *maximum transmission unit (MTU)*. For example, the MTU is 1,500 bytes for an Ethernet, 4,472 bytes for an FDDI Ring, and 4,444 bytes for a Token Ring. So, routers have to be able to fragment datagrams as they go through networks of decreasing MTUs. Fragments are reassembled at the IP level by the destination host. For example, a 2,500-byte packet crossing from the

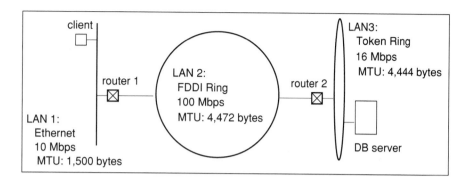

Figure 8.6. Connectivity Between a Client and a Server.

FDDI network to the Ethernet has to be fragmented into two *fragments* by router 1.

Each protocol layer adds its own header and sometimes a trailer. Table 8.3 lists the PDU name, maximum size of the PDU, header plus trailer overhead, and the maximum size of the data area, which is equal to the maximum size of the PDU minus the overhead, for various important protocols [4]. When a TCP connection is established, each side has the option of announcing the largest "chunk" of data it expects to receive [15]. This is called the maximum segment size (MSS). The MSS plus the size of the TCP and IP headers cannot exceed the MTU at the network layer. For example, if Ethernet is used at the network layer and IP version 4 is used, MSS cannot exceed 1,460 (= 1,500 - 20 - 20) bytes.

The service time of a message at a network is the time it takes to transmit the message over the network. This time is equal to the ratio of the number of bytes needed to transmit the message—including protocol header and trailer overhead—divided by the network bandwidth. The protocol overhead depends on the protocols involved and on the fragmentation that may be needed at the network layer.

To illustrate how a message service time is computed, let us consider the following example. The client of Fig. 8.7 (a) sends a three-hundred-byte long request to the database server and receives a ten-thousand-byte long reply.

Table 8.3. Characteristics of Various Network Protocols.

Protocol	PDU Name	Max. PDU Size (bytes)	Overhead (bytes)	Max. Data Area (bytes)
TCP	segment	65,515	20	65,495
UDP	datagram	65,515	8	65,507
IP version 4	datagram	65,535	20	65,515
IP version 6	datagram	65,535	40	65,495
ATM	cell	53	5	48
Ethernet	frame	1,518	18	1,500
IEEE 802.3	frame	1,518	21	1,497
IEEE 802.5 Token Ring	frame	4,472	28	4,444
FDDI (RFC 1390)	frame	4,500	28	4,472

The interaction between the client and the server takes place over a TCP connection (see Fig. 8.7 (a)).

The request from the client to the server is placed into the data area of a TCP segment, which travels in the data area of an IP datagram. The IP datagram is encapsulated by an Ethernet frame, by an FDDI frame, and by a Token Ring frame as it travels in LANs 1, 2, and 3, respectively (see Fig. 8.7 (b)). So, the three-hundred-byte request receives twenty bytes of TCP and twenty bytes of IP header, plus eighteen bytes of frame overhead in LAN1, twenty-eight bytes of frame overhead in LAN 2, and twenty-eight bytes of frame overhead in LAN3. So, the three-hundred-byte request becomes a 358 (= 300 + 20 + 20 + 18) byte frame in LAN 1 and a 368 (= 300 + 20 + 20 + 28) byte frame in LANs 2 and 3. The time to transmit a frame over a network is equal to the size of the frame in bits divided by the network's bandwidth in bps. So, the frame transmission times for the

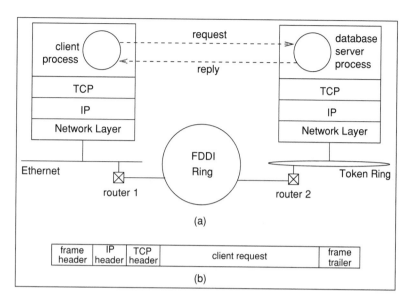

Figure 8.7. Interaction Between Client and Server over a TCP Connection.

frames containing the client request at LANs 1, 2, and 3 are given by

$$\frac{358 \times 8}{10,000,000} = 0.000286 \ \ \text{sec},$$

$$\frac{368 \times 8}{100,000,000} = 0.00002944 \ \ \text{sec, and}$$

$$\frac{368 \times 8}{16,000,000} = 0.000184 \ \ \text{sec, respectively.}$$

Let us now turn our attention to the reply from the server to the client. Assume that when the TCP connection was established, the MSS used is 1,460 bytes. This means that the server will have to send seven TCP segments to the client in order to send its ten-thousand-byte reply. The first six segments have 1,460 bytes of data each plus the twenty-byte TCP header. The last segment has $1,240 \ (= 10,000 - 6 \times 1,460)$ bytes. Each segment receives an IP header and a frame header in each of the networks it travels from the server to the client.

We compute now the service times of the reply in LANs 1, 2, and 3. We start with LAN 3, the Token Ring LAN. Each of the first six segments generate 1,528-byte frames because each of these frames has 1,460 bytes worth of TCP data, twenty bytes of TCP header, twenty bytes of IP header, and twenty-eight bytes of Token Ring frame header. The last segment generates a 1,308-byte frame. Thus, the service time of the reply in LAN 3 is

$$\frac{(6 \times 1,528 + 1,308) \times 8}{16,000,000} = 0.00524 \text{ sec.} \tag{8.4.5}$$

The frame header and bandwidth in LANs 1 and 2 are different than for LAN 3, giving rise to different service times. The service times for LANs 1 and 2 are given by

$$\frac{[6 \times (1,460 + 20 + 20 + 18) + (1,240 + 20 + 20 + 18)] \times 8}{10,000,000} = 0.00832 \text{ sec and}$$

$$\frac{[6 \times (1,460 + 20 + 20 + 28) + (1,240 + 20 + 20 + 28)] \times 8}{100,000,000} = 0.000838 \text{ sec,}$$

respectively. Note that since the MSS is smaller than or equal to the MTU of all networks involved, there is no fragmentation. Current IP standards recommend that a source host discovers the minimum MTU along a path before choosing the initial datagram size [4]. This avoids fragmentation and reassembly altogether and speeds up packet processing time at intermediate routers and at the destination host.

In what follows, we provide general equations for the average service time of a message at a network for the case when there is no fragmentation.

Let

- N = number of networks between the client and the server,

- MessageSize = size, in bytes, of a message exchanged between client and server,

- MTU_n = MTU, in bytes, of network n,

- TCPOvhd = overhead, in bytes, of the TCP protocol,

- IPOvhd = overhead, in bytes, of the IP protocol,

- MSS $=$ maximum segment size in bytes (since there is no fragmentation, we assume that MSS $\leq \min_{n=1}^{N}$ MTU$_n$ − TCPOvhd − IPOvhd),

- FrameOvhd$_n$ $=$ overhead, in bytes, of the frames in network n,

- Overhead$_n$ $=$ total overhead (TCP + IP + frame), in bytes, for all frames necessary to carry a message on network n,

- Bandwidth$_n$ $=$ bandwidth, in Mbps, of network n, and

- NDatagrams$_n$ $=$ number of IP datagrams transmitted over network n to carry a message.

In the case of no fragmentation, the sender host (client or server) generates datagrams whose size is less than or equal to the minimum MTU over all N networks. Each datagram only carries MSS bytes worth of message data. Thus, the number of datagrams needed to transmit the message over any of the N networks is

$$\text{NDatagrams} = \left\lceil \frac{\text{MessageSize}}{\text{MSS}} \right\rceil. \tag{8.4.6}$$

The total protocol overhead involved in transmitting a message over network n is given by

$$\text{Overhead}_n = \text{NDatagrams} \times (\text{TCPOvhd} + \text{IPOvhd} + \text{FrameOvhd}_n). \tag{8.4.7}$$

Finally, the service time at network n for a message is equal to the total number of bits needed to transmit the message (including overhead) divided by the bandwidth in bps. Hence,

$$\text{ServiceTime}_n = \frac{(\text{MessageSize} + \text{Overhead}_n) \times 8}{10^6 \times \text{Bandwidth}_n}. \tag{8.4.8}$$

The utilization of network n is given by the arrival rate of messages to the network multiplied by the average service time of a message in the network.

Example 8.2

The client in Fig. 8.6 submits transactions to the database server at a rate of three transactions per minute, i.e, 0.05 transactions/sec. The average size of the request message is four hundred bytes. Eighty percent of the replies are 8,092 bytes long and the remaining 20% are 100,000 bytes long on average. Assuming that there is no fragmentation, we want to compute the average service time of requests and replies at each of the three networks, as well as the utilization of each network assuming an MSS of 1,460 bytes.

Using Eq. (8.4.6), we compute the number of datagrams for requests, short replies, and long replies, as

$$\lceil 400/1,460 \rceil = 1 \text{ for requests,}$$

$$\lceil 8,092/1,460 \rceil = 6 \text{ for short replies, and}$$

$$\lceil 100,000/1,460 \rceil = 69 \text{ for long replies.}$$

The overhead per network, computed using Eq. (8.4.7), and the average service time, computed from Eq. (8.4.8), for the request and the two types of replies are shown in Table 8.4. The average network utilization at each network is obtained by multiplying the average arrival rate of e-commerce transactions by the average service time for the messages involved in a transaction. The average service time per transaction at any network is equal to the average service time for the request plus the average service time for the reply. The average service time for the reply is 0.8 times the average service time for short replies plus 0.2 times the average service time for long replies. Using the values of Table 8.4, we can compute the utilization of each network. The results are shown in Table 8.5. Network utilization values are given for various values of the number of clients. The overall arrival rate of transactions at each network is equal to the number of clients multiplied by the arrival rate of transactions per client.   ∎

The expressions for network service times and utilizations are summarized in Fig. 8.8. Another popular component in communication networks

Table 8.4. Network Computations for Ex. 8.2.

		Request	Short Reply	Long Reply
LAN 1	NDatagrams	1	6	69
	Overhead (bytes)	58	348	4002
	ServiceTime (msec)	0.366	6.75	83.2
LAN 2	NDatagrams	1	6	69
	Overhead (bytes)	68	408	4692
	ServiceTime (msec)	0.0374	0.680	8.38
LAN 3	NDatagrams	1	6	69
	Overhead (bytes)	68	408	4692
	ServiceTime (msec)	0.234	4.25	52.3

is a router. It is a communications processor that is used to determine the route that a datagram will follow from the source host to the destination host. Datagrams incoming into a router are queued up until the router processor is available to inspect the packet. The datagram's destination address is used by the router to determine the next best outgoing link, based on routing tables at the router. The datagram is then placed at the output queue for the next link in its path to the destination. The time taken by a router to process a datagram is known as *router latency* and is usually provided by router vendors in μsec per packet. The total service time of a message at a router is then given by

$$\text{RouterServiceTime} = \text{NDatagrams} \times \text{RouterLatency}, \qquad (8.4.13)$$

where NDatagrams is given by Eq. (8.4.6).

Example 8.3

Consider the simple example of Section 8.2, where the Web server and database server exchange messages as shown by the dashed rectangle of the

Table 8.5. Network Utilizations for Ex. 8.2.

	Service Times (sec)		
	LAN 1	LAN 2	LAN 3
	0.0224	0.00223	0.0141
	Percent Utilization		
No. Clients	LAN 1	LAN 2	LAN 3
40	4.5	0.4	2.8
80	9.0	0.9	5.6
120	13.4	1.4	8.5
160	17.9	1.8	11.3
200	22.4	2.3	14.1
240	26.9	2.7	16.9
280	31.4	3.2	19.7

CSID of Fig 8.9. Consider that the size of the request message is $m_3 = 400$ bytes and the size of the reply is $m_4 = 9,150$ bytes. The Web server uses CGI stubs to send transaction requests over a TCP connection with a MSS equal to 1,460 bytes to the database server, as shown in the configuration of Fig. 8.1. The network is a 100BASE-T Ethernet. What is the network utilization?

From Table 8.1 and Section 8.3.3, we know that the throughput in searches/sec is

$$35,000 \times 2.5/3,600 = 24.3 \text{ tps.}$$

Using Eq. (8.4.6), we compute the number of datagrams for requests and replies as

$$\lceil 400/1,460 \rceil = 1 \text{ for requests and}$$
$$\lceil 9,150/1,460 \rceil = 7 \text{ for replies.}$$

Number of datagrams generated by a message (no fragmentation):

$$\text{NDatagrams} = \left\lceil \frac{\text{MessageSize}}{\text{MSS}} \right\rceil \quad (8.4.9)$$

Total protocol overhead of a message over network n:

$$\text{Overhead}_n = \text{NDatagrams} \times (\text{TCPOvhd} + \text{IPOvhd} + \text{FrameOvhd}_n) \quad (8.4.10)$$

Message service time at network n:

$$\text{ServiceTime}_n = \frac{(\text{MessageSize} + \text{Overhead}_n) \times 8}{10^6 \times \text{Bandwidth}_n} \quad (8.4.11)$$

Utilization of network n:

$$U_n = \sum_{\text{messages } j} \lambda_j \times \text{ServiceTime}_n^j, \quad (8.4.12)$$

where λ_j is the arrival rate of messages of type j and ServiceTime_n^j is the average service time for messages of type j on network n

Figure 8.8. Network Equations.

Using Eqs. (8.4.7) and (8.4.8) we compute the service times for the request and reply as 0.366 and 7.64 msec, respectively. Then, the network

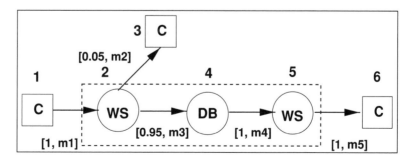

Figure 8.9. CSID for the Online Toy Store.

utilization is $U_{\text{network}} = 24.3 \times (0.366 + 7.64) \times 10^{-3} = 19.5\%$.   ■

8.4.3   Revisiting the Simple Problem

In this section, we learned how to compute service time and service demands for different resources of a system. So let us now revisit the simple example and calculate the service times and service demands for the Search transactions that are executed at the online toy store. From Table 8.2, we know that each customer session generates 2.5 Searches on average. Moreover, each Search visits the Web server 1.95 times and the database server 0.95 times. Therefore, $V_{\text{WS}} = 1.95$ and $V_{\text{DB}} = 0.95$. The total number of searches in the measurement period and the service demands are given by

$$\text{TotalNumberOfSearches} = \text{NumberOfSessions} \times \text{SearchesPerSession}$$
$$= 35,000 \times 2.5$$
$$= 87,500 \text{ and}$$

$$D_{\text{WS}} = \frac{\text{WS TotalBusyTime}}{\text{TotalNumberOfSearches}}$$
$$= \frac{1,200 \text{ sec}}{87,500} = 13.71 \text{ msec.} \qquad (8.4.14)$$

Similarly, we obtain the service demand for the database server, $D_{\text{DB}} = (2,100/87,500) = 24$ msec. Once we have obtained the service demands and the visit ratios per search, we can calculate the service times per visit using the equation, $S_i = D_i/V_i$. Thus, $S_{\text{WS}} = 13.71/1.95 = 7.03$ and $S_{\text{DB}} = 24/0.95 = 25.26$.

8.5   Queues, Waiting Time, and Response Time

During its execution, a transaction in e-commerce systems is serviced by many different resources, such as Web servers, database servers, and payment servers. Each time a transaction or request visits a resource, it may need to queue for the use of the resource. Figure 8.10 (a) shows the graphical

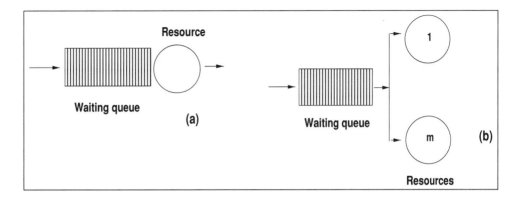

Figure 8.10. Graphical Representations of a Resource and Its Queue.

notation used to represent a resource (a circle) and its queue (striped rectangle). The resource in the case of Fig. 8.10 (a) could be an authentication server, and the striped rectangle would represent the queue of transactions waiting to be authenticated by the server. From Fig. 8.10-a, we notice that

$$\text{Response Time} = \text{Waiting Time} + \text{Service Time}, \qquad (8.5.15)$$

where response time is the time spent by an e-commerce transaction per visit to the resource, queuing and receiving service.

In some cases, there may be multiple resources for the same queue. Consider the example of an e-commerce site with multiple servers and some sort of load balancing mechanism, used to distribute the requests among the servers. In this case, there is a common queue of requests waiting to be scheduled to any of the servers, as shown in Fig. 8.10 (b).

There are situations in which a resource is dedicated to a request or an ample number of resources exist so that no queuing takes place. We call these resources *delay resources* since they only impose a delay to the flow of a request. The graphical representation of a delay resource is a circle without the striped rectangle (the queue). Delay resources can be used to represent the time needed by a third party (e.g., payment authorization or ad generation) to service a request from an e-commerce site.

As the load on a resource increases, more requests will be queued for the resource. At light loads, however, the total queuing time may be negligible when compared with the service time at the resource. In these cases, we may want to represent the resource as a delay resource to simplify the model. We now define the notation used throughout this book to represent performance variables for queues in e-commerce systems. Some of the concepts presented here were already introduced, albeit more informally, in the previous sections. We will call *queue* the waiting queue plus the resource or resources associated with the waiting queue. Let us use the following notation.

- V_i is the average number of visits to queue i by an e-commerce transaction.

- S_i is the average service time of an e-commerce transaction at resource i per visit to the resource.

- W_i is the average waiting time of an e-commerce transaction at queue i per visit to the queue.

- R_i is the average response time of an e-commerce transaction at queue i, defined as the sum of the average waiting time plus average service time per visit to the queue. Therefore,

$$R_i = W_i + S_i. \tag{8.5.16}$$

- λ_i is the average arrival rate of requests to queue i.

- X_i is the average throughput of queue i, defined as the average number of transactions that complete from queue i per unit time. We will assume that any queue is observed during a large period such that the number of arrivals and departures to the queue are almost the same. This assumption is known as *Flow Equilibrium Assumption* [7] [13] and implies that $\lambda_i = X_i$.

- X_0 is the average system throughput, defined as the average number of transactions that complete per unit time.

- N_i^w is the average number of transactions waiting at queue i.

- N_i^s is the average number of transactions receiving service at any of the resources of queue i. In the case of a single resource queue (see Fig. 8.10-a), N_i^s is a number between zero and one that can be interpreted as the fraction of time that the resource is busy, or in other words, the utilization of the resource.

- N_i is the average number of transactions at queue i waiting or receiving service from any resource at queue i. Therefore,

$$N_i = N_i^w + N_i^s. \qquad (8.5.17)$$

8.6 Performance Laws

The relationships presented in this section are very simple and general, and they are known as operational results [7]. To understand the validity of these results, we do not need to resort to any complex mathematical formulation. Consider first the system of Fig. 8.11, which may be composed of a number of resources. Consider that the system was observed during $\mathcal{T}$ seconds and the counters registered the following measurements: i) the system was busy during B_0 seconds, ii) the number of arrivals of requests was A_0, and iii) the number of completed requests was C_0. From these simple measurement data, we can derive a series of other measurements, such as arrival rate, completion rate, utilization, and mean service time. The whole set of measurements is called *operational quantities*.

Example 8.4

During a measurement interval of 1,200 sec, the number of requests that arrived at the Web server was 24,000. What is the arrival rate (λ)?

$$\lambda = \frac{\text{number of request arrivals}}{\text{measurement interval}} = \frac{A_0}{\mathcal{T}} = \frac{24,000}{1,200} = 20 \text{ tps.}$$

∎

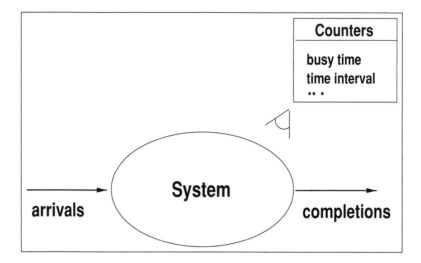

Figure 8.11. Operational Analysis Approach.

Example 8.5

During a measurement interval of 1,200 sec, the number of requests executed by the Web server was 27,300. What is the completion rate (X_0)?

$$X_0 = \frac{\text{number of completed requests}}{\text{measurement interval}} = \frac{C_0}{\mathcal{T}} = \frac{27,300}{1,200} = 22.75 \text{ tps.}$$

■

Example 8.6

During a measurement interval of 1,200 sec, the processor of a Web server was busy for 1,040 sec. What is the processor mean service time (S) per request?

$$S = \frac{\text{busy interval}}{\text{number of completed requests}} = \frac{1,040}{27,300} = 0.038 \text{ sec per request.}$$

■

8.6.1   Utilization Law

Let us start with a very simple relationship called *Utilization Law*. The utilization U_i of resource i of a system is defined as the fraction of time that the resource is busy. So, if we monitor queue i during $\mathcal{T}$ seconds and find out that the resource was busy during B_i seconds, its utilization, U_i, is $B_i/\mathcal{T}$. Assume that during the same interval $\mathcal{T}$, C_0 transactions completed from the system. This means that the average throughput from the queue is $X_i = C_0/\mathcal{T}$. Combining this relationship with the definition of utilization, we obtain the relationship

$$U_i = B_i/\mathcal{T} = B_i/(C_0/X_i) = (B_i/C_0) \times X_i = S_i \times X_i. \qquad (8.6.18)$$

Note that in Eq. (8.6.18) we used the fact that the average service time S_i per transaction is equal to the total time the resource was busy (B_i) divided by the number of transactions that were served during the monitoring period. In equilibrium, $\lambda_i = X_i$, and we can write that

$$U_i = X_i \times S_i = \lambda_i \times S_i. \qquad (8.6.19)$$

Example 8.7

During an observation interval, a database server executed forty-five Search transactions per second. Each transaction takes an average of 19.0 msec to execute. What was the utilization of the server during the interval?

From the Utilization Law, the utilization of the database server is $45 \times 0.019 = 0.855 = 85.5\%$.   ∎

8.6.2   Forced Flow Law

By definition of the average number of visits V_i, each completing transaction has to pass V_i times, on average, by queue i. So, if X_0 transactions complete per unit time, $V_i \times X_0$ transactions will visit queue i per unit time. So, the average throughput of queue i, X_i, is $V_i \times X_0$. This simple result is known as the *Forced Flow Law* and is written as

$$X_i = V_i \times X_0. \tag{8.6.20}$$

Example 8.8

During a measurement interval of 1,200 sec, an e-commerce site was monitored, and during this period, 4,800 transactions were executed. From the CSID of a typical interaction, we know that a transaction visits the Web server 5.2 times and the database server 3.8 times. The database service time is 59 msec and the Web service time is 35 msec. What is the average throughput of the database server and of the Web server?

The e-commerce site throughput, X_0, is equal to $4,800/1200 = 4$ transactions per sec (tps). The average number of visits to the DB server and Web server are $V_{\mathrm{DB}} = 3.8$ and $V_{\mathrm{WS}} = 5.2$, respectively. Using Eq. 8.6.20, we have that

$$X_{\mathrm{DB}} = V_{\mathrm{DB}} \times X_0 = 3.8 \times 4 = 15.2 \text{ tps and}$$

$$X_{\mathrm{WS}} = V_{\mathrm{WS}} \times X_0 = 5.2 \times 4 = 20.8 \text{ tps.}$$

■

8.6.3 Service Demand Law

The service demand D_i, previously defined as $V_i.S_i$, can easily be related to the system throughput and utilization by combining the Utilization and Forced Flow laws as follows.

$$D_i = V_i \times S_i = (X_i/X_0) \times (U_i/X_i) = U_i/X_0. \tag{8.6.21}$$

Example 8.9

Consider again Ex. 8.8. Now, we want to know what the service demands are at the two components of the e-commerce site, the Web server and database server. We also want to calculate the utilization of the two resources.

The service demands are calculated directly from the definition and the utilizations from Eq. (8.6.21).

$$D_{\text{WS}} = V_{\text{WS}} \times S_{\text{WS}} = 5.2 \times 0.035 = 0.182 \text{ sec.}$$

$$D_{\text{DB}} = V_{\text{DB}} \times S_{\text{DB}} = 3.8 \times 0.059 = 0.224 \text{ sec.}$$

$$U_{\text{WS}} = D_{\text{WS}} \times X_0 = 0.182 \times 4 = 0.728 = 72.8\%.$$

$$U_{\text{DB}} = D_{\text{DB}} \times X_0 = 0.224 \times 4 = 0.896 = 89.6\%.$$

∎

The utilization can also be interpreted as the average number of transactions in the resource since there is one transaction using the resource during U_i percent of the time and zero transactions during $(1 - U_i)$ percent of the time. For the case of a multiple resource queue, as in Fig. 8.10-b, the utilization is defined as the average number of transactions using any of the resources normalized by the number of resources. So, the utilization of an m-resource queue is

$$U_i = X_i \times S_i / m. \tag{8.6.22}$$

We will see in the next subsection why $X_i \times S_i$ is also the average number of transactions using any resource in a multiple resource queue. Since this number is less than or equal to the number of resources m, the utilization of an m-resource queue must be less than or equal to one.

8.6.4 Little's Law

Little's Law is quite simple and widely applicable to performance analysis of computing systems. In what follows, we present a very simple derivation of this result [12]. Consider the box in Fig. 8.12 (a).

This box could contain anything from a very simple device such as a disk to something as complex as an entire e-business site. For the purpose of this discussion, we assume that customers that arrive at the black box spend an average of R seconds in the black box and leave. The average departure rate, i.e., the throughput of the black box, is X customers/sec and the average number of customers in the black box is N. We want to show that $N = X \times R$. Consider that Fig. 8.12 (b) shows a graph of the number of customers, $n(t)$, in the black box at time t. Suppose we observe the flow of customers from time zero to time $\mathcal{T}$. Then, the average number of customers in that interval is simply equal to the sum of all products of the form $k \times f_k$, where k is the number of customers in the black box and f_k is the fraction of time k customers are in the black box. But f_k is simply $r_k/\mathcal{T}$, where r_k is the total time during which k customers were in the black box (see Fig. 8.12 (b)). So,

$$N = \sum_k k \times f_k = \sum_k k \times \frac{r_k}{\mathcal{T}}. \tag{8.6.23}$$

Let us multiply and divide the right-hand side of Eq. (8.6.23) by the number of customers, C_0, that departed from the black box in the interval $[0, \mathcal{T}]$ and

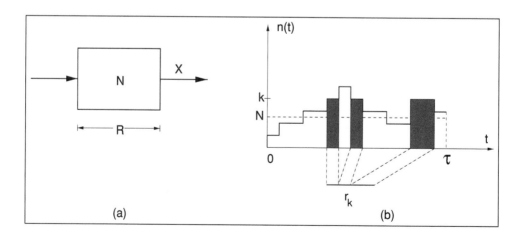

Figure 8.12. (a) Box for Little's Law (b) Graph of n (t) vs. t.

rearrange the equation. Hence,

$$N = \frac{C_0}{\mathcal{T}} \cdot \frac{\sum_k k.r_k}{C_0}. \qquad (8.6.24)$$

Note that $C_0/\mathcal{T}$ is the throughput X. The summation in Eq. (8.6.24) is the total number of (customer $\times$ seconds) accumulated in the system. If we divide this number by the total number C_0 of customers completed, we get the average time, R, each customer spent in the black box. So,

$$N = X \times R. \qquad (8.6.25)$$

Example 8.10

Consider a large portal service that offers free email services to its users. Suppose the number of registered users is two million. During the peak hour, 30% of the users send mails through the portal. Let us assume that each mail takes 5.0 sec, on average, to be processed and delivered to the destination's mailbox. Let us also assume that during this busy period, each user sends 3.5 mails on average. Analysis of the mail log file indicates that the average message size is 7,120 bytes. What should be the capacity of the spool for outgoing mails during the peak period?

From Little's Law, the average number of mails is given by

$$\begin{aligned} \text{AverageNumberOfMails} &= \text{Throughput} \times \text{Response Time} \\ &= \frac{(2,000,000 \times 0.30 \times 5.0)}{3,600} \\ &= 833.3 \text{ mails.} \end{aligned}$$

Based on the average mail size, the spool file should be

$$833.3 \times 7,120 \text{ bytes} = 5.9 \text{ Mbytes.}$$

∎

Little's Law is quite powerful and can be applied to any black box provided it does not create nor destroy customers. If we now apply Little's Law to the waiting queue, to the set of m resources, and to the entire queue of Fig. 8.10 (b), we get, respectively, that

$$N_i^w = X_i \times W_i, \tag{8.6.26}$$

$$N_i^s = X_i \times S_i, \text{ and} \tag{8.6.27}$$

$$N_i = X_i \times R_i. \tag{8.6.28}$$

Equation (8.6.27) gives the average number of transactions at the set of m resources. So, the average number of transactions per resource, also defined as the utilization, is $X_i \times S_i/m$.

Example 8.11

A Web-based brokerage company runs a three-tier site, as shown in Fig. 8.13. The application servers convert business functions from the Web servers into transactions that are submitted to the mainframes in the backend. The Web trading system services are used by 1.1 million customers. During the peak hour, twenty thousand users are logged in simultaneously. The e-commerce site processes 3.6 million business functions per hour on a peak-load hour. What is the average response time of an e-commerce function during the busiest hour?

Let us consider the entire e-commerce site as the "black box" for applying the Little's Law, as indicated by the dashed box in Fig. 8.13. Hence,

$$\begin{aligned} \text{Average Response Time} &= \frac{\text{Average Number of Users}}{\text{Site Throughput}} \\ &= \frac{20,000}{3,600,000/3,600} = 20 \text{ sec.} \end{aligned}$$

■

Example 8.12

Let us consider again Ex. 8.11. Based on the CSID diagrams of the business functions, we found that each function generates an average of 1.4

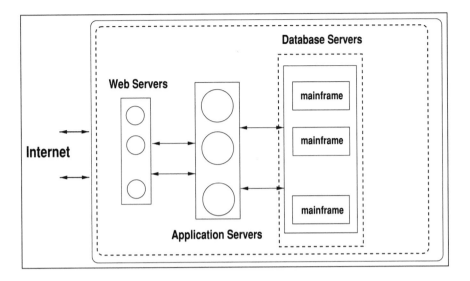

Figure 8.13. Web-Site Architecture.

transactions to the database system, that resides on the mainframes. We also know that the aggregate capacity of the mainframes is 11,500 transactions per sec. What percentage of the customer average response time is spent on the mainframes?

In this example, we consider the mainframes as the "black box" represented by a dashed box in Fig. 8.13. Applying Little's Law to the dashed box, we have that

$$\text{Average Response Time} = \frac{\text{Average Number of Transactions}}{\text{Mainframe Throughput}}$$

$$= \frac{20,000 \times 1.4}{11,500} = 2.43 \text{ sec.}$$

Considering that each business function generates 1.4 transactions, the time spent on the mainframes is 3.4 ($= 2.43 \times 1.4$) sec. This corresponds to 17.0% ($= 3.40 \ / \ 20.0$) of the business function average response time. ∎

8.6.5   Revisiting the Simple Problem

Let us go back to the problem of Section 8.2 and retrieve the questions that our simple model has to answer.

> The company managers are concerned with the increase of visitors during the peak hour. So, they posed the following general questions about the performance of the site. What will the online store performance if the number of customer sessions doubles during the peak hour? What is the LAN utilization if the size of the catalog pages increases by 100% due to new high-resolution pictures? What is the impact on performance if customers change their navigational pattern and the number of catalog searches increases by 50%?

The basic problem is quantitatively described by the data in Table 8.6. In the first question, our model should be able to predict the performance of the online store if the number of customer sessions doubles during the peak hour. In fact, this question is not stated precisely. What does management mean by "performance of the online store?" It could mean many things, such as the site response time, the user perceived response time, the utilization of the site's resources, or the rate of refused customers. Because we are working with simple performance laws, we will concentrate on computing the resource utilization when the number of customer sessions doubles during the peak hour.

The first step to answering the question is to change the model parameters to reflect the future scenario. In this case, we have to double the number of completed customer sessions, i.e., $2 \times 35,000 = 70,000$. Assuming that the customer behavior does not change, the total number of searches is $70,000 \times 2.5 = 175,000$, which yields a system throughput of $175,000 / 3,600 = 48.61$ tps. The utilization of the two servers is calculated as follows:

$$U_{\text{WS}} = X_0 \times D_{\text{WS}} = 48.61 \times 0.01371 = 66.67\% \text{ and} \qquad (8.6.29)$$

Table 8.6. Input Data for the Simple Problem.

Type of Data	Value
Number of completed customer sessions	35,000
Web server busy period (sec)	1,200
Database server busy period (sec)	2,100
Measurement interval (sec)	3,600
Number of searches per customer session	2.5
Number of visits to the Web server per search	1.95
Number of visits to the database server per search	0.95
Web server service demand in msec (D_{WS})	13.71
Database server service demand in msec (D_{DB})	24.00
Web server service time in msec (S_{WS})	7.03
Database server service time in msec (S_{DB})	25.26

$$U_{\mathrm{DB}} = X_0 \times D_{\mathrm{DB}} = 48.61 \times 0.024 = 116.7\%. \qquad (8.6.30)$$

From Eq. (8.6.30), we notice that the system will not support the forecast number of customer sessions because the utilization of any resource cannot exceed 100%.

The second question is, "What is the LAN utilization if the size of the catalog pages increases by 100%?" Example 8.3 shows the solution for this question. We know that the size of the request message is $m_3 = 400$ bytes and the size of the replies is $m_4 = 9,150$ bytes. To reflect the future scenario in the parameters of our model, we have to change the size of the replies accordingly. The new size of the replies is equal to $m_4 = 9,150 \times 2 = 18,300$ bytes. Redoing the calculations of Ex. 8.3, we obtain a network utilization of 36.0% assuming the number of sessions does not change.

The last question is, "What is the impact on performance if customers change their navigational pattern and the number of catalog searches increases by 50%?" In this case, we have to change the average number of searches per session to 3.75 ($= 2.5 \times 1.5$). Assuming that the number of customer sessions does not change, we can then calculate the new system throughput as

$$X_0 = 35,000 \times 3.75/3,600 = 36.46 \text{ tps.}$$

Using the new throughput, we calculate the new utilizations and we can notice that the system is capable of supporting the change in customer behavior. Although the database server's utilization is very high, it did not exceed 100%.

$$U_{\text{WS}} = X_0 \times D_{\text{WS}} = 36.45 \times 0.01371 = 49.97\%.$$
$$U_{\text{DB}} = X_0 \times D_{\text{DB}} = 36.45 \times 0.024 = 87.48\%.$$

8.7 Bottlenecks and Scalability Analysis

Performance bounding analysis [7] [11] [13] is a key technique to understanding scalability problems in electronic business. Because it is hard to estimate traffic, e-business sites must be designed with scalability in mind. In other words, a designer of an online business must know a priori what are the limits of the system. For instance, a designer must know the maximum number of transactions per second the system is capable of processing (i.e., an upper bound on the throughput) or the minimum response time that can be achieved by the business site (i.e., a lower bound on the response time). Performance bounding techniques allow us to calculate optimistic and pessimistic bounds. The former refers to the best possible performance values. Throughput upper bounds and response time lower bounds are optimistic bounds. Pessimistic bounds refer to the worst possible performance values. The resources that limit the overall performance of a system are called *bottlenecks*. Scalability analysis refers to techniques that find a single bottleneck that cannot be sped up. When a bottleneck cannot be removed, the system is considered non-scalable in terms of performance.

E-commerce sites with their unpredictable traffic spikes bring new challenges to performance modeling. Detailed and costly modeling analysis may not be worthwhile when the capacity planning analyst faces a large number of possible future scenarios. Quick bounding studies may be the right solution for these cases. Consider an e-commerce site that is preparing for a surge of customers due to a special event, such as the Olympic Games, the World Soccer Cup, or an ad campaign. Management does not know how many customers would be attracted to the site. Some analysts estimate that the campaign could add a number of customers that varies between a hundred thousand and a million new visitors per day. Developing a detailed model to calculate that the proposed system will be able to serve 34.722 customers per sec may be an overkill. Simply knowing that the site is able to serve approximately twenty customers per sec for one alternative or thirty-eight for another alternative is the right level of information to select one option over another. The options could be adding eight or fifteen additional application servers to the current site configuration.

8.7.1 Asymptotic Bounds

A very simple bounding technique is known as asymptotic bound analysis (ABA) [7] [11]. The technique determines bounds on throughput and response time for systems under extreme load conditions, i.e., light load or heavy load. The load may be defined by the intensity of the request arrival rates or by the number of simultaneous customers in an online store. At this point, it is necessary to characterize two classes of model representations for systems: *open* and *closed*. Open models allow requests to arrive, go through the various resources (e.g., servers in an e-commerce site), and leave the system. For instance, imagine an e-commerce site with no limit on the number of customers that can login simultaneously. An open model would represent this system nicely. Closed models are characterized by having a fixed number of requests. In most online stores, there is a limitation on the maximum number of simultaneous customers logged in the system. Usually, this is due to the maximum number of TCP connections that the system can accept. Suppose an online store that, during peak hours, operates under very heavy load in which the number of customers simultaneously logged in is constantly near the maximum. These situations can be adequately represented by closed models.

The models considered in this section are represented by a few parameters and their solution requires only a few arithmetic operations. As in every phenomenon of life, there is a price to be paid for all these good characteristics of asymptotic techniques. The price is a loss of accuracy of the results that simply establish maximum and minimum values for the performance metrics. The parameters of the models used by the asymptotic techniques are

- K, the number of resources of the system;
- D_i, the service demand of resource i;
- D_{max}, the largest service demand among all resources; and
- D_{total}, the sum of the service demands of all resources.

8.7.1.1   Open Models

For open models, the bound on throughput indicates the maximum possible arrival rate of customers that the system can service [11]. In an online store, if the arrival rate of customers exceeds the limit on throughput, customers may experience extremely long delays and may even get disconnected from the store.

For systems in equilibrium, the number of arrivals is equal to the number of transactions completed during an interval $\mathcal{T}$. As a consequence, the arrival rate (i.e., λ) equals the throughput (i.e., X_0) of the system and $\lambda_i = X_i$. From the Utilization Law, we have that for each resource i,

$$U_i = X_i \times S_i = \lambda_i \times S_i. \tag{8.7.31}$$

Using the Service Demand Law, we can rewrite Eq. (8.7.31) as

$$U_i = D_i \times X_0 = D_i \times \lambda. \tag{8.7.32}$$

Under heavy load conditions, resource utilizations tends to be high but cannot exceed 100%. This observation can be used to derive an upper bound on throughput for each resource. These are good bounds under heavy load conditions, i.e., as the resource utilizations approach 100%. Thus, for a *saturated* resource i, i.e., one in which its utilization U_i approaches 100%, Eq. (8.7.32) becomes

$$\lambda \times D_i = 1$$
$$\lambda = 1/D_i. \tag{8.7.33}$$

Considering that for any resource i, $U_i \leq 1$, then $\lambda \leq 1/D_i$. Thus, the largest value of D_i (i.e. D_{max}) will be the first to approximate 100% under heavy load conditions. So, the maximum arrival rate (i.e., λ_{max}) is limited by the resource that has the largest value of D_i, which is called *bottleneck* because it limits the system's overall performance.

$$\lambda_{max} \leq 1/D_{max}. \tag{8.7.34}$$

Example 8.13

Consider a three-tier site, like the one depicted in Ex. 8.11. The execution of a typical business function involves various visits to the servers. Based on the CSID diagrams of several business functions, the performance analyst came up with Table 8.7, which shows the quantitative data about the "typical business function." It is worth mentioning that the number of visits in the table assumes that only one instance of each server is available. Let us assume that the different transactions that compose the typical business function are equally spread among the servers of each layer of the architecture. What is the maximum arrival rate of business functions that the site accepts?

Table 8.7. Data for a Typical Business Function.

Layer	Number of Servers	Number of Visits	Mean Service Time
Web Server	5	1.8	110 msec
Application Server	3	2.5	230 msec
Database Server	2	2.3	180 msec

Since we have more than one of each type of server and since we are assuming that the load is equally distributed among all of them, the number of visits in Table 8.7 has to be divided by the corresponding number of servers of each type. Thus, the service demand for each server is given below.

$$D_{\text{web}} = (V_{\text{web}}/N_{\text{web}}) \times S_{\text{web}} = (1.8/5) \times 0.110 = 0.0396 \text{ sec.}$$

$$D_{\text{appl}} = (V_{\text{appl}}/N_{\text{appl}}) \times S_{\text{appl}} = (2.5/3) \times 0.230 = 0.192 \text{ sec.}$$

$$D_{\text{DB}} = (V_{\text{DB}}/N_{\text{DB}}) \times S_{\text{DB}} = (2.3/2) \times 0.180 = 0.207 \text{ sec.}$$

Therefore, we have $D_{\text{max}} = D_{\text{DB}} = 0.207$ sec, which means that the application servers are capable of processing

$$\lambda \leq 1/0.207 = 4.83 \text{ tps.}$$

Note that the maximum throughput due to the Web servers would be 25.25 (= 1/0.0396) tps and due to the application servers would be 5.21 (= 1/0.192) tps. However, the database layer limits the site throughput at 4.83 tps. Since each e-commerce function visits a database server 2.3 times on the average, we can compute an upper bound on the site throughput, measured in terms of e-commerce functions, by using the Forced Flow Law (i.e., $X_i = V_i \times X_0$):

$$X_0 \leq X_{\text{DB}}/V_{\text{DB}} = 4.83/2.3 = 2.1 \text{ functions/sec.}$$

■

8.7.1.2   Closed Models

For closed models, the bounds on throughput can be obtained by varying the number of transactions in the system (N). What is the best throughput a system can achieve? Let us think of an ideal situation, where the N transactions in the system are processed in such a way that none of them faces a queue. We then have a situation that is called "no queuing" case upper bound. In this case, the response time equals D_{total} since there is no waiting time in the system. Combining Little's Law and the "no queuing" situation, the system throughput is given by

$$X_0(N) \ \leq \ \frac{N}{D_{\text{total}}}. \tag{8.7.35}$$

However, we know that the utilization of any resource in the system cannot exceed 100%. Thus, from the Service Demand Law, we have the following:

$$
\begin{aligned}
X_0(N) &= \frac{U_i(N)}{D_i}, \\
U_i(N) &\leq 1, \\
X_0(N) &\leq \frac{1}{D_i}.
\end{aligned}
\tag{8.7.36}
$$

Since the bottleneck is the first resource that saturates, we have

$$X_0(N) \ \leq \ \frac{1}{D_{\text{max}}}. \tag{8.7.37}$$

Combining Eqs.(8.7.35), (8.7.36) and (8.7.37), the asymptotic upper bounds are

$$X_0(N) \ \leq \ \min\left[\frac{N}{D_{\text{total}}}, \frac{1}{D_{\text{max}}}\right]. \tag{8.7.38}$$

Example 8.14

Let us consider a three-tier online site, with one Web server, one application server, and one database server. The maximum number of customers simultaneously connected is one hundred. The site offers a set of business functions to its customers. To plan the site capacity, the performance analyst decided to average all business functions to obtain a "typical function." This function is executed through transactions that are processed by each server. What is the maximum throughput of the site?

The service demands at the three servers are the following: $D_{\text{web}} = 0.121$ sec, $D_{\text{appl}} = 0.545$ sec, and $D_{\text{DB}} = 0.656$ sec. From the description of the problem, we have the following data:

- $N = 100$,

- $D_{\text{total}} = D_{\text{web}} + D_{\text{appl}} + D_{\text{DB}} = 0.121 + 0.545 + 0.656 = 1.322$ sec, and

- $D_{\text{max}} = D_{\text{DB}} = 0.656$ sec.

Using Eq. (8.7.38), we have:

$$X_0(100) \leq \min \left[\frac{100}{1.322}, \frac{1}{0.656} \right],$$
$$X_0(100) \leq \min \left[75.64, 1.52 \right],$$
$$X_0(100) \leq 1.52 \text{ tps.}$$

So, the site is capable of executing at most 1.52 business functions per sec. ∎

8.8   Summary

Performance is a key issue in electronic business. The emphasis of this chapter was to introduce concepts of system performance modeling, applied to electronic business. As a matter of fact, this chapter provided a framework to develop, solve, and use simple performance models to gain an understanding of the behavior of complex systems such as e-commerce. Instead of relying on ad hoc procedures and rules of thumb, this chapter presented a uniform way of quantitatively analyzing system performance. Simple models based on "operational analysis" were developed throughout the chapter. Operational analysis is not a replacement for stochastic analysis, which is based upon random variables characterized by given distributions (e.g., Poisson, exponential, and hyperexponential). Operational analysis is based on measured or known data. The operational analysis approach developed a series of laws and formulas that can be used to construct performance models of distributed computer systems.

A performance model can be developed at different levels of detail. In this chapter, we view an electronic business system as a network of servers. An e-commerce transaction was defined as a request from a customer to execute a business function. By its turn, a business function is implemented through various client/server interactions that may involve many different servers. Thus, we looked at performance models from a server-level point of view. A server-level approach considers the server being modeled as a "black box." In this case, the internal details of the box (i.e., processor, disks, and network interface) are not modeled explicitly. More powerful models that lead to more accurate system representations and detailed results are treated in Chapter 9. The following points summarize what we learned from this chapter.

- A model is a representation of a system and should be simple and capable of capturing the most relevant characteristics of the system under study. In particular, performance models represent the way system resources are used by the workload and capture the main factors determining system performance.

- We use analytical performance models that specify the interaction among the various components of a system via formulas.

- Performance models are useful for infrastructure design, resource allocation problems, system tuning, and capacity planning.

- An e-commerce transaction uses various servers. The total response time of a transaction is composed of two main components: service time and waiting time.

- Many formulas were given to obtain average service time at communication networks.

- Several important relationships, including the Utilization Law, Service Demand Law, Forced Flow Law and Little's Law were derived and their use described through simple and realistic examples in e-commerce.

Bibliography

[1] V. A. F. Almeida, A. Bestavros, M. Crovella, and A. Oliveira, "Characterizing Reference Locality in the WWW," *Proc. Fourth International Conference on Parallel and Distributed Information Systems (PDIS)*, IEEE Computer Society, Dec. 1996, pp. 92–106.

[2] M. Arlitt and C. Williamson, "Web Server Workload Characterization," *Proc. 1996 ACM SIGMETRICS Conference on Measurement of Computer Systems*, Philadelphia, PA, May 1996.

[3] L. Breslau et al, "Web Caching and Zipf-like Distributions: Evidence and Implications," *Proc. IEEE Infocom'99* , New York, March 1999.

[4] D. Comer, *Computer Networks and Internet*, Prentice Hall, Upper Saddle River, NJ, 1997.

[5] M. Crovella and A. Bestavros, "Self-similarity in World Wide Web Traffic: Evidence and Possible Causes," *Proc. 1996 ACM SIGMETRICS Conference on Measurement of Computer Systems*, Philadelphia, PA, May 1996.

[6] C. Cunha, A. Bestavros, and M. Crovella, "Characteristics of WWW Client-based Traces," *Technical Report TR-95-010*, Department of Computer Science, Boston University, April 1995.

[7] P. Denning and J. P. Buzen, "The Operational Analysis of Queuing Network Models," *Computing Surveys*, vol. 10, no. 3, Sept. 1978, pp. 225–261.

[8] J. Heidemann, K. Obraska, and J. Touch, "Modeling the Performance of HTTP Over Several Transport Protocols," *IEEE/ACM Transactions on Networking*, vol. 20, no. 4, pp. 604–623, Oct. 1998.

[9] R. Jain, *The Art of Computer System Performance: Analysis, Techniques for Experimental Design, Measurement, Simulation and Modeling*, Wiley, New York, 1991.

[10] L. Kleinrock, *Queueing Systems, Vol. I: Theory*, Wiley, New York, 1975.

[11] E. Lazowska, J. Zahorjan, G. Graham, and K. Sevcik, *Quantitative System performance: Computer System Analysis Using Queuing Network Models*, Prentice Hall, Upper Saddle River, NJ, 1984.

[12] J. Little, "A proof of the Queuing Formula $L = \lambda W$," *Operations Research*, vol. 9, 1961, pp. 383–387.

[13] D. A. Menascé, V. A. F. Almeida, and L. W. Dowdy, *Capacity Planning and Performance Modeling: From Mainframes to Client-Server Systems*, Prentice Hall, Upper Saddle River, NJ, 1994.

[14] D. A. Menascé and V. A. F. Almeida, *Capacity Planning for Web Performance: Metrics, Models and Methods*, Prentice Hall, Upper Saddle River, NJ, 1998.

[15] W. R. Stevens, *TCP/IP Illustrated, Vol. 1*, Addison-Wesley, Reading, MA, 1994.

[16] G. Zipf, *Human Behavior and the Principle of Least Effort*, Addison-Wesley, Cambridge, MA, 1949.

Chapter 9

Solving Performance Models of E-Business Sites

9.1 Introduction

There are many types of performance models and various analytic solution techniques in the literature [6] [10]. What makes one solution technique different from another? How does one select a solution method that is well-suited for a specific modeling problem? These are questions that might be intriguing the reader. Simplicity, accuracy, computational cost, and availability of information about the system under analysis are some of the issues to be considered when choosing a solution technique. The modeling approach used in this book favors simplicity, so that the user can understand the model and use it to uncover essential aspects of actual systems.

This chapter starts by introducing very simple models. Complexity is progressively introduced and the solution to each model is presented using first principles and intuitive concepts. Two broad categories of models are covered in this chapter: system- and component-level models. System-level models treat the actual system as a black box. Only the input, represented by the arrival rate of requests, and the output behavior, represented by the throughput, are considered at this level. For example, in a multi-tier business site, the database layer could be represented by a system-level model. In this case, the database servers are modeled as a single black box that receives database requests, processes them, and returns the results. On the other hand, to examine the impact of a new database management system (DBMS) or a new model of RAID disks on the request response time, one needs to explicitly represent the internal components of the servers, LANs, and other hardware and software components. This can be accomplished by a component-level model, based on queuing networks, in which components are represented by queues. Both types of techniques are used to solve performance models of e-business systems.

9.2   A Simple Example

Consider a small toy store that sells wooden toys. The company decided to go online and set up its site a year ago. Because of its reduced customer base, management had a limited budget to develop the online project. As a result, the site came up with a very simple configuration. The e-commerce server setup consists of a Web server and a DB server that provide both the catalog content and the order forms. The technique used to connect the Web server and the application logic is Common Gateway Interface (CGI).

The following business functions are available at the site of the toy store: Welcome, Search, Browse, Product Information, Shopping Cart, and Check-out. By examining the logs of the site, we found that Search constitutes approximately 85% of all transactions. Thus, to simplify the problem, we assume that customers have only one navigational pattern: they visit the home page and then do a number of catalog searches for their favorite toys. The CBMG (*Customer Behavior Model Graph*) that models the navigational pattern and the CSID (*Client/Server Interaction Diagram*) of the search function are displayed in Fig. 9.1. It is worth recalling that the CSID describes the logical architecture of e-business functions, which are implemented by software entities called servers. In the CSID of Fig. 9.1, the search function is implemented by the Web and database servers, which run on a single machine.

Due to an international weekly magazine's article that described its unique handmade toys, the store's site is attracting the attention of online customers from all over the world. The company managers learned from others that doing business on the Web means dealing with potentially high traffic volumes at highly unpredictable times. Thus, they want to be proactive. In particular, management wants to know what the response time would be if the number of requests during the peak hour grew by a factor of four. To answer this what-if question, a performance model will be de-

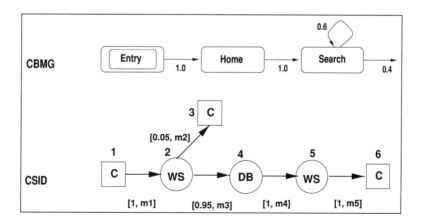

Figure 9.1. CBMG and CSID Models for the Customer of the Online Toy Store.

veloped to represent the system behavior during the peak hour. Table 9.1 summarizes information regarding the system usage, collected during the peak hour.

9.3   First Cut: the Single Queue Approach

What is the best model to represent the system of the simple example? This is a common question that arises when one faces real problems. Figure 9.2 illustrates this typical performance modeling question. Performance models can be developed at different levels of detail. The level of detail of a given model depends on what questions one wants to answer with the model. As a first cut, we look at performance models from a system-level point of view as opposed to a component-level point of view. A *system-level* performance model views the system being modeled as a "black box." In this case, the internal details of the box are not modeled explicitly. Only the throughput function of the box is considered. The throughput function, $X_0(k)$, gives the average throughput of the box as a function of the number of requests, k, present in the box. In other words, we are simplifying the problem by abstracting the internal details of the site architecture.

A starting point to represent the behavior of the site is the use of a single queue model, which is the most elementary form of a queuing model. Figure 9.3 depicts a single queue model characterized by the arrival process, the

Table 9.1. Input Data for the Simple Problem.

Type of Data	Value
Number of completed searches	18,000
Measurement interval	3,600 sec
Average time to execute a search	48 msec

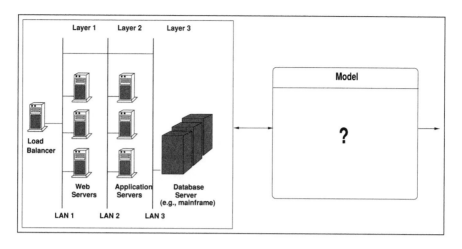

Figure 9.2. A Performance Modeling Question.

service process, the space for holding the queue of waiting requests, and the number of resources that render the service. The term *queue* stands for a resource (e.g., processor, I/O, and network) and the queue of requests waiting to use the resource. A queue is characterized by a function $S(n)$ that represents the average service time per request when there are n requests at the queue. Remember that the term queue stands for the waiting queue plus the resource itself; the number of requests, n, at the queue is called the *queue length*. There are three categories of resources in a queuing network, and they vary according to whether or not there is queuing and whether or not the average service time, $S(n)$, depends on the queue length n. The resource types are described below.

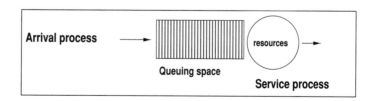

Figure 9.3. Single Server Model.

- *Load-independent resources* represent resources where there is queuing but the average service time does not depend on the load; that is, $S(n) = S$ for all values of n.

- *Load-dependent resources* are used to represent resources where there is queuing and the average service time depends on the load, that is, $S(n)$ is an arbitrary function of n.

- *Delay resources* indicate situations where there is no queuing. Thus, the total time spent by a request at a delay resource is the request's service time. The average service time function does not depend on the number of requests present at the resource, that is, $S(n) = S$ for all values of n.

Let us understand each of these characteristics of a single queue in the context of the following example. Consider a server accessible to a very large population. One could imagine that this is the search engine server of an online newspaper. The number of people in the user population is unknown and very large. By "very large" we mean that the arrival rate of requests for the search service is not influenced by the number of requests that arrived already and are being processed. From now on, we will refer to this as the *infinite population* case. The arrival process to the search server is then characterized by requests arriving at an average arrival rate of λ requests/sec. We also assume that all requests are statistically indistinguishable. This implies that the requests present in the server are not important, only the number of requests that are present counts. This is the case of single class or *homogeneous workload* assumption [9].

Since this is our first and simplest example, we assume that the average service function is very simple. It is a constant, that is, it does not depend on the number of requests in the system. What could be simpler? The service function specifies the rate at which requests are serviced by the server. In other words, it is the server throughput. So, the average throughput of the search engine server is given by $X_0 = \mu$ requests/sec. It should be noted that the server's service rate is not just a function of its physical characteristics (e.g., number and type of processors and disk speeds), but also of the demands of the workload (e.g., database management system, complexity of the search operation, and size of the database).

At first in this example, we also assume that the search engine server does not refuse any requests. All arriving requests are queued for service. This assumption is known as *infinite queue*, i.e., there is enough space for all waiting requests. The analyses presented in this section and in the rest of the chapter assume that the systems being analyzed are in *operational equilibrium* [3]. This means that the number of requests present in the system at the start of an observation interval is equal to the number of requests present at the end of the interval. The number of requests in the system may vary between the start and end of the interval. For reasonably large intervals, the number of departures tends to approach the number of arrivals and therefore the operational equilibrium assumption holds with negligible error.

Requests arrive at the search engine server at a rate of λ requests/sec, queue for service, receive service at a rate of μ request/sec, and depart. It should be noted that the service rate is equal to the inverse of the service time, i.e., $\mu = 1/S$. We want to compute p_k, which is the probability that there are k $(k = 0, 1, \cdots)$ requests in the server, the average number of requests present, the average response time of a request at the search engine server, and the server's utilization and throughput.

9.3.1 Model Solution

Solving the single queue model is being able to calculate performance metrics such as queue length, average response time, and utilization. To provide the reader with some taste of queuing theory, we take the approach of developing the general solution for this case. In our other performance books [9] [10], the reader can find the development of the solution for various models not covered here, such as the finite queue case, that illustrates the case where a server can only handle a maximum number of requests.

We start by deciding how to describe the *state* of the search server. Given the assumptions presented thus far, the state description for our search server is a *single* parameter, the number of requests present in the server—waiting or receiving service. It turns out that by choosing such a simple state description, we are implicitly making the additional assumption that the past is irrelevant. This means that it does not matter how the system arrived at a certain state k nor does it matter for how long the system has been in this state. The only thing that matters is that the system is at state k. This is also known as the *memoryless* or *Markovian* assumption.

The possible states are then given by the integers $0, 1, 2, \cdots, k, \cdots$. Due to the infinite population and infinite queue length assumptions used in this example, we have an infinite, but enumerable, number of states. We then draw a state transition diagram (STD), where each state is represented by a circle (see Fig. 9.4). Transitions between states correspond to physical events in the system and are represented by arrows between states. For example, an arrival of a new request when the server has k requests will take the server to state $k + 1$. This type of transition happens upon request arrivals, and therefore the rate at which these transitions occur is λ transitions/sec, the arrival rate. Similarly, if the database server has k requests and one of them completes, the new state is $k - 1$. These transitions occur at rate μ, the request completion rate.

We start by obtaining the values of p_k ($k = 0, 1, \cdots$). Since we are assuming operational equilibrium, the flow of transitions going into a state k has to be equal to the flow of transitions going out of that state. For a more formal discussion on this, see Buzen's paper [3]. This is called the *flow equilibrium equation* or the *flow-in = flow-out* principle and can be applied to any set of states. Consider Fig. 9.5 that shows a sequence of boundaries (dashed lines) around states. Each boundary contains one more state than

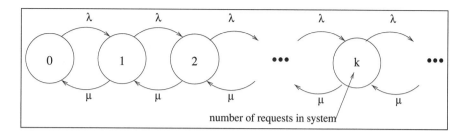

Figure 9.4. State Transition Diagram—Infinite Population/Infinite Queue.

the previous. The first boundary contains state 0 only. The next includes states 0 and 1. The next boundary includes states 0, 1, and 2, and so on. The flow-in = flow-out principle applies to any of these boundaries.

The flow out of a boundary is computed by considering all transitions that go from a state within the boundary to a state outside the boundary. The flow into a boundary includes all transitions that come from a state outside the boundary to a state inside the boundary. The following is the set of flow-in = flow-out equations for Fig. 9.5.

$$\text{flow} - \text{in} = \text{flow} - \text{out}$$

$$\mu \, p_1 = \lambda \, p_0 \tag{9.3.1}$$

$$\mu \, p_2 = \lambda \, p_1 \tag{9.3.2}$$

.

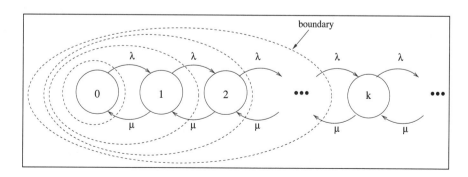

Figure 9.5. State Transition Diagram with Boundaries.

.

.

.

$$\mu \, p_k = \lambda \, p_{k-1} \qquad (9.3.3)$$

.

.

.

Note that if we combine Eqs. (9.3.1) through (9.3.3), we get

$$p_k = \frac{\lambda}{\mu} \, p_{k-1} = \frac{\lambda}{\mu} \left(\frac{\lambda}{\mu} \, p_{k-2} \right) = \cdots = p_0 \, \left(\frac{\lambda}{\mu} \right)^k , \quad k = 1, 2, \cdots . \qquad (9.3.4)$$

We now have p_k as a function of p_0 for all values of $k = 1, 2, \cdots$. We just need to find p_0. Our database server has to be in one of the possible states at any time. So, the sum of the fractions of time that the server is at any possible state, from 0 to ∞, equals one. Hence,

$$p_0 + p_1 + p_2 + \cdots + p_k + \cdots = \sum_{k=0}^{\infty} p_k = \sum_{k=0}^{\infty} p_0 \, \left(\frac{\lambda}{\mu} \right)^k = 1. \qquad (9.3.5)$$

This leads to

$$p_0 = \left[\sum_{k=0}^{\infty} \left(\frac{\lambda}{\mu} \right)^k \right]^{-1} = 1 - \frac{\lambda}{\mu}. \qquad (9.3.6)$$

Note that the infinite sum in Eq. (9.3.6) is the sum of a geometric series. This series only converges (i.e., has a finite sum) if $\lambda/\mu < 1$. This means that an equilibrium solution to the system can be found only if the average arrival rate of requests is smaller than the service rate. This makes a lot of sense!

Example 9.1

Going back to the search engine problem, consider that the server gets 144,000 requests per hour from the home page servers. The server takes 0.02 sec to process each search request. What is the server utilization? How many search requests are on average on the server? What is the fraction of time that k $(k = 0, 1, \cdots)$ search requests are found in the server?

Let us map the input information into the parameters of the formulae that solve the model. If the server can process μ requests in 1 sec, one request takes an average of $1/\mu$ seconds to complete. Then, the average service rate μ is the inverse of the average service time per request. So, $\mu = 1/0.02 = 50$ requests/sec. The average arrival rate is $\lambda = 144,000$ requests/hour or forty search requests per second (i.e., $40 = 144,000/3,600$). So, the fraction of time that the search server is idle, i.e., p_0, is $1 - (\lambda/\mu) = 1 - (40/50) = 1 - 0.8 = 20\%$. Then, the server is utilized $1 - p_0 = \lambda/\mu = 80\%$ of the time. The fraction of time that there are k requests at the server is given by

$$p_k = (1 - \lambda/\mu)(\lambda/\mu)^k = 0.2 \times 0.8^k \quad k = 0, 1, \cdots. \tag{9.3.7}$$

The equation above shows that p_k decays rapidly with k. This is a geometric distribution. ∎

So, from what we saw in Ex. 9.1, the utilization U of the server is

$$U = 1 - p_0 = \lambda/\mu. \tag{9.3.8}$$

This means that $p_k = (1 - U) U^k$ for $k = 0, 1, \cdots$. The state distribution depends only on the utilization and not on the individual values of the arrival and service rates!

Now that we know p_k, we can easily find the average number of requests $\overline{N}$ at the server by using the definition of average. Thus,

$$\overline{N} = \sum_{k=0}^{\infty} k \times p_k = \sum_{k=0}^{\infty} k \times (1 - U) U^k = (1 - U) \sum_{k=0}^{\infty} k \times U^k, \tag{9.3.9}$$

where the summation $\sum_{k=0}^{\infty} k \times U^k = U/(1 - U)^2$ for $U < 1$. Making the proper substitutions we get

$$\overline{N} = U/(1 - U). \tag{9.3.10}$$

So, using the parameters of Ex. 9.1 in Eq. (9.3.10), we get that the average number of requests at the server is $0.8/(1 - 0.8) = 4.0$.

The throughput of the server is μ when there is at least one request being processed—this occurs during a fraction of time equal to U. The throughput equals zero when the server is idle. So, the average throughput, X, of the server is

$$X = U \times \mu + 0 \times (1 - U) = (\lambda/\mu)\,\mu = \lambda. \qquad (9.3.11)$$

This is an expected result since no requests are being lost at the server. So, in equilibrium, the average arrival rate will be equal to the average departure rate.

We now compute the average response time, R, at the server by using Little's Law (see Section 8.6.4). The black box in this case is the server. So, given the throughput X, computed in Eq. (9.3.11), and the average number of requests $\overline{N}$ given by Eq. (9.3.10), we get that

$$R = \overline{N}/X = (U/\lambda)/(1 - U) = (1/\mu)/(1 - U) = S/(1 - U), \qquad (9.3.12)$$

where $S = 1/\mu$ is the average service time of a request at the server. Let us understand what Eq. (9.3.12) is telling us. First, when the utilization of the server is very low, i.e., U is close to zero, the average response time is equal to the average service time. This is expected since no time is spent queuing due to the presence of other requests. When the utilization is very high, i.e., U is close to 1, the denominator of Eq. (9.3.12) goes to zero and R goes to infinity! In fact, R goes to infinity quickly as U gets close to 100%.

Example 9.2

Consider again the input parameters of Ex. 9.1. What is the average response time at the server? What would the average response time be if the search engine server were replaced with a server twice as fast? What would the response time be if the arrival rate were doubled when the server became twice as fast?

Using Eq. (9.3.12), the average search response time is $R = (1/50)/(1 - 0.8) = 0.1$ sec. If the server is twice as fast, $\mu = 100$ requests/second, and the server utilization becomes $U = 40/100 = 0.4$. So, $R = (1/100)/(1 - 0.4) = 0.017$ sec. So, by using a server that is twice as fast, the response time is reduced to about 17% of its original value. If both the arrival rate and the service rate are doubled, the utilization remains the same, $U = 0.8$. Using Eq. (9.3.12), we get that $R = (1 / 100)/(1 - 0.8) = 0.05$ sec.   ∎

Example 9.3

Consider the mail server of a company in which the employees make intense use of e-mail services. The mail server processes about 35,000 requests (e.g., **sendmail**) during working days. However, the mail service requests are not uniformly spread over the twenty-four hours and there is a concentration of requests during a peak hour. Mail service requests are characterized by the following:

- average interarrival time = 2.50 sec,
- average interarrival time during the peak hour = 0.80 sec,
- average message size = 8.2 Kbytes,
- average message size during the peak hour = 7.1 Kbytes.

On average, the SMTP (i.e., Simple Mail Transfer Protocol) service processes 2.2 typical messages per second. By typical, we mean a message of average size. What is the average response time during the peak hour? What is the average response time if the average mail size is twice as big?

From the description of the problem, we have the following parameters for a single queue model:

$$\lambda = 1/(\text{interarrival time}) = 1/0.80 = 1.25 \text{ messages/sec}$$

and $\mu = 2.2$ messages/sec. The mail server utilization is

$$U = \lambda/\mu = 1.25/2.2 = 0.568.$$

Using Eq. (9.3.12), the average request response time is given by

$$R = (1/2.2)/(1 - 0.568) = 1.05 \text{ sec.}$$

To answer the second question, we need to know the impact of the message size on the service time. From measurements taken at the mail server, we learn that doubling the mail size increases the service time by 35%. The effect of modeling the mail size increase is captured by the 35% increase in the service time.

$$\text{New service time} = (1/\mu) \times 1.35 = 0.454 \times 1.35 = 0.613 \text{ sec.}$$

The utilization becomes $U = 1.25 \times 0.613 = 0.766$ and the response time becomes

$$R = (0.613)/(1 - 0.766) = 2.62 \text{ sec.}$$

So, by doubling the average mail size, the response time increases by 149%. ■

9.3.2   Revisiting the Simple Example

Figure 9.6 illustrates the use of a single queue model. It means that the "whole" e-business site is viewed as a black box that receives business requests and processes them one at a time. This assumption is pessimistic when compared to the actual system because we are assuming that only one request is serviced at a time by the system. As a matter of fact, Web servers are capable of servicing many requests simultaneously in a multiprogrammed manner.

The formulas provided by the solution of the single queue model will be used to answer the following question posed in Section 9.2.

What would the response time be if the number of requests during the peak hour grew by a factor of four?

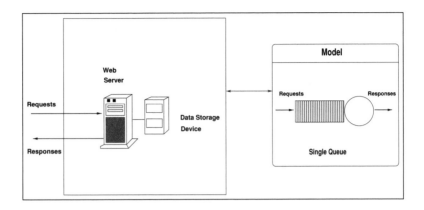

Figure 9.6. Single Queue Model.

The input parameters required to calculate response time are the average service time and the average arrival rate. From Table 9.1, we know that $S = 0.048$ sec and the average arrival rate is $\lambda = 18,000/3,600 = 5$ requests/sec. Using the operational laws from Chapter 8, we know that utilization is given by $U = S \times \lambda$, where S denotes average service time and λ is the average arrival rate. Thus, the average response time of the online toy store is

$$U = S \times \lambda = 0.048 \times 5 = 0.24$$

$$R = S/(1 - U) = 0.048/(1 - 0.24) = 0.063 \text{ sec.}$$

To answer the management question, we need to calculate the average response time for the new arrival rate.

$$\lambda_{New} = 4 \times \lambda = 4 \times 5 = 20 \text{ request/sec.}$$

$$U = S \times \lambda = 0.048 \times 20 = 0.96.$$

$$R = S/(1 - U) = 0.048/(1 - 0.96) = 1.2 \text{ sec.}$$

Thus, by multiplying the arrival rate by four, the response time increases by 1,900%.

9.4   A More Realistic Approach: A Queuing Network

As discussed in Chapter 4, a typical e-business site architecture is composed of a number of interconnected servers including Web servers, application servers, and database servers. Suppose that one wants to know what the site performance would be if five new Web servers were added to a given configuration of an e-business site. Can this question be answered by a single queue model? When one models the whole site as a single queue, one loses the ability to represent the role of each server in the system. Thus, the above question would hardly be answered by a system-level model. In capacity planning, models are essential because they are able to predict adequately the performance of a system with different configurations. Therefore, a more realistic approach to modeling a system would explicitly represent the most relevant components of the system. In this section, we look at the components that make up a networked system and examine how we can build models that take into consideration the interaction of these components.

9.4.1   Queuing Network Models

The various queues that represent a system are interconnected, giving rise to a network of queues called a queuing network (QN). The level of detail at which resources are depicted in the QN depends on the reasons to build the model and the availability of detailed information about the operation and detailed parameters of specific resources. A *queue* in a QN stands for a resource (e.g., Web server, database server, processor, disk, network, etc.) and the queue of requests waiting to use the resource.

A queuing network model (QNM) is a collection of single queues arranged in the same configuration as a real system, as shown in Fig. 9.7. Component-level models use queuing networks to represent systems. Connections between queues reflect the system architecture and the flow of requests between the components. The component-level models presented here are able to capture the essential behavior of the main elements of a network-

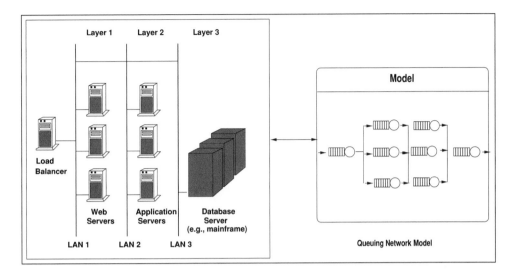

Figure 9.7. Queuing Network Model.

based environment and represent the contention for shared resources. A queue is characterized by a function $S(n)$ that represents the average service time per request when there are n requests at the queue. The parameters of a queuing network are the service demands at each queue of the model and workload intensity parameters.

At this point, let us assume that all requests have similar characteristics and they form a single class of requests. We will revisit this assumption in the next section, when we look at more general types of models. QNMs can also be grouped into two categories: closed and open models. Models that have a fixed number of requests per class are called *closed models*. On the other hand, *open models* do not place any limits on the number of requests present in the system. Open models allow requests to arrive, go through the various resources of the site, and leave the system.

9.4.2   Single-Class Open Models

Let us examine first the case of a single open class QN where all resources are either delay or load-independent resources. Consider the following notation:

- λ: average arrival rate of requests to the QN,

- K: number of queues,

- X_0: average throughput of the QN, and in the case of open systems with operational equilibrium, the average throughput is the same as the average arrival rate, i.e., $X_0 = \lambda$,

- V_i: average number of visits to queue i by a request,

- S_i: average service time of a request at queue i per visit to the queue,

- W_i: average waiting time of a request at queue i per visit to the queue,

- X_i: average throughput of queue i,

- R_i: average response time of a request at queue i, defined as the sum of the average waiting time plus average service time per visit to the queue, i.e., $R_i = W_i + S_i$,

- R_i': average residence time of a request at queue i, defined as the total waiting time (i.e., the queuing time) plus the total service time (i.e., the service demand) over all visits to queue i, so, $R_i' = V_i \times R_i$,

- R_0: average response time and equal to the sum of the residence times over all queues, i.e., $R_0 = \sum_{i=1}^{K} R_i'$,

- n_i: average number of requests at queue i waiting or receiving service from any resource at queue i,

- N: average number of requests in the QN.

We start by obtaining the average response time R_i at queue i. We note that the average response time is equal to the average service time S_i plus the average waiting time of a request. The average waiting time is equal to the average number of requests *seen* at queue i by an arriving request to the queue multiplied by the average service time S_i per request. An important result, known as the Arrival Theorem [11] [12] and applied to open QNs, says that the average number of requests seen upon arrival to queue i is equal to the average number, n_i, of requests in the queue. Thus,

$$R_i = S_i + n_i \times S_i. \tag{9.4.13}$$

But, from Little's Law, $n_i = X_i \times R_i$. Combining this result with Eq. (9.4.13) and noting from the Utilization Law that $U_i = X_i \times S_i$, we get that

$$R_i = S_i/(1 - U_i). \tag{9.4.14}$$

From Eq. (9.4.14), we can get the residence time at queue i as

$$R'_i = V_i \times R_i = \frac{V_i \times S_i}{1 - U_i} = \frac{D_i}{1 - U_i}. \tag{9.4.15}$$

Using Little's Law, Eq. (9.4.14), and the Utilization Law again, we can obtain the average number of requests at queue i as

$$n_i = U_i/(1 - U_i). \tag{9.4.16}$$

Example 9.4

Consider an online investment company that is planning a site to support a financial investment transaction application. The site architecture has three layers, as shown in part (a) of Fig. 9.8. The first one consists of a Web server accessed by Internet clients through a browser. The second layer is an application server that receives transaction requests generated at the Web server. To carry out the transaction, the application server communicates with the database server and requests specific database information. The Web server provides static HTML documents (e.g., welcome pages and input forms) to customers, collects data, and transfers them to the application

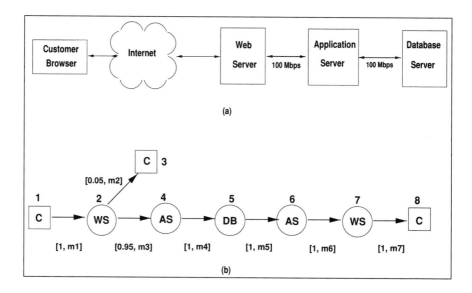

Figure 9.8. Financial Site: Architecture and CSID.

server. The application server gets requests from the Web server, parses them, and activates the processes that carry out the requested e-business function (e.g., Login, User Information, Show Portfolio, and Sell Stocks).

In particular, we want to analyze one class of transactions, represented by the business function Show Portfolio and used by customers to request information about their portfolio of investments. The logical architecture of the Show Portfolio business function is depicted by the CSID diagram in part (b) of Fig. 9.8. After receiving the request, the Web server sends it to the application server, which validates the customer identification and parses the request. The application server communicates with the database server to obtain the portfolio information of that specific customer. At this initial phase of the project, management is first concerned about scalability. In other words, the project manager wants to know how the site's response time will evolve with the growth of the transaction arrival rate. To answer this question, an open queuing network model of the financial transaction site was developed, as shown in Fig. 9.9.

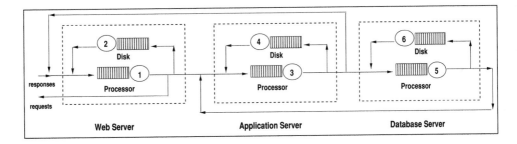

Figure 9.9. Open QN of the Financial Site.

To obtain the input parameters of the analytical model, the analysts ran a series of tests that executed the Show Portfolio transaction. The site was instrumented and monitored during the test period. The performance information collected was used to calculate the service demands of the Show Portfolio transaction and are displayed in Table 9.2.

Using Eqs. (9.4.14) and (9.4.15), we obtain the response time of the Show Portfolio transaction (R_{sp}) for different values of the arrival rate (λ). As an example, let us show the calculations for $\lambda = 9$. We know that the average transaction response time R is equal to the sum of residence times at each queue that makes up the model of Fig. 9.9. So,

$$R_{\text{sp}} = R_1' + R_2' + R_3' + R_4' + R_5' + R_6'.$$

$$R_i' = \frac{D_i}{1 - U_i}.$$

Table 9.2. Input Data for the Financial Site.

Server	Processor Demand	I/O Demand
Web (WS)	19 msec	12 msec
Application (AS)	40 msec	48 msec
Database (DB)	35 msec	56 msec

We also know from Chapter 8 that $U_i = X_0 \times D_i$ and $X_0 = \lambda$ for open models. Thus,

$$U_1 = \lambda \times D_1 = 9 \times 0.019 = 0.171.$$

$$R'_1 = \frac{0.019}{1 - 0.171} = 0.023 \text{ sec.}$$

Similarly, we obtain $R'_2 = 0.013$, $R'_3 = 0.063$, $R'_4 = 0.085$, $R'_5 = 0.051$, $R'_6 = 0.113$, and $R_{\text{sp}} = 0.347$. Figure 9.10 shows how the response time increases as a function of the business transaction arrival rate. ∎

9.4.3 Single-Class Closed Models

The open-queuing network models we studied in the previous section do not place any limits on the maximum number of requests present in the system. There are situations in which we want to model systems with a fixed and finite number of requests in the system. These situations arise when we

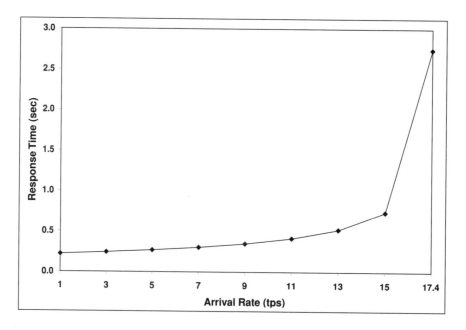

Figure 9.10. Response Time of the Financial Site.

want to model a system with a maximum level of multiprogramming under heavy load, such as a multithreaded Web server or an intranet system with a known number of clients sending requests to a Web server.

The technique presented here to solve closed queuing networks is called Mean Value Analysis (MVA) [11]. It is rather elegant and intuitive. The first efficient technique to solve closed queuing network models is the convolution algorithm due to Buzen [4]. The notation used for closed QN models is similar to the one used for open models except that we denote the variables as a function of the number of requests, n, in the system. So, for instance, $R_i'(n)$ stands for the residence time at queue i when there are n requests in the system.

Mean Value Analysis is based on recursively using three equations: the residence time equation, the throughput equation, and the queue length equation. We derive here these equations from first principles. Consider a closed queuing network with n requests. Let us start by computing the response time, $R_i(n)$, per visit to resource i. As we know, the response time is the sum of the service time S_i, plus the waiting time $W_i(n)$. The waiting time is equal to the time to serve all requests found in the queue by an arriving request. This is equal to the average number, $n_i^a(n)$, of requests found in the queue by an arriving request multiplied by the average service time per request. So,

$$R_i(n) = S_i + W_i(n) = S_i + n_i^a(n) \times S_i = S_i\left[1 + n_i^a(n)\right]. \qquad (9.4.17)$$

The Arrival Theorem [11] [12], applied to closed QNs says that the average number of requests seen upon arrival to queue i when there are n requests in the QN is equal to the average number of requests in queue i in a QN with $n - 1$ requests, i.e., with the arriving request to queue i removed from the queuing network. After all, the arriving request cannot find itself in the queue! Thus, from the Arrival Theorem we have that

$$n_i^a(n) = n_i(n - 1). \qquad (9.4.18)$$

Combining Eqs. (9.4.17) and (9.4.18), we get that

$$R_i(n) = S_i \left[1 + n_i(n-1)\right]. \tag{9.4.19}$$

Multiplying both sides of Eq. (9.4.19) by V_i, we get the first equation of MVA:

$$R'_i(n) = D_i \left[1 + n_i(n-1)\right]. \tag{9.4.20}$$

If we add the residence time $R'_i(n)$ for all queues i, we get the response time $R_0(n)$. Applying Little's Law to the entire QN, we obtain MVA's throughput equation:

$$X_0(n) = \frac{n}{R_0(n)} = \frac{n}{\sum_{i=1}^{K} R'_i(n)}. \tag{9.4.21}$$

To obtain the third equation of MVA, the queue length equation, we apply Little's Law and the Forced Flow Law to queue i. Hence,

$$n_i(n) = X_i(n) \times R_i(n) = X_0(n) \times V_i \times R_i(n) = X_0(n) \times R'_i(n). \tag{9.4.22}$$

We repeat the three equations for single-class MVA in Fig. 9.11.

The residence time for n requests in the QN, $R'_i(n)$, requires that we know the value of the queue length for a QN with one less request, $n_i(n-1)$. But $n_i(n-1)$ depends on $R'_i(n-1)$, which depends on $n_i(n-2)$, which depends on $R'_i(n-2)$, and so on. This indicates that we need to start with $n = 0$ and work our way up to the value of n we are interested in. Fortunately, the results for $n = 0$ are trivial because when there are no requests in the QN, the queue lengths are zero at all queues. So, $n_i(0) = 0$ for all is. This allows us to compute $R'_i(1)$ for all is. With the residence times for $n = 1$ we can use the throughput equation to obtain the throughput for $n = 1$. From the queue length equation we can obtain $n_i(1)$ since we now have $R'_i(1)$ and $X_0(1)$, and so on. The computation sequence required by the MVA algorithm is illustrated in Fig. 9.12.

Residence time equation:

$$R_i'(n) = \begin{cases} D_i & \text{delay resource} \\ D_i \left[1 + n_i(n-1)\right] & \text{queuing resource} \end{cases} \quad (9.4.23)$$

Throughput equation:

$$X_0(n) = \frac{n}{\sum_{i=1}^{K} R_i'(n)} \quad (9.4.24)$$

Queue length equation:

$$n_i(n) = X_0(n) \times R_i'(n) \quad (9.4.25)$$

Figure 9.11. Formulas for Single-Class MVA with No Load-Dependent Resources.

Example 9.5

Let us consider a three-tier configuration similar to that of the e-business site of Ex. 9.4. The third layer of Fig. 9.9 consists of a database server (DB). Every request to a database requires the use of a database connection. As traffic to an e-business site grows, a common bottleneck is database connectivity, which may not scale up to handle thousands of customers simultaneously. During the peak hour, the database server handles the maximum number of simultaneous connections, which in this example is set to five. Let us assume that the database server consists of a processor and two

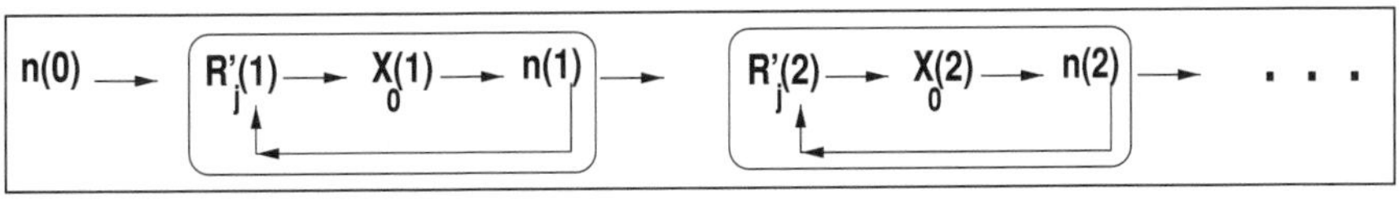

Figure 9.12. Sequence of Computations for Mean Value Analysis.

disks. The service demands of a Search transaction are $D_{\text{proc}} = 21$ msec, $D_{\text{disk1}} = 17$ msec, and $D_{\text{disk2}} = 28$ msec. What is the throughput of the database server during the peak hour? And what is the average response time of the Search transaction?

Considering that the number of transactions being executed by the database server during the peak period is constant, we can model the server as a closed queuing network model. Thus, we use the MVA algorithm of Fig. 9.11 to calculate the performance metrics for $n = 5$. Table 9.3 shows how the throughput, in transactions per second, varies as a function of the number of concurrent requests in the database server. The manager has one more question about the future performance of the database server: what would the server throughput be if the number of database connections increased to 10, 20, and 30? To answer the question, we changed the value of n to 30 and used again the MVA algorithm to compute the following throughputs: $X_0(10) = 34.09$ tps, $X_0(20) = 35.29$ tps, and $X_0(30) = 35.52$ tps. So, we see that increasing the number of connections does not increase the server throughput beyond a given limit, which is determined by the bottleneck of the server. In this particular case, the bottleneck is disk2, which sets an upper bound for the server equal to $X_{\text{max}} = 1/28 = 35.71$ tps. ∎

Table 9.3. Residence Time (in msec), Response Times (in msec), and Throughput (in tps) Results for Ex. 9.5.

n	$R'_{\text{processor}}$	R'_{disk1}	R'_{disk2}	R_0	X_0
0	0.00	0.00	0.00	0.00	0.00
1	21.00	17.00	28.00	66.00	15.15
2	27.00	21.00	41.00	89.00	22.41
3	33.00	24.00	55.00	113.00	26.52
4	39.00	27.00	72.00	138.00	29.07
5	43.00	29.00	90.00	163.00	30.75

9.4.4   Revisiting the Simple Example

In Section 9.3.2, we solved the toy store example using a single queue model. The results provided us the following information about the system behavior: if the current arrival rate is multiplied by four, then the system utilization reaches 96% and the response time increases by 1,900%, changing from 0.063 to 1.2 sec. Although the single queue model provided some useful results, it did not answer another management question: What should be changed in the site configuration so that the average response time does not exceed 1 sec during the peak hour? To answer this question, we need to understand the behavior of the two main components of the server: the processor and the disk subsystem. In other words, we need to develop and solve a queuing network model of the e-business server. Figure 9.13 depicts the open queuing network model with two queues, one for the processor and another one for the disk subsystem. The input parameters for the model are the transaction arrival rates and service demands of the Search transaction. From measurements taken at the site, the analyst calculated the following values for the service demands: $D_{\text{proc}} = 0.014$ sec and $D_{\text{disk}} = 0.034$. The current average arrival rate during the peak hour is five transactions per second.

Using the solution technique presented in Section 9.4.2, we calculated the following performance metrics for the e-business server: $U_{\text{proc}} = 7\%$, $U_{\text{disk}} = 17\%$, $n_{\text{proc}} = 0.075$, $n_{\text{disk}} = 0.205$, $R_{\text{proc}} = 0.015$ sec, $R_{\text{disk}} = 0.041$ sec. Now, we use the model to predict the average response time of the online toy store when the arrival rate grows by a factor of four.

$$\lambda_{\text{New}} = 4 \times \lambda = 4 \times 5 = 20 \text{ request/sec.}$$

$$U_{\text{proc}} = D_{\text{proc}} \times \lambda = 0.014 \times 20 = 0.28.$$

$$U_{\text{disk}} = D_{\text{disk}} \times \lambda = 0.034 \times 20 = 0.68.$$

$$R'_{\text{proc}} = D_{\text{proc}}/(1 - U_{\text{proc}}) = 0.014/(1 - 0.28) = 0.019 \text{ sec.}$$

$$R'_{\text{disk}} = D_{\text{disk}}/(1 - U_{\text{disk}}) = 0.034/(1 - 0.68) = 0.106 \text{ sec.}$$

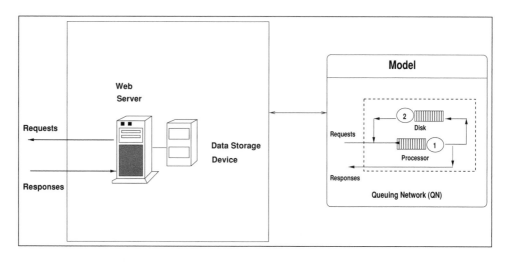

Figure 9.13. Queuing Network Model.

The average response time is then $R = R'_{\text{proc}} + R'_{\text{disk}} = 0.126$ sec and we observe that the disk is the server bottleneck. Using Eq. (9.4.16), we compute the average number of transactions at each queue.

$$n_{\text{proc}} = U_{\text{proc}}/(1 - U_{\text{proc}}) = 0.28/(1 - 0.28) = 0.389 \text{ sec.}$$

$$n_{\text{disk}} = U_{\text{disk}}/(1 - U_{\text{disk}}) = 0.68/(1 - 0.68) = 2.125 \text{ sec.}$$

9.5   Refining the Approach: Multiple Classes

The real power of performance models becomes evident when they are used for predictive purposes. In capacity planning of e-business, models are essential, because of their ability to adequately predict performance of a particular site under different workloads. E-business sites have a wide variety of customers (e.g., heavy buyers, impulsive buyers, opportunistic buyers, patient buyers, and analytical buyers that perform substantial product research before purchasing something), that exhibit different navigational patterns with different demands on the site resources. The transactions associated with each e-business function are the basic components of the e-business workload. Thus, actual workloads would hardly be considered as a single class of homogeneous transactions. Typically, each transaction differs from every other transaction. Because it is impractical to represent each individual transaction in a model, they are grouped into classes of somehow similar transactions.

Usually, what-if questions that appear in capacity planning are associated with individual classes of transactions. As an example, one could ask what the performance of a given site would be if the arrival rate of Search transactions were to increase by 80% or if the average number of simultaneous shoppers during the peak hour is multiplied by ten? Single-class models are unable to answer most of the capacity planning questions related to specific classes of the workload; they are limited in their predictive capability. Therefore, we need techniques to solve multi-class performance models.

Although multiple class models are more useful and natural for describing workloads of real e-business sites, they present some difficulties to the modeler. For instance, it is harder to obtain parameters for multi-class models than for single class queuing network models. Usually, monitoring tools do not provide measurements on a per-class basis. Inferences have to be made to parameterize each workload class and to apportion the system overhead among the classes.

Readers interested in the detailed derivations of algorithms for multi-class open and closed queuing network models should refer to our previous publications [9] [10]. The solution to these models is implemented in the MS Excel workbook `OpenQN.XLS` and `ClosedQN.XLS`, for open and closed queuing networks, respectively. These workbooks can be downloaded from the website associated with this book (see Preface) by following the link called `Chapter 9`.

9.5.1   Revisiting the Simple Example

When we started analyzing the online toy store, our tendency was to keep the model simple, i.e., with few parameters. One of the assumptions we made to simplify the modeling problem was to consider the workload as a collection of just one type of transaction: the Search transaction. The rationale for that assumption was that Search constitutes approximately 85% of all transactions executed by the site. But now that the online store is luring new customers, management wants to increase revenue. One new project is to make the site more attractive to customers. Therefore, the Product Information business function will be redesigned to provide nice pictures of the toys. Management estimates that the new version of Product Information will represent 10% of the total requests in the near future. The question is: what will be the impact of the new business function on the site performance?

To answer the question, we use a two-class queuing network model. One class represents the Search transactions and the other one is composed of the Product Information transactions. Using the CSIDs specified in Section 9.2 and the results of run tests of the Product Information transaction, we were able to calculate its service demands, which are displayed in Table 9.4. The forecast arrival rates are 20 tps and 2.4 tps for Search and Product Information, respectively. Using the `OpenQN.XLS` MS Excel workbook, we obtained the response time for the two classes of transactions:

$$R_{\text{Search}} = 0.269 \text{ sec},$$

$$R_{\text{Product Information}} = 0.613 \text{ sec}.$$

Although the average response time of Search has increased 113% due to

Table 9.4. Service Demands (in sec) for the Two-Class Model of the Simple Problem.

Queue	Search	Product Information
Processor	0.014	0.038
Disk	0.034	0.076

the work generated by the new transaction, the site will still have acceptable response times for the forecast traffic.

9.6   Summary

This chapter introduced powerful techniques to solve performance models of e-business sites. These techniques are based on open and queuing network models. Some of the important results in the theory of queuing networks are worth noting here. One of them is the BCMP theorem [2], developed by Baskett, Chandy, Muntz, and Palacios, that specifies the combination of service time distributions and scheduling disciplines that yield multi-class product-form queuing networks with any combination of open and closed classes. Buzen developed the Convolution Algorithm—the first computationally efficient method to solve QNs [4]. Sevcik and Mitrani [12] developed the arrival theorem and Reiser and Lavenberg [11] developed Mean Value Analysis, which is based on the arrival theorem. Several approximations to QNs for the non-product-form case were developed and reported in the literature. Some aspects of actual e-business sites such as priority at processor scheduling or at load balancing systems are not amenable to modeling with the exact queuing network models presented here. Readers interested in solution techniques for approximate models should refer to Agrawal [1], Lazowska et al [7], and Menascé et al [9].

Detailed performance models for the Web, either client-side models or server-side models, are available in Menascé and Almeida [10] as are specific issues of Web performance modeling, such as modeling of burstiness and heavy-tailed distributions. The algorithms discussed in this chapter are implemented in the MS Excel `OpenQN.XLS` and `ClosedQN.XLS` workbooks available at the site associated with this book. They solve multi-class open and closed queuing networks, respectively, and provide results, such as utilization, residence times, and queue lengths, per class and per device, as well as response times and throughputs per class.

Bibliography

[1] S. Agrawal, *Metamodeling: A Study of Approximations in Queuing Models*, Cambridge, MA, MIT Press, 1985.

[2] F. Baskett, K. Chandy, R. Muntz, and F. Palacios, "Open, Closed, and Mixed Networks of Queues with Different Classes of Customers," *J. ACM*, vol. 22, no. 2, Apr. 1975.

[3] J. P. Buzen, "Operational Analysis: an Alternative to Stochastic Modeling," in *Performance of Computer Installations*. North Holland, June 1978, pp. 175–194.

[4] J. P. Buzen, "Computational Algorithms for Closed Queuing Networks with Exponential Servers," *Comm. ACM*, vol. 16, No. 9, Sept. 1973.

[5] P. Denning and J. P. Buzen, "The Operational Analysis of Queuing Network Models," *Computing Surveys*, vol. 10, no. 3, Sept. 1978, pp. 225-261.

[6] L. Kleinrock, *Queueing Systems, Vol. I: Theory*, Wiley, New York, 1975.

[7] E. Lazowska, J. Zahorjan, G. Graham, and K. Sevcik, *Quantitative System Performance: Computer System Analysis Using Queuing Network Models*, Prentice Hall, Upper Saddle River, NJ, 1984.

[8] J. Little, "A proof of the queuing formula $L = \lambda W$," *Operations Research*, vol. 9, 1961, pp. 383-387.

[9] D. A. Menascé, V. A. F. Almeida, and L. W. Dowdy, *Capacity Planning and Performance Modeling: from Mainframes to Client-Server Systems*, Prentice Hall, Upper Saddle River, NJ, 1994.

[10] D. A. Menascé and V. A. F. Almeida, *Capacity Planning for Web Performance: Metrics, Models and Methods*, Prentice Hall, Upper Saddle River, NJ, 1998.

[11] M. Reiser and S. Lavenberg, "Mean-value Analysis of Closed Multi-Chain Queuing Networks," *J. ACM*, vol. 27, no. 2, 1980.

[12] K. Sevcik and I. Mitrani, "The Distribution of Queuing Network States at Input and Output Instants," *J. ACM*, vol. 28, no. 2, Apr. 1981.

Chapter 10

Modeling Contention for Software Servers

10.1 Introduction

The previous two chapters discussed models that show the effect of contention for hardware resources (e.g., processors, I/O devices, routers, and LAN segments) on the response time of requests to execute functions of an e-business site. Besides hardware resources, other resources, such as software resources (e.g., threads of a software server, database locks, and semaphores), can add to the delay experienced by requests and transactions.

This chapter illustrates the effects of software contention through some examples. Performance models that deal with software contention may be based on approximate analytic queuing network models or on simulation techniques. We briefly describe here how these techniques can be used to model software contention, and we provide reference sources so readers can obtain additional and more detailed information on these methods.

10.2   A Simple Example

Consider a Web server with a fixed number m of threads. When a request arrives, it can be handled directly by a thread if one is available. Otherwise, it has to wait in a queue for threads as shown in Fig. 10.1. When a thread is executing a request, it may use the CPU and I/O resources. In the process of doing so, the thread may have to wait in the queue for the CPU and I/O. So, the total response time for a Web request can be decomposed into three types of components:

- *Software contention:* time spent by a request waiting to obtain a software resource (e.g., access to a server thread, a semaphore, or a database lock),

- *Hardware contention:* time spent waiting to use a hardware resource such as the CPU or an I/O device,

- *Usage of hardware resources:* time spent using hardware resources such as the CPU or I/O devices, i.e., the sum of the service demands at all hardware resources.

Example 10.1

Consider an HTTP server configured with five threads. Each request requires, on average, 0.050 sec of CPU time and 0.065 sec of I/O time. There is no limit on the size of the queue for threads. We want to investigate the impact of contention for threads as the arrival rate, λ, of requests increases.

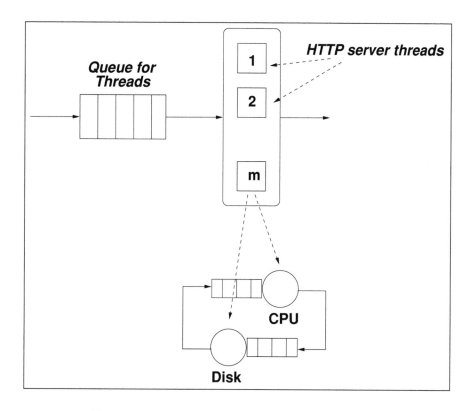

Figure 10.1. Example of Contention for Server Threads.

Figure 10.2 shows the variation of the response time as the arrival rate increases from one to twelve requests/sec (top curve). The bottom curve indicates the variation of the time spent by a request waiting for a thread to become available. The horizontal line indicates the sum of the CPU plus I/O service demands, i.e., 0.115 sec (=0.050 + 0.065). This line represents a lower bound on the response time.

We can use Little's Law (see Section 8.6.4) to calculate the average number of requests in execution and the average number of requests in the queue for threads. Consider first that the "black box" to which we apply Little's Law is the entire HTTP server, including the queue for threads. For $\lambda = 12$ requests/sec, the response time is 0.487 sec. Then, according to Little's Law, the average number of requests in the HTTP server, including the queue for

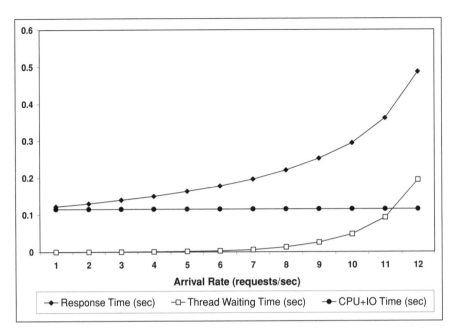

Figure 10.2.   Response Time and Waiting Time for Threads for the Case of Unlimited Thread Queue Size.

threads, is 5.84 ($= 12 \times 0.487$). Let us now apply Little's Law to the queue for threads. The throughput of the queue for threads is still λ because all requests that join the queue for threads leave that queue. The average time spent in that queue for $\lambda = 12$ requests/sec is 0.194 sec. So, the average number of requests waiting for a thread is 2.33 ($= 12 \times 0.194$).

The difference between the response time and the thread waiting time is the request execution time, i.e., the time spent using the CPU and I/O plus the time spent waiting for these resources. For $\lambda = 12$ requests/sec, the execution time is 0.293 ($= 0.487 - 0.194$) sec. Since 0.115 sec are spent using the CPU and I/O, the time spent waiting for these resources is 0.063 ($= 0.293 - 0.115$) sec.   ■

Consider now the case in which the queue for threads is limited as illustrated in Fig. 10.3. A maximum of J requests can be in the queue for threads

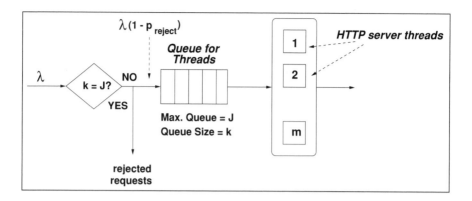

Figure 10.3. Contention for Server Threads with Finite Queue.

at any time. A request that finds J requests in the queue is rejected. One of the motivations for placing such limits is to control the load on the system and limit the response time for the requests that are not rejected. These limits are also useful in preventing denial of service attacks from completely flooding an e-business site.

Example 10.2

Consider the same situation of Ex. 10.1, but now the number of requests allowed to queue for threads is limited to J requests. We want to explore the influence of the value of J on the response time, thread waiting time, and request execution time. We define request execution time as the sum of all the processing time plus I/O time plus all the time spent waiting for hardware resources.

We assign values of 1, 3, 5, 7, and 9 to J and model the system to watch the behavior of the response time, thread waiting time, and request execution time. The result, obtained with a simulation model, is depicted in Fig. 10.4 for $\lambda = 12$ requests/sec. The picture shows that each of the three metrics grows with the maximum queue size but approaches the value each of the metrics would have in the unlimited thread queue size case. For example, for $\lambda = 12$ and for the unlimited queue size case (see Ex. 10.1), the average

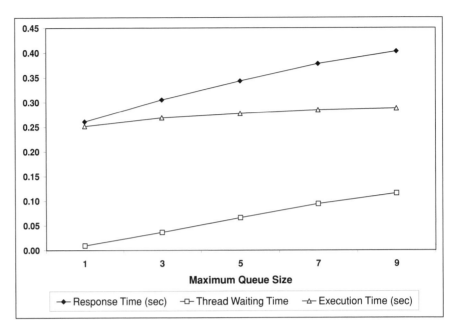

Figure 10.4. Response Time, Waiting Time for Threads, and Execution Time for the Case of Limited Queue Size.

response time is 0.487 sec. This is the limit value of the response time when J goes to infinity in Fig. 10.4. The thread waiting time increases as the maximum queue size increases because requests that are not rejected tend to find more requests in the queue for threads as J increases. The execution time increases at the beginning and then saturates when the maximum queue size is large enough to keep all threads (five in this case) busy most of the time.

When there is a limit on the number of requests allowed to wait in the queue, some requests may be rejected. An important question is what the probability is that a request is rejected? In the case of Ex. 10.1, the system throughput was equal to the arrival rate λ because all requests that arrived went through the system and completed. Here, the throughput is equal to the arrival rate of requests that are not rejected (see Fig. 10.3). In other words,

$$\text{Throughput} = \lambda \times (1 - P_{\text{reject}}), \qquad (10.2.1)$$

where P_{reject} is the probability that a request is rejected. The reject probability is shown in Table 10.1 for $\lambda = 12$ requests/sec. As shown in Table 10.1, the reject probability decreases very fast: from about 10.3% when $J = 1$ to a little below 1.6% for $J = 9$.   ∎

10.3   Contention for Software in E-Business Sites

Consider now a slightly more complex situation. As discussed in previous chapters, e-business sites are organized in a multi-tiered fashion, both in terms of hardware and software architecture. Figure 10.5 illustrates the software and hardware queues for an e-business site. The top part of the figure illustrates the software queues. The Web server (WS) is multithreaded with m threads, the application server (AS) has n threads, and the database server (DS) is multithreaded with p threads. The queue for Web server threads is limited. So, requests may be rejected if that queue is full to its capacity. A Web server thread processes an incoming request and determines which application (e.g., a search in the store's catalog) must be executed. A request is then sent to the application server and placed in the queue for application server threads. The application server will need to request

Table 10.1. Reject Probability for Ex. 10.2.

Maximum Queue Size	Reject Probability
1	0.1027
3	0.0605
5	0.0345
7	0.0227
9	0.0159

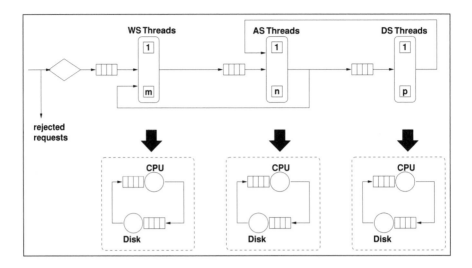

Figure 10.5. Software and Hardware Queues in an E-Business Site.

the database server to perform one or more database accesses. So, requests are sent to the database server and placed in the queue for database server threads. The application server thread continues to be assigned to the request until the application completes. At this point, the result is sent back to the Web server and the original Web server thread completes the execution. Note that the Web server thread is allocated to the request since the request was first processed by the Web server until the application server returned the generated results and the request was completed.

So, as shown in the equations below, the response time for a request to execute an e-business function is the sum of the software contention at the three servers plus the execution time at the three servers. Execution time is the sum of service demands plus time spent waiting for hardware resources, i.e., hardware contention.

$$\mathrm{ResponseTime} = \mathrm{SoftwareContention} + \mathrm{ExecutionTime}.$$

$$\mathrm{SoftwareContention} = \mathrm{Wait_{WS}} + \mathrm{Wait_{AS}} + \mathrm{Wait_{DS}}.$$

$$\mathrm{ExecutionTime} = \mathrm{HardwareContention} + \mathrm{TotalDemands}.$$

$$\text{HardwareContention} = \text{HdwWait}_{\text{WS}} + \text{HdwWait}_{\text{AS}} + \text{HdwWait}_{\text{DS}}.$$

$$\text{TotalDemands} = \text{Demands}_{\text{WS}} + \text{Demands}_{\text{AS}} + \text{Demands}_{\text{DS}}.$$

$$(10.3.2)$$

The bottom part of Fig. 10.5 shows the hardware resources and their queues, assuming that the Web server, application server, and database server execute on different machines.

Example 10.3

Consider an e-business site such as the one illustrated in Fig. 10.5. The maximum queue size for Web server threads is fifty requests. The number of threads and service demands at the CPU and I/O for the three servers are given in Table 10.2. We want to investigate how the response time, software contention, execution time, and hardware contention vary as a function of the arrival rate of requests.

The results, obtained with a simulation model, are shown in Fig. 10.6. The first observation drawn from the figure is that response time, software contention, execution time, and hardware contention grow at the beginning with the arrival rate and then saturate when the queue for threads is filled with fifty requests. Another observation is that hardware contention represents the largest component of execution time. The difference between execution time and hardware contention is the sum of all service demands, which in this case is 0.107 ($= 0.010 + 0.015 + 0.012 + 0.020 + 0.020 + 0.030$) sec, according to Table 10.2.

Table 10.2. Parameters for Ex. 10.3.

Server Type	Number of Threads	D_{CPU} (sec)	$D_{\text{I/O}}$ (sec)
Web Server	15	0.010	0.015
Application Server	10	0.012	0.020
Database Server	5	0.020	0.030

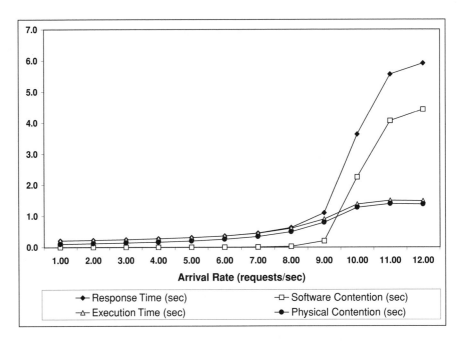

Figure 10.6. Response Time, Software Contention, Hardware Contention, and Execution Time for an E-Business Site.

As a result of the model, we also obtain the average number, N_{site}, of requests at the e-business site, including the three servers and all queues for threads. For $\lambda = 12$ requests/sec, this number is 59.7 requests and the response time is 5.92 sec. According to Little's Law,

$$N_{site} = \text{Throughput} \times \text{ResponseTime}$$
$$= \lambda \, (1 - P_{reject}) \times \text{ResponseTime}. \tag{10.3.3}$$

So, the reject probability, P_{reject}, is

$$P_{reject} = 1 - \frac{N_{site}}{\lambda \times \text{ResponseTime}}$$
$$= 1 - 59.7/(12 \times 5.92) = 0.16. \tag{10.3.4}$$

It is also worth noting that software contention is negligible for low arrival rates and exceeds execution time by far as traffic increases. In the case of $\lambda = 12$, software contention represents 75% of the response time. ∎

10.4   Modeling Software Contention

The previous sections illustrated the effects of software contention on response time. This section briefly describes three approaches that can be used to build performance models that reflect the effect of software contention. The first two approaches are analytic and the last is based on discrete event simulation.

10.4.1   Simultaneous Resource Possession

The type of queuing networks (QNs) described in Section 9.4, can be solved exactly under a certain set of conditions. When these conditions hold, the QNs are said to have a *product-form* solution [3] [9] [11]. Product-form QNs do not allow a request to simultaneously hold more than one resource. This situation, called *simultaneous resource possession*, can be modeled only through approximate analytic models based on QNs.

Software contention can be modeled through simultaneous resource possession as illustrated in Fig. 10.7. In this case, both software and hardware resources are part of the QN. The solid bars in Fig. 10.7 illustrate periods when a resource is being held by a request and the hashed bars indicate time spent waiting to seize a resource. The figure shows five time axes for the following resources: Web server thread, application server thread, database server thread, CPU at the database server, and I/O at the database server. The first three resources are software resources and the last two are hardware resources. A request arrives at time 1 at the Web server and queues for service by a Web server thread. Then, the request receives some processing at the Web server, which uses the CPU and I/O devices at the Web server machine. These two resources are used while simultaneously holding the Web server thread resource. Then, at time 3, the request joins the queue for service by an application server thread. While holding the application server thread, the request alternates holding the CPU and I/O resources at the application server machine (not shown in the picture). Then, at time

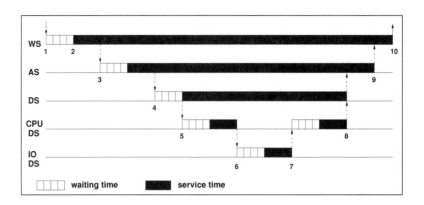

Figure 10.7. Simultaneous Resource Possession of Software and Hardware Resources.

4, the request joins the queue for a database server thread. At this point, the request is already holding the Web server and application server threads simultaneously. When the request obtains a database server thread, at time 5, it alternates between waiting and using the CPU and I/O resources as shown in the figure. For example, when the request is using the CPU at the database server machine, it is simultaneously holding the following resources: a Web server thread, an application server thread, a database server thread, and the CPU at the database server machine. In other words, the request is holding the three software resources and one hardware resource at the same time.

Various approximations have been proposed to deal with the issue of simultaneous resource possession in QNs and software delays [1] [6] [8] [10] [16].

10.4.2   Method of Layers

Due to its multi-tier architecture, e-business sites are suitable for representation by models composed of multiple layers. An extension to QNs, called *Layered Queuing Networks (LQNs)*, is quite suitable for representing the software and hardware hierarchy in an e-business site [13] [17]. LQNs are queuing network models that combine contention for both software and hardware components, such as processors, disks, and networks.

In a LQN model, processes with similar behavior form a group or a class of processes. These processes may invoke services from lower level processes, which may represent software and/or hardware resources. For example, Fig. 10.8 shows a layered queuing model of an e-business site. We assume in the figure that the Web server is running on a machine of its own and that the application and database servers share another machine. However, the application server uses disk 2 and the database server uses disks 3 and 4. Web server threads are at level 1 of the LQN model and request services from CPU 1, disk 1, and application server threads, which are at level 2 of the LQN. The application server threads use disk 2 and the database server threads at level 3. Finally, the database server threads use CPU 2 and disks 3 and 4, which are at level 4.

Approximate analytic techniques based on Mean Value Analysis (MVA) are used to estimate performance measures of layered queuing models with L levels. Two of these techniques are the Method of Layers [13] (MOL) and Stochastic Rendez-vous Networks (SRNs) [17]. The MOL is an iterative technique that decomposes an LQN into a sequence of two-level QN submodels

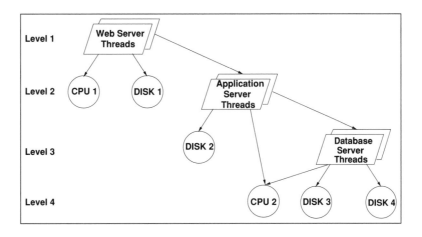

Figure 10.8. Layered Queueing Network (LQN) Model.

that are solved using MVA-based solution techniques. Performance estimates for the QN at each submodel are calculated and used as input for subsequent QN models. The goal of the MOL is to obtain a fixed point where mean performance measures (i.e., response time, utilization, and queue length) are consistent across all levels. The MOL solution method consists of an iterative algorithm that begins by assuming no hardware or software contention. The algorithm iterates until the response times of successive groups reach a fixed point [13]. A tool that implements these techniques is described in a paper by Franks et al [5].

Although SRNs are similar to MOLs in modeling capability, its solution technique differs from the approach used by the MOL. A SRN generalizes the client/server relationship to multiple layers of servers with send-and-wait interactions (rendez-vous). In a SRN, tasks represent software and hardware resources that may execute concurrently. Random execution times and communication patterns are associated with the tasks of a SRN [17].

10.4.3   Simulation

Simulation is the modeling technique of choice when obtaining exact or adequately accurate analytic models is very difficult for the system to be modeled. Simulation models mimic the behavior of a real system through computer programs that randomly generate events such as arrivals of requests and move these requests around through the various simulated queues. Several counts accumulate metrics of interest such as total waiting time in a queue and total time a resource was busy. These counts can be used at the end of the simulation to obtain average waiting times, average response times, and utilization of the various resources [7].

Simulation programs can be written in general purpose programming languages (e.g., C or C++), in general purpose programming languages augmented by simulation libraries (e.g., CSIM 18 [12] or SimPack [4]), in special purpose simulation languages (e.g., GPSS/H [2] or Simscript II.5 [15]), or in graphical languages supported by simulation packages that offer a GUI through which resources and flow of requests are described (e.g., SES/workbench [14]). To provide readers with an example of simulation programs, GPSS/H programs that model the situations depicted in the examples of the previous section are available at the book's website (see the `Chapter 10` link).

Simulation is usually much more computationally intensive than analytic models. On the other hand, simulation models can be made as accurate as desired. However, more detailed simulation models tend to require more detailed data and more time for execution, thus increasing the cost of using simulation. Analytic models, even approximate ones, are, in general, the technique of choice for scalability analysis and for capacity planning.

10.5   Concluding Remarks

The response time for a request to execute an e-business function can be broken down in three components: software contention, hardware contention, and hardware resource usage. Software contention includes the time spent by a request waiting to get access to a software resource such as a thread of a server, a database lock, or a semaphore. Hardware contention is the component of the response time that accounts for all the time spent waiting to use a hardware resource, such as a processor, an I/O device, or a LAN segment. Finally, hardware usage time is the time during which one of the hardware resources is being used by the request.

Models that include software contention can be solved by approximate analytic models or with the use of simulation techniques. While simulation models can be built to be as accurate and detailed as desired, they tend to be more time-consuming to develop and validate as well as more computationally expensive than analytic models.

Bibliography

[1] S. Agrawal and J. P. Buzen, "The Aggregate Server Method for Analyzing Serialization Delays in Computer Systems," ACM TOCS, vol. 1, no. 2, 1983, pp. 116–143.

[2] J. Banks, J. S. Carson II, and J. N. Sy, *Getting Started with GPSS/H*, 2nd. ed., Wolverine Software Corporation, Annandale, VA, 1995.

[3] F. Baskett, K. Chandy, R. Muntz, and F. Palacios, "Open, Closed, and Mixed Networks of Queues with Different Classes of Customers," *J. ACM*, vol. 22, no. 2, Apr. 1975.

[4] P. Fishwick, *Simulation Model Design and Execution*, Prentice Hall, Upper Saddle River, NJ, 1995.

[5] G. Franks, A. Hubbard, S. Majumdar, D. Petriu, J. Rolia, and C. M. Woodside, "A Toolset for Performance Engineering and Software Design of Client-Server Systems," *Performance Evaluation J.*, vol. 24, no. 1-2, 1996, pp. 117–135.

[6] P. A. Jacobson and E. Lazowska, "Analyzing Queueing Networks with Simultaneous Resource Possession," *Comm. ACM*, vol. 25, no. 2, 1982.

[7] A. Law and W. Kelton, *Simulation Modeling and Analysis*, McGraw Hill, NY, 1995.

[8] D. A. Menascé and V. A. F. Almeida, "Performance of Client/Server Systems," *Performance Evaluation - Origins and Directions*, eds. G. Haring, C. Lindemann, and M. Reiser, LNCS Series of Springer-Verlag, 2000.

[9] D. A. Menascé and V. A. F. Almeida, *Capacity Planning for Web Performance: Metrics, Models, and Methods*, Prentice Hall, Upper Saddle River, NJ, 1998.

[10] D. A. Menascé, O. Pentakalos, and Y. Yesha, "An Analytic Model of Hierarchical Mass Storage Systems with Network-Attached Storage Devices," *Proc. 1996 ACM Sigmetrics Conference*, Philadelphia, PA, May 1996.

[11] D. A. Menascé, V. A. F. Almeida, and L. W. Dowdy, *Capacity Planning and Performance Modeling: From Mainframes to Client-server Systems*, Prentice Hall, Upper Saddle River, NJ, 1994.

[12] *CSIM User Guide*, Mesquite Software, Inc., Austin, TX, www.mesquite.com.

[13] J. A. Rolia and K. C. Sevcik, "The Method of Layers," *IEEE Tr. Software Eng.*, vol. 21, no. 8, 1995, pp. 689–700.

[14] SES/workbench, SES Inc., Austin, TX, www.ses.com.

[15] *Simscript II.5 User's Manual*, CACI, www.simscript.com.

[16] Thomasian, A., "Queuing Network Models to Estimate Serialization Delays in Computer Systems," *Performance'83*, eds. A. K. Agrawal and S. K. Tripathi, North-Holland Publishing Company, 1983, pp. 61–81.

[17] C. M. Woodside, J. E. Neilson, D. C. Petriu, and S. Majumdar, "The Stochastic Rendez-vous Network Model for Performance of Synchronous Client-Server-like Distributed Software," *IEEE Tr. Computers*, vol. 44, no. 1, 1995.

Chapter 11

Characterizing E-Business Workloads

11.1 Introduction

Chapter 7 described the general methodology for characterizing the workload of e-commerce sites. As described in that chapter, a key issue is the characterization of customer behavior. In Chapter 2 we discussed two models for customer behavior characterization: the Customer Behavior Model Graph (CBMG) and the Customer Visit Model (CVM). The former captures the navigational pattern of a customer during a visit to the site and the latter is a less detailed representation and only captures the number of times a customer executes each of the e-business functions per session.

In this chapter, we show how CBMGs and CVMs can be obtained from HTTP logs and describe methods, based on clustering analysis, to derive small groups of CBMGs or CVMs that accurately represent the workload. We also show how the parameters for the resource models (e.g., queuing network models) can be derived from customer behavior models.

11.2   Workload Characterization of Web Traffic

There is a significant body of work on workload characterization of Web traffic. A very helpful survey can be found in a paper by Pitkow [22]. The workload characterization studies described in that paper attempt at detecting invariants, i.e., regular and predictable patterns, of Web traffic from measurements taken at clients, proxy servers, servers, and the Web as a whole. Even though the focus of this chapter is on workload characterization for e-commerce, it is important to review some of the results obtained in the analysis of information retrieval Web servers.

The file popularity was shown to follow a Zipf distribution, which means that the number of accesses, P, to a document is inversely proportional to the document rank r [2] [7] [12] as discussed in Chapter 8. So, $P = k/r$ where k is a constant. The rank of the most popular document is one, the second most popular is two, and so on and so forth (see Ex. 11.1).

Example 11.1

The HTTP log of a Web site shows 1,800 requests for files during a five-minute period. These requests are directed to twelve unique files. Assuming, Zipf's Law, what is the estimated number of accesses to each of the twelve files?

Let us number the files from 1 to 12 according to their rank; file 1 is the most popular and 12 the least popular. The number of accesses to each of these files is k/r. The total number of accesses can then be written as

$$1,800 = k \times (\frac{1}{1} + \frac{1}{2} + \cdots + \frac{1}{12}) = k \times 3.1032. \qquad (11.2.1)$$

Therefore, $k = 1,800/3.1032 = 580.05$. So, the estimated number of accesses to the most popular file is $k/1 = 580$ and to the least popular file is $k/12 = 580.05/12 = 48$. Figure 11.1 shows how the number of references varies from the most to the least popular file.   ■

Several empirical studies have found that many of the distributions related to Web traffic (e.g., distribution of file sizes retrieved from a Web server, reading time per page) are heavy-tailed. A heavy-tailed distribution for a random variable X is one in which the tail of the distribution, i.e., the probability that $X > x$, decreases with $x^{-\alpha}$ for large values of x and for $0 < \alpha < 2$. For these distributions, the probability that a large value occurs is small but non-negligible. A good example of a heavy-tailed distribution

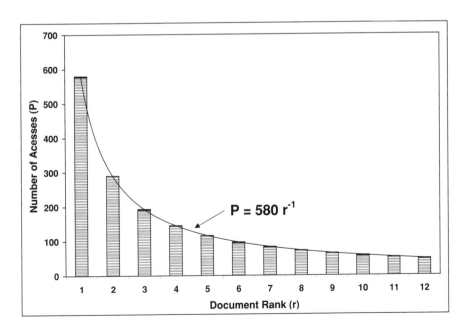

Figure 11.1. Example of Zipf's Law.

is the Pareto distribution. The cumulative distribution function (CDF) for the Pareto distribution is given by

$$F(x) = P[X \le x] = 1 - \left(\frac{k}{x}\right)^{\alpha} \quad \alpha, k > 0 \qquad (11.2.2)$$

and the tail of the distribution is given by

$$P[X > x] = \left(\frac{k}{x}\right)^{\alpha}. \qquad (11.2.3)$$

On the Web, while most files retrieved from a Web server are small, there is a non-negligible probability of large files (e.g., images and video clips) being retrieved. The next example illustrates the properties of heavy-tailed distributions.

Example 11.2

Suppose that the HTTP log for a website was analyzed to estimate the distribution of the sizes of the files retrieved from the site. Suppose that the file size X is distributed according to a Pareto distribution. If we plot the logarithm of the tail of the distribution, i.e., $log\ P[X > x]$, versus the logarithm of the file size, we obtain the straight line

$$log\ P[X > x] = -\alpha \times log\ x + \alpha \times log\ k. \qquad (11.2.4)$$

So, the logarithm of the tail of the distribution decreases linearly with the logarithm of the file size with a slope of $-\alpha$. This is a very simple test for verifying that a distribution has a heavy tail. You just plot the tail of the distribution in a log-log scale. If you get a straight line for large values of x, then you are dealing with a heavy-tailed distribution. Other, more formal methods are described by Crovella and Bestavros [11]. Figure 11.2 shows such a log-log plot for $\alpha = 0.5$ and $k = 1$ for a Pareto distribution. ∎

Some Web traffic features that were found to be heavy-tailed include the size of files requested from Web servers [4] [12] and from the entire

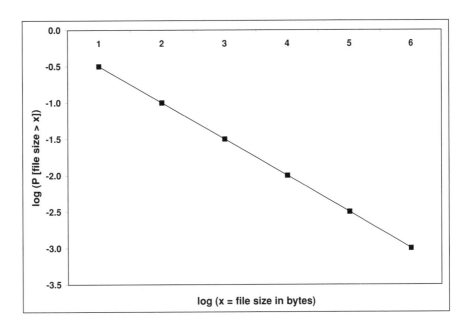

Figure 11.2. Log-Log Plot of the Tail of the Pareto Distribution.

Web [6] [25], the number of pages requested per site [10] [12] [17], and the reading time per page [10] [12].

It has been demonstrated in many empirical studies that small images account for the majority of the traffic and that document size is inversely related to request frequency [4] [12]. HTTP traffic was shown to be self-similar, i.e., it exhibits similar patterns of burstiness across several time scales ranging from microseconds to minutes [1] [11].

As reported in the summary by Pitkow [22], studies of WWW queries showed that 99% of the queries did not use any Boolean or other advanced operators.

A study by Arlitt et al [3] looks at proxy server workloads in a cable modem environment. That study showed that 40% of the total size of the unique HTTP files retrieved is due to the presence of a few very large file types (e.g., audio, video, compressed, and executable). Due to the higher bandwidth of cable modems when compared to 56 kbps modems, users become more willing to download larger files. This poses additional stress on server resources.

The invariants described here were derived by analyzing logs of websites that do not involve e-commerce activities. The basic component for workloads of information retrieval websites is an individual HTTP request. The remainder of this chapter deals with workload characterization methods for e-commerce sites. In this case, the basic component is a session.

11.3   Characterizing Customer Behavior

Chapter 2 introduced Customer Behavior Model Graphs (CBMGs) and the Customer Visit Model (CVMs) as examples of models that characterize customer behavior. That chapter described how the static portion of the CBMG can be built. We describe in this section how the dynamic portion of the CBMG is obtained from HTTP logs. A good part of this description is adapted from a paper by Menascé et al [19].[1]

We start by reviewing and extending the definition of the CBMG presented in Chapter 2. The CBMG can be used to capture the navigational pattern of a customer through an e-commerce site. This pattern includes two aspects: a transitional and a temporal one. The former determines how a customer moves from one state (i.e., an e-business function) to the next. This is represented by the matrix of transition probabilities. The temporal aspect has to do with the time it takes for a customer to move from one state to the next. This time is measured from the server's perspective and is called *server-perceived think time* or just think time. This is defined as the average time elapsed since the server completes a request for a customer until it receives the next request from the same customer during the same session. Figure 11.3 illustrates this definition. As it can be seen, the server-side think time is given by $t_3 - t_2$ and is equal to $2 \times \text{nt} + Z_b$, where nt

---

[1] © 1999 ACM.

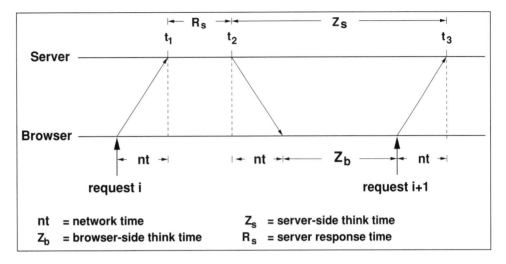

Figure 11.3. Browser-Side and Server-Side Think Times. Reprinted from [19] © 1999 ACM.

represents the network time and Z_b is the browser-side think time. A think time can be associated with each transition in the CBMG.

So, a CBMG can be defined by a pair (P, Z) where $P = [p_{i,j}]$ is an $n \times n$ matrix of transition probabilities between the n states of the CBMG and $Z = [z_{i,j}]$ is an $n \times n$ matrix that represents the average think times between the states of the CBMG. Recall that state 1 is the Entry state and n is the Exit state. In Chapter 2, we discussed metrics derived from the CBMG. We revisit these here in a more formal way.

Example 11.3

Consider the CBMG of Fig. 11.4. This CBMG has seven states; the Exit state, state seven, is not explicitly represented in the figure. Let V_j be the average number of times that state j of the CBMG is visited for each visit to the e-commerce site, i.e., for each visit to the state Entry. Consider the Add to Cart state. We can see that the average number of visits (V_{Add}) to this state is equal to the average number of visits to the state Select (V_{Select})

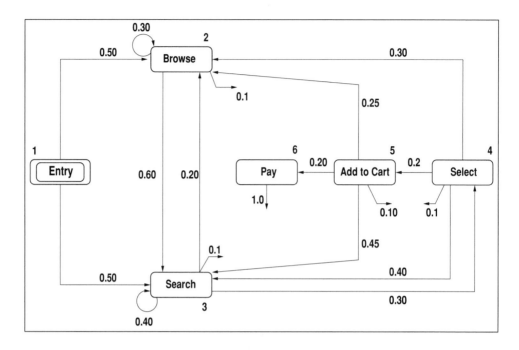

Figure 11.4. CBMG for Ex. 11.3

multiplied by the probability (0.2) that a customer will go from Select to Add Cart. We can then write the relationship

$$V_{\text{Add}} = V_{\text{Select}} \times 0.2. \tag{11.3.5}$$

Consider now the Browse state. The average number of visits (V_{Browse}) to this state is equal to the average number of visits to state Search (V_{Search}) multiplied by the probability (0.2) that a customer will go from Search to Browse, plus the average number of visits to state Select (V_{Select}) multiplied by the probability (0.30) that a customer will go from Select to Browse, plus the average number of visits to the state Add to Cart (V_{Add}) multiplied by the probability (0.25) that a customer will go from Add to Cart to Browse, plus the average number of visits to the state Browse (V_{Browse}) multiplied by the probability (0.30) that a Customer will remain in the Browse state, plus the number of visits to the Entry state multiplied by the probability (0.5) of going from the Entry state to the Browse state. Hence,

$$V_{\text{Browse}} = V_{\text{Search}} \times 0.20 + V_{\text{Select}} \times 0.30 + V_{\text{Add}} \times 0.25 +$$
$$V_{\text{Browse}} \times 0.30 + V_{\text{Entry}} \times 0.5. \tag{11.3.6}$$

∎

So, in general, the average number of visits to a state j of the CBMG is equal to the sum of the number of visits to all states of the CBMG multiplied by the transition probability from each of the other states to state j. Thus, for any state j ($j = 2, \cdots, n-1$) of the CBMG, one can write the equation

$$V_j = \sum_{k=1}^{n-1} V_k \times p_{k,j}, \tag{11.3.7}$$

where $p_{k,j}$ is the probability that a customer makes a transition from state k to state j. Note that the summation in Eq. (11.3.7) does not include state n (the Exit state) since there are no possible transitions from this state to any other state. Since $V_1 = 1$ (because state 1 is the Entry state), we can find the average number of visits V_j by solving the system of linear equations

$$V_1 = 1 \tag{11.3.8}$$

$$V_j = \sum_{k=1}^{n-1} V_k \times p_{k,j} \quad j = 2, \cdots, n-1. \tag{11.3.9}$$

Note that $V_n = 1$ since, by definition, the Exit state is only visited once per session. This system of linear equations can be solved using the MS Excel workbook `cbmg.xls` found on this book's website or by using any other package (e.g., SAS, Mathematica, Matlab).

As mentioned in Chapter 2, we can obtain useful metrics from the CBMG. Once we have the average number of visits (V_j) to each state of the CBMG, we can obtain the average session length as

$$\text{AverageSessionLength} = \sum_{j=2}^{n-1} V_j. \tag{11.3.10}$$

For the visit ratios of Ex. 11.3, the average session length is

$$\mathrm{AverageSessionLength} = V_{\mathrm{Browse}} + V_{\mathrm{Search}} + V_{\mathrm{Select}} + V_{\mathrm{Add}} + V_{\mathrm{Pay}}$$
$$= 2.498 + 4.413 + 1.324 + 0.265 + 0.053$$
$$= 8.552. \tag{11.3.11}$$

The buy to visit Ratio is simply given by V_{Pay}.

11.4   From HTTP Logs to CBMGs

Each customer session can be represented by a CBMG. We show here how we can obtain the CBMGs that characterize customer sessions from HTTP logs. We then show how we can group CBMGs that originate from "similar" sessions and represent each group by a CBMG. The goal is to characterize the workload by a relatively small and representative number of CBMGs as opposed to having to deal with thousands or even hundreds of thousands of CBMGs.

We discuss in what follows a process by which a small number of CBMGs can be obtained from HTTP logs. Figure 11.5 illustrates these steps. The first step consists of merging and filtering HTTP logs from the various HTTP servers of the e-commerce site to discard irrelevant entries such as image requests, errors, and others. These logs can be merged into a single log using the timestamp. Clock synchronization services such as the ones available in Linux and NT can be used to facilitate merging of distributed logs. This first step generates a *request log* $\mathcal{L}$. Each line in this log is assumed to have the following entries:

- UserID (u): identification of the customer submitting the request. Cookies, dynamic URLs, or even authentication mechanisms can be used to uniquely identify requests as coming from the same browser during a session [24].

- RequestType (r): indicates the type of request. Examples include a

GET on the home page, a browse request (i.e., a GET on another page), a request to execute a search, a selection of one of the results of a search, a request to add an item to the shopping cart, or a request to pay. It is assumed that requests to execute CGI scripts or other types of server applications can be easily mapped into request types, i.e., states of the CBMG.

- RequestTime (t): time at which the request arrived at the site.

- ExecTime (x): execution time of the request. Even though this value is not normally recorded in the HTTP log, servers can be configured and/or modified to record this information.

From now on, we represent a line of the request log $\mathcal{L}$ by the four-tuple (u, r, t, x).

The second step of the methodology, called GetSessions, takes as input the request log and generates a session log $\mathcal{S}$ described below. The next step, called GetCBMGs, takes as input the session log $\mathcal{S}$ and performs a clustering analysis that results in a set of CBMGs that can be used as a compact representation of the sessions in the log $\mathcal{S}$. We now describe the steps GetSessions and GetCBMGs in turn.

11.4.1 GetSessions Algorithm

Before we describe the step GetSessions, we need to describe the session log $\mathcal{S}$. The k-th entry in this log is composed of the two-tuple (C_k, W_k) where $C_k = [c_{i,j}]$ is an $n \times n$ matrix of transition counts between states i and j of the CBMG for one session, and $W_k = [w_{i,j}]$ is an $n \times n$ matrix of accumulated think times between states i and j of the CBMG for one session.

To illustrate the notation, consider that for a given session, there were three transitions between states s and t and the think times for each of the transitions were 20 sec, 45 sec, and 38 sec, respectively. Then, $c_{s,t} = 3$ and $w_{s,t} = 20 + 45 + 38 = 103$ sec.

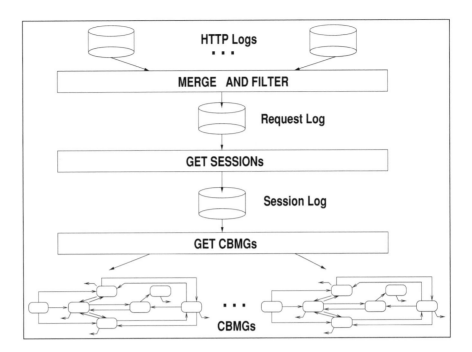

Figure 11.5.   Customer Behavior Characterization Methodology.   Reprinted from [19] © 1999 ACM.

The algorithm GetSessions is presented in Fig. 11.6. It consists of three major steps. In the first one, the request log is sorted so that all the requests with the same UserID are put together in order of RequestTime. This creates one subsequence in the log per UserID. The second step extracts sessions from subsequences using a session threshold time. Finally, the last step scans the requests of each session and accumulates the number of transitions and think times between states in the matrices C and W for that session.

Some precautions need to be taken when using HTTP logs [13]. For example, recording request times with millisecond accuracy may not be sufficient as processors and networks become faster. For this reason, a higher precision timestamp was recorded in Apache's HTTP log in a capacity planning study [18]. One may also want to clean the log from crawler activity. Having the browser identification recorded in the log is useful in this case [13]. Most proxy and origin servers record, by default, only a small

1. Sort the request log $\mathcal{L}$ by UserID and then by RequestTime to generate a sorted log $\mathcal{L}_s$ composed of subsequences, one per UserID, of the form:

$$\overbrace{(u_1, \cdots), \cdots, (u_1, \cdots)}^{\text{subsequence for } u_1}, \overbrace{(u_2, \cdots), \cdots, (u_2, \cdots)}^{\text{subsequence for } u_2}, \cdots \overbrace{(u_k, \cdots), \cdots, (u_k, \cdots)}^{\text{subsequence for } u_k}.$$

2. Each subsequence may represent one or more sessions. For example, a customer may generate a sequence of requests and return to the site one hour later for another session. Thus, subsequences need to be broken into sessions using a time threshold $\mathcal{T}$ (e.g., thirty minutes [13]). If the time between two consecutive requests R_1 and R_2 in a subsequence exceeds $\mathcal{T}$, R_1 is considered to be the last request of a session and R_2 the first of the following session.

3. Subsequences are now broken down into sessions and requests within sessions are in chronological order. Let Q be the number of requests in a given session for UserID u and let $(u, r_1, t_1, x_1), \cdots, (u, r_Q, t_Q, x_Q)$ be the requests of this session as they appear in the sorted log $\mathcal{L}_s$. Repeat the following procedure for each session.

   $C[i, j] \leftarrow 0$ for all $i, j = 1, \cdots, n$.
   $W[i, j] \leftarrow 0$ for all $i, j = 1, \cdots, n$.
   For $k = 2$ to Q do
     Begin
       $C[r_{k-1}, r_k] \leftarrow C[r_{k-1}, r_k] + 1$;
       $W[r_{k-1}, r_k] \leftarrow W[r_{k-1}, r_k] + (t_k - t_{k-1} - x_{k-1})$;
     End;
   $C[r_Q, n] \leftarrow 1$; {transition to the Exit state}

Figure 11.6. Algorithm GetSessions.

portion of each HTTP request and/or response. However, most support an extended log format and can be configured to provide a lot more information.

11.4.2   GetCBMGs Algorithm

Once the session log $\mathcal{S}$ is generated, we need to perform a clustering analysis on it to generate a synthetic workload composed of a relatively small number of CBMGs. The centroid of a cluster determines the characteristics of the CBMG. Any type of clustering algorithms can be used. An example of such an algorithm is the k-means clustering algorithm [14] [15] [20] [21]. This algorithm begins by selecting k points in the space of points, which act as an initial estimate of the centroids of the k clusters. The remaining points are then allocated to the cluster with the nearest centroid. The allocation procedure iterates several times over the input points until no point switches cluster assignment or a maximum number of iterations is performed. Clustering algorithms require a definition of a distance metric to be used in the computation of the distance between a point and a centroid. Assume that the session log is composed of M points $X_m = (C_m, W_m), m = 1, \cdots, M$ where C_m and W_m are the transition count and accumulated think time matrices defined previously. Our definition of distance is based on the transition count matrix only since this is a factor that more clearly defines the interaction between a customer and an e-commerce site. We define the distance d_{X_a, X_b} between two points X_a and X_b in the session log as the Euclidean distance

$$d_{X_a, X_b} = \sqrt{\sum_{i=1}^{n} \sum_{j=1}^{n} (C_a[i,j] - C_b[i,j])^2}. \qquad (11.4.12)$$

At any point during the execution of the k-means clustering algorithm we have k centroids. The clustering algorithm needs to keep track of the number of points, $s(k)$, represented by centroid k. We show now how the coordinates of a new centroid, i.e, the new values of the matrices C and W, are obtained when a new point is added to a cluster. Suppose that point $X_m = (C_m, W_m)$ is to be added to centroid k represented by point (C, W). The new centroid will be represented by the point (C', W'), where the elements of the matrices C' and W' are computed as

$$C'[i,j] = \frac{s(k) \times C[i,j] + C_m[i,j]}{s(k) + 1} \tag{11.4.13}$$

$$W'[i,j] = \frac{s(k) \times W[i,j] + W_m[i,j]}{s(k) + 1}. \tag{11.4.14}$$

Once all the clusters have been obtained, we can derive the matrices P and Z, which characterize the CBMG associated with each cluster, as

$$p_{i,j} = C[i,j]/\sum_{k=1}^{n} C[i,k] \tag{11.4.15}$$

$$z_{i,j} = W[i,j]/C[i,j]. \tag{11.4.16}$$

The arrival rate, λ_k^s, of sessions represented by the CBMG of cluster k is given by $\lambda_k^s = s(k)/T$, where T is the time interval during which the request log $\mathcal{L}$ was obtained. Once we have the matrices P and Z for each cluster, we can obtain the metrics we discussed previously for each type of session.

Example 11.4

Consider that an HTTP log was analyzed for an e-commerce site that has a static CBMG equal to the static CBMG of Fig. 11.4. The GetSessions algorithm generated 20,000 sessions out of the 340,000 lines in the request log. After running the k-means clustering algorithm on the session log using $k = 6$, we obtained the six clusters described in Table 11.1. The first line shows the percentage of sessions that fall into each cluster. For instance, cluster 1 represents almost half of all the sessions. Line 2 shows the *buy to visit ratio* (BV), which represents the percentage of customers who buy from the Web store. Session length indicates the average number of shopper operations requested by a customer for each visit to the electronic store. Line 4 exhibits the Add to Shopping Cart Visit Ratio (V_a), which represents the average number of times per session that a customer adds an item to the shopping cart. However, this operation does not necessarily imply a buy operation, as can be noticed from the comparison between its values and the

Table 11.1. Clusters for Ex. 11.4. Reprinted from [19] © 1999 ACM.

Cluster	1	2	3	4	5	6
% of the Sessions	44.28	28	10.6	9.29	6.20	1.5
BV Ratio (%)	5.7	4.5	3.7	4	3.5	2
Session Length	5.6	15	27	28	50	81
V_a	11	15	21	20	32	50
$V_b + V_s$	3.6	11.4	20	23	39	70

BV's values. The last line of the table indicates the number of browse and search operations associated with customers of each cluster. ■

The natural question that arises now is what kind of conclusions we can draw from the above characterization of the e-commerce workload. We can note two very different behavior patterns. Cluster 1, which represents the majority of the sessions (44.28%), has a very short average session length (5.6) and the highest percentage of customers that buy from the store. On the other extreme, we notice that cluster six represents a small portion of the customers and exhibits the longest session length and the smallest buying ratio. In an attempt to correlate these parameters, we plot in Fig. 11.7 the percentage of customers who buy as a function of the average session length. We can observe that for this sample, an interesting pattern emerges: the longer the session, the less likely it is for a customer to buy an item from the Web store. Moreover, the buy to visit ratio decreases, in a quadratic fashion, with the session length.

An alternative approach to the one discussed above is to first partition the workload and then apply clustering techniques. For example, one may partition the HTTP log into sessions that resulted in sales and those that did not. Then, we can apply clustering techniques to analyze separately the behavior of buyers and non-buyers. This approach would have the advantage

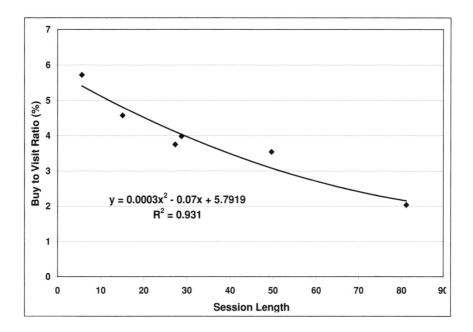

Figure 11.7. Buy to Visit Ratio vs. Session Length. Reprinted from [19] © 1999 ACM.

of giving a special treatment to buyers who typically constitute a small percentage of the sessions.

11.4.3   How Many Clusters to Choose?

A common question when dealing with clustering algorithms is how many clusters accurately represent the workload. This question can be answered by examining the variation of two metrics: the average distance between points of a cluster and its centroid—the intracluster distance—and the average distance between centroids—the intercluster distance. This variation can be characterized by the coefficient of variation (CV), i.e., the ratio between the average and the standard deviation. In general, the purpose of clustering is to minimize the intracluster CV while maximizing the intercluster CV. It is clear that if the number of clusters is made equal to the number of points, we will have achieved this goal. On the other hand, we want a compact representation of the workload. So, we need to select a relatively small number of clusters such that the intracluster variance is small and the intercluster variance is large. The ratio between the intracluster and intercluster CV, denoted β_{CV}, is a useful guide in determining the quality of a clustering process.

Figure 11.8 plots the intercluster and intracluster coefficient of variation as well as β_{CV} versus the number of clusters k. As it can be seen in the figure, CV_{intra} does not vary much with the number of clusters. On the other hand, CV_{inter} increases with k. The important observation is that β_{CV} drops significantly from $k = 3$ to $k = 6$ and then exhibits a much slower rate of decrease. This is an indication that we should select $k = 6$ as the number of clusters in our workload.

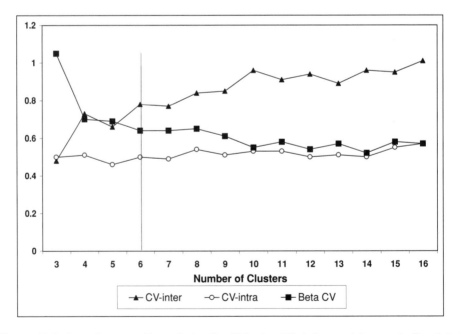

Figure 11.8. Intercluster and Intracluster Coefficients of Variation and β_{CV} vs. k. Reprinted from [19] © 1999 ACM.

11.5　From HTTP Logs to CVMs

Chapter 2 discussed two types of customer behavior models: CBMGs and Customer Visit Models (CVMs). In a CVM, each session is characterized by the number of visits to each state of the CBMG. For example, consider Table 11.2 that shows the CVM for twelve sessions for the same states as in the CBMG of Fig. 11.4. We do not include V_{Entry} and V_{Exit} in the table because they are always equal to one.

Sessions represented by a CVM instead of a CBMG can be obtained from an HTTP log through the algorithm GetCVMSessions shown in Fig. 11.9.

Again, as in the case of sessions characterized by CBMGs, we need to group sessions in smaller and representative groups. Clustering techniques can also be applied here. The distance metric is the distance between to visit ratio vectors. Consider sessions a and b characterized by the visit ratio

Table 11.2. Customer Visit Model with Twelve Sessions.

Session	V_{Browse}	V_{Search}	V_{Add}	V_{Select}	V_{Pay}
1	4	10	2	4	1
2	15	20	1	18	0
3	5	8	3	5	1
4	16	18	3	16	1
5	10	8	0	5	0
6	3	10	2	8	1
7	5	11	3	8	1
8	10	15	0	12	0
9	8	6	3	4	1
10	7	10	1	8	1
11	10	20	0	15	0
12	5	4	1	2	1

1. Execute steps 1 and 2 of the algorithm GetSessions.

2. At this point, subsequences are broken down into sessions and requests within sessions are in chronological order. Let Q be the number of requests in a given session for UserID u and let $(u, r_1, t_1, x_1), \cdots, (u, r_Q, t_Q, x_Q)$ be the requests of this session as they appear in the sorted log $\mathcal{L}_s$. Repeat the following procedure for each session.

   $V_i \leftarrow 0$ for all $i = 2, \cdots, n - 1$.

   $V_1, V_n \leftarrow 1$;

   For $k = 1$ to Q do

   $\quad V_{r_k} \leftarrow V_{r_k} + 1$;

Figure 11.9. Algorithm GetCVMSessions.

vectors $V_a = (V_2^a, \cdots, V_{n-1}^a)$ and $V_b = (V_2^b, \cdots, V_{n-1}^b)$. Note that we left out the visit ratios for states 1 and n. The distance between sessions A and B is

$$d_{V_a, V_b} = \sqrt{\sum_{i=2}^{n-1} (V_i^a - V_i^b)^2}. \tag{11.5.17}$$

Table 11.3 shows the results of applying the k-means clustering algorithm to the values of Table 11.2 for $k = 2, 3$, and 4. One can see for example that cluster 4 in the $k = 4$ case captures the customers who do not buy anything from the site while cluster 1 represents people who always buy.

11.6   Characterizing the Workload at the Resource Level

To be able to perform capacity planning and sizing studies of an e-commerce site, we need to map each CBMG resulting from the workload characterization process described above to IT resources as described in Section 7.7.2 and depicted in Fig. 11.10. The figure shows an e-business function search being mapped to a CSID. With each server in the CSID, we associate service

Table 11.3. Customer Visit Model with Twelve Sessions.

Cluster	V_{Browse}	V_{Search}	V_{Add}	V_{Select}	V_{Pay}
1	5.875	8.375	1.875	5.500	0.875
2	12.750	18.250	1.000	15.250	0.250
1	4.750	10.250	2.000	7.000	1.000
2	12.750	18.250	1.000	15.250	0.250
3	7.000	6.500	1.750	4.000	0.750
1	4.750	10.250	2.000	7.000	1.000
2	15.500	19.000	2.000	17.000	0.500
3	7.000	6.500	1.750	4.000	0.750
4	10.000	17.500	0.000	13.500	0.000

demands at the various components (e.g., processors and disks) of the server.
Also, to each arc of the CSID, we associate service demands for the networks
involved in the exchange of messages represented by the arc. Consider the
following example.

Example 11.5

The characterization of the customer behavior for an e-commerce site
generated two CBMGs. One is more characteristic of heavy buyers, i.e.,
customers who will buy from the site with higher probability and the other
characterizes occasional buyers. These customers tend to search more than
heavy buyers and buy less. Let us focus on the e-business function Search,
which represents a state of the CBMG. Assume that the database server
(DS) has one CPU and two disks with service demands 0.006 sec, 0.020
sec, and 0.018 sec, respectively, for one execution of the search transaction.
Table 11.4 displays the session arrival rate for each of the two CBMGs and
the average number of visits to the state Search for each one. What is the
service demand per session for Search functions at each component of the

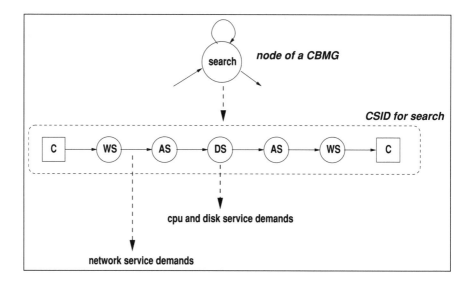

Figure 11.10. From CBMGs to IT Resources.

DS for each CBMG? What is the utilization of each resource of the database server due to the Search function?

Consider the CBMG for occasional buyers. Each session of this type executes 6.76 searches on the average. Each search uses 0.006 sec of CPU at the database server. So, the CPU service demand due to Search functions executed during sessions from occasional buyers is

$$D_{\mathrm{CPU,OccasionalBuyers}}(\mathrm{Search}) = 6.76 \times 0.006 = 0.0406 \text{ sec.} \qquad (11.6.18)$$

In general, the service demand at a resource i (e.g., CPU or disk) due to sessions of type r (e.g., heavy buyers, occasional buyers) for all executions of the e-business function f (e.g., Search, Browse) is

$$D_{i,r}(f) = V_{f,r} \times D_i(f), \qquad (11.6.19)$$

where $V_{f,r}$ is the average number of executions of function f per session of type r and $D_i(f)$ is the service demand of a single execution of function f at resource i. Table 11.4 shows the results of the computations, using Eq. (11.6.19), of the service demands for all resources and for the two types of CBMGs.

Let us now compute the utilizations. As we saw in Chapter 8, the utilization of a resource is equal to the product of the service demand at that resource multiplied by the throughput (or arrival rate in equilibrium). Thus,

$$U_{i,r}(f) = D_{i,r}(f) \times \lambda_r(f), \qquad (11.6.20)$$

where $U_{i,r}(f)$ is the utilization of resource i due to the execution of function f for sessions of type r, and in which $\lambda_r(f) = \lambda_r^s \times V_{f,r}$ is the rate of execution of function f due to sessions of type r and in which λ_r^s is the arrival rate of sessions of type r. So,

$$\lambda_{\text{OccasionalBuyers}}(\text{Search}) = 0.8 \times 6.76 = 5.408 \text{ searches/sec}$$
$$U_{\text{CPU,OccasionalBuyers}}(\text{Search}) = 0.0406 \times 5.408 = 0.2193 = 21.93\%.$$

Table 11.4 presents the computation of the utilization for the CPU, disks 1 and 2, for heavy and occasional buyers due to the execution of the Search. It also presents the total utilization of each resource due to the Search function. For example, the total CPU utilization due to the execution of Search functions is 22.82%.   ∎

11.7   E-Business Benchmarks: TPC-W

Accurate workload characterizations can be used to build benchmark suites that can be used to evaluate and compare competing systems. Several workload generators exist for Web servers: Mindcraft's Webstone, SPEC's SPECWeb96 and SPECWeb99, and SURGE [5]. The Transaction Processing Performance Council (TPC) has just released TPC-W, the first benchmark aimed at evaluating sites that support e-business activities [23]. We provide in this section a brief description of this benchmark and refer the reader to the TPC-W specification for more details [23].

Table 11.4. Table for Example 11.5

CBMG Type	Arrival rate (sessions/sec)	V_{Search}	Database Server		
			CPU	Disk 1	Disk 2
			Service Demands (sec)		
Heavy Buyers	0.2	2.71	0.0163	0.0542	0.0488
Occasional Buyers	0.8	6.76	0.0406	0.1352	0.1217
			Utilizations		
Heavy Buyers			0.0088	0.0294	0.0264
Occasional Buyers			0.2193	0.7312	0.6580
Total Utilization			0.2282	0.7605	0.6845

11.7.1 TPC-W's Business Model

The business model of TPC-W is a B2C e-tailer that sells products and services over the Internet. The site provides e-business functions that allow customers to browse through selected products (e.g., best sellers or new products), search information on existing products, see product detail, place an order, or check the status of a previous order. Interactions related to placing an order are encrypted through SSL with RSA, RC4, and MD5 as the cipher suites (see Chapter 5). Customers need to register with the site before they are allowed to buy.

The site maintains a catalog of items that can be searched by a customer. Each item has a description and a 5K-byte thumbnail image associated with it. TPC-W specifies that the site maintains a database with information about customers, items in the catalog, orders, and credit card transactions. All database updates must have the ACID (Atomicity, Consistency, Isolation, and Durability) property [16]. The size of the catalog is the major scalability parameter for TPC-W. The number of items in the catalog may be one of the following: 1,000, 10,000, 100,000, 1,000,000, or 10,000,000.

11.7.2   TPC-W's Customer Behavior Model

TPC-W specifies that the activity with the site being benchmarked is driven by *emulated browsers (EBs)*. These EBs generate *Web interactions*, which represent a complete cycle that starts when the EB selects a navigation option from the previously displayed page and ends when the requested page has been completely received by the EB. EBs engage in *user sessions*, defined similarly to Chapter 2, i.e., sequences of Web interactions that start with an interaction to the home page.

Sessions in TPC-W can be described by the CBMG shown in Fig. 11.11. This is a simplified version of the actual CBMG for TPC-W. We left out interactions to inquire about the status of previous orders as well as site administration interactions. We have also grouped into the Browse state two types of browse interactions specified by TPC-W: requests for best sellers and requests for new product information. The CBMG of Fig. 11.11 does not show the transitions to the Exit state explicitly. The Entry state can only lead to the Home state, which can be reached from any other state. The Shopping Cart state represents a state in which items can be added or deleted from the shopping cart. Customers have to go through the Login state before they can reach the Buy Request state. This is the state in which a customer provides billing information (e.g., credit card and billing address information) and shipping address. From the Buy Request state a customer can move to the Buy Confirm state which completes the buying process.

TPC-W classifies Web interactions into two broad categories:

- *Browse* interactions involve browsing and searching but no product ordering activity. States of the CBMG that fall in this category are Home, Browse, Select, Product Detail, and Search.

- *Order* interactions involve product ordering activities only and include the following states of the CBMG: Shopping Cart, Login, Buy Request, and Buy Confirm.

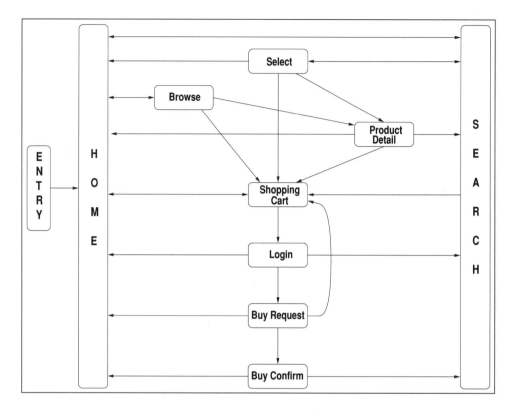

Figure 11.11. Customer Behavior Model Graph for TPC-W.

TPC-W specifies three different types of sessions according to the percentage of Browse and Order Web interactions found in each session.

- *Browsing mix*: 95% of Browse Web interactions and 5% of Order Web interaction. These sessions are characterized by a 0.69% buy to visit ratio.

- *Shopping mix*: 80% of Browse Web interactions and 20% of Order Web interaction. The buy to visit ratio in these sessions is 1.2%.

- *Ordering mix*: 50% of Browse Web interactions and 50% of Order Web interaction. These sessions have a buy to visit ratio of 10.18%.

11.7.3 TPC-W Performance Metrics

TPC-W has two types of performance metrics: a throughput metric and a cost/throughput metric as explained in what follows. There are three throughput metrics depending on the type of session. The main throughput metric for TPC-W is called WIPS (Web Interactions Per Second) and measures the average number of Web Interactions completed per second during an interval in which all the sessions are of the shopping type. There are two secondary throughput metrics. One, called WIPSb, measures the average number of Web Interactions per second completed during an interval in which all sessions are of the browsing type. The other, called WIPSo, measures the average number of Web Interactions per second completed during an interval in which all sessions are of the ordering type.

The cost related metric specified by TPC-W is $/WIPS and indicates the ratio between the total cost of the system under test and the number of WIPS measured during a shopping interval. Total cost includes purchase and maintenance costs for all hardware and software components for the system under test.

11.8 Concluding Remarks

Workload characterization is the process of describing a workload by means of quantitative parameters in a way that captures the most important features of the workload [8]. A workload characterization can be static or dynamic. A static workload characterization describes the consumption of hardware and software resource, while a dynamic characterization consists of parameters related to the behavior of user requests [8].

In this chapter, we described dynamic workload models, in the form of CBMGs and CVMs, as well as the processes used to obtain these characterizations from HTTP logs. These dynamic characterizations need to be mapped to resources at the IT level to generate a static workload description. This is achieved by mapping customer behavior models to client/server interaction diagrams (CSIDs) and obtaining the service demands at each of the servers and networks of the CSID.

Accurate workload characterizations can be used to build benchmark suites that can be used to evaluate and compare competing systems. The Transaction Processing Council (TPC) released recently TPC-W, a benchmark for e-commerce sites engaged in B2C activities [23]. This benchmark is designed to mimic operations of an e-business site and it measures Web Interactions Per Second (WIPS) and cost/performance. The transactions of the benchmark are designed to reproduce five types of operations: Browse, Shopping Cart, Buy (using SSL), Register, and Search.

Bibliography

[1] G. Abdulla, "Analysis and Modeling of World Wide Web Traffic," Doctoral Thesis, Department of Computer Science, Virginia Polytechnic Institute and State University, Blacksburg, VA, 1998.

[2] V. A. F. Almeida, A. Bestavros, M. Crovella, and A. Oliveira, "Characterizing Reference Locality in the WWW," *Proc. Fourth International Conference on Parallel and Distributed Information Systems (PDIS)*, IEEE Computer Society, Dec. 1996, pp. 92–106.

[3] M. Arlitt, R. Friedrich, and T. Jin, "Workload Characterization of a Web Proxy in a Cable Environment," *ACM Performance Evaluation Review*, 27 (2), Aug. 1999, pp. 25–36.

[4] M. Arlitt and C. Williamson, "Web Server Workload Characterization: the Search for Invariants," *Proc. 1996 ACM Sigmetrics Conference on Measurement & Modeling of Computer Systems*, Philadelphia, PA, May 23-26, pp. 126–137.

[5] P. Barford and M. Crovella, "Generating Representative Web Workloads," *Proc. 1998 ACM Sigmetrics Conference on Measurement & Modeling of Computer Systems*, Madison, WI, June 22-26, pp. 151–160.

[6] T. Bray, "Measuring the Web," *The World Wide Web J.*, 1(3), http://www5conf.inria.fr/fich_html/papers/P9/Overview.htm.

[7] L. Breslau et al., "Web Caching and Zipf-Like Distributions: Evidence and Implications," *Proc. IEEE Infocom'99* , New York, March 1999.

[8] M. Calzarossa, L. Massari, and D. Tessera, "Workload Characterization Issues and Methodologies," *Performance Evaluation - Origins and Directions*, eds. G. Haring, C. Lindemann, and M. Reiser, LNCS Series, Springer-Verlag, 2000.

[9] M. Calzarossa and G. Serazzi, "Workload Characterization: a Survey," *Proc. IEEE*, vol. 81, no. 8, Aug. 1993, pp. 1136–1150.

[10] L. D. Catledge and J. E. Pitkow, "Characterizing Browsing Strategies in the World Wide Web," *Comp. Networks and ISDN Syst.*, 26 (6), pp. 1065–1073.

[11] M. Crovella and A. Bestavros, "Self-Similarity in World Wide Web Traffic: Evidence and Possible Causes," *Proc. 1996 ACM Sigmetrics Conference on Measurement & Modeling of Computer Systems*, Philadelphia, PA, May 23-26, pp. 160–169.

[12] C. Cunha, A. Bestavros, and M. Crovella, "Characteristics of WWW Client-Based Traces," *Technical Report TR-95-010*, Department of Computer Science, Boston University, April 1995.

[13] B. D. Davidson, "Web Traffic Logs: an Imperfect Resource for Evaluation," *Proc. INET'99 Conf.*, Internet Society, San Jose, CA, June 1999.

[14] B. Everitt, *Cluster Analysis*, Halsted Press, New York, 1980.

[15] D. Ferrari, G. Serazzi, and A. Zeigner, *Measurement and Tuning of Computer Systems*, Upper Saddle River, Prentice Hall, NJ, 1983.

[16] J. Gray and A. Reuter, *Transaction Processing: Concepts and Techniques*, Morgan Kaufman, San Mateo, CA, 1993.

[17] B. Huberman, P. Pirolli, and R. Lukose, "Strong Regularities in WWW Surfing," *Science*, vol. 280, 1998.

[18] Menascé, D. A., B. Peraino, N. Dinh, and Q. Dinh, "Planning the Capacity of a Web Server: An Experience Report," *Proc. 1999 Comp. Measurement Group (CMG) Conf.*, Reno, NV, Dec. 5-10, 1999.

[19] Menascé, D. A., V. A. F. Almeida, R. C. Fonseca, and M. A. Mendes, "A Methodology for Workload Characterization for E-commerce Servers," *Proc. 1999 ACM Conference in Electronic Commerce*, Denver, CO, Nov. 1999.

[20] D. A. Menascé and V. A. F. Almeida, *Capacity Planning for Web Performance: Metrics, Models and Methods*, Prentice Hall, Upper Saddle River, NJ, 1998.

[21] D. A. Menascé, V. A. F. Almeida, and L. W. Dowdy, *Capacity Planning and Performance Modeling: From Mainframes to Client-Server Systems*, Prentice Hall, Upper Saddle River, NJ, 1994.

[22] J. E. Pitkow, "Summary of WWW Characterization," *Proc. World Wide Web Conf.*, 2(1), Jan. 1999, pp. 3–13.

[23] Transaction Processing Council, TPC-W, http://www.tpc.org.

[24] G. W. Treese and L. C. Stewart, *Designing Systems for Internet Commerce*, Addison Wesley, Reading, MA, 1998.

[25] A. Woodruff, P. Aoki, E. Brewer, P. Gauthier, and L. Rowe, "An Investigation of Documents from the World Wide Web," *The World Wide Web J.*, 1(3), http://www5conf.inria.fr/fich_html/papers/P7/Overview.htm.

Chapter 12

Preparing E-Business for Waves of Demand

12.1 Introduction

A computer game company was forced to shut down its e-commerce site due to heavy traffic. The site went down early on Monday right after the new version of its popular video game went online. The site received 200,000 hits in just one minute, fifteen times more than the expected volume of traffic. "We have been victims of our own success!" said the vice president for online operations. This undesirable scenario shows how demand forecasting is critical for e-business and emphasizes the importance of good planning

355

and forecasting for online business environments.

In electronic business, companies must meet customer's expectations in terms of products (i.e., selection, price, and customer service), usability, availability, and performance. Studies of online customer behavior indicate a low tolerance for complicated designs or slow sites. If the e-business site is slow due to poor capacity or overload, customers may not return. Online customers expect "always-on" service and consistent quality of service. The Internet offers low switching costs. Choices on the Web are numerous and users can easily turn to another e-commerce site. Therefore, providing high level quality of service during peak periods matters. Companies do not want to lose customers who arrive at busy times.

Performance and availability may suffer when an e-business site is not prepared to receive the workload generated by its customers. Being proactive and anticipating performance problems and waves of demand is a key aspect of managing online environments. It is important to improve the methods used to forecast customer demand behavior in time scales that stretch from hours to months. These forecasts can be useful in many ways. For example, system administrators and capacity planners can use demand forecasts to decide how to respond (e.g., by reconfiguring the site or adding extra servers) to surges in traffic volume. Management can rely on demand forecasts to plan and build (e.g., by improving networking capacity or planning a second site) a robust IT infrastructure for an online business that is prepared for any contingency.

Because the lead time to enhance the capacity of an e-business IT infrastructure could take weeks, it is important to anticipate traffic bursts and plan ahead of time to enable fast response to crises. This chapter discusses issues and methods that deal with demand forecast for e-business.

12.2   Customer Demand and Workload

Customer demand generates workload to e-business sites. Online customers see an online store as a set of functions and services. The execution of services and functions requested by customers creates the workload processed by the site. Therefore, customer demands translate into system workload. Let us then understand why demands change in light of the reference model introduced in Chapter 1 and shown in Figure 12.1.

As demands change, so do workloads; they may grow or shrink suddenly, depending on many factors. Demands on an e-business site vary with traffic to the site and with the functionality offered to customers. Demand expansion should be analyzed along the four layers of the reference model. Major changes in demand occur due to events that happen at the business layer. Examples of decisions or plans set at the business model layer include a new

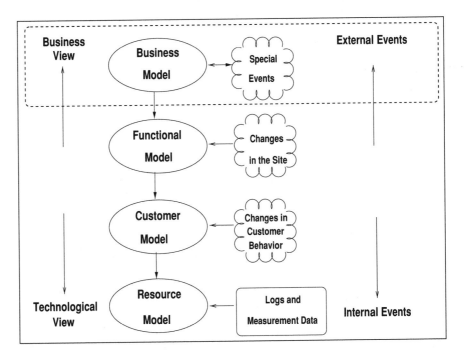

Figure 12.1. Revisiting the Reference Model.

TV campaign, the launch of a new product, low price offerings, a new security policy, and special plans for events such as Christmas and Valentine's Day. At the functional layer, changes in demand are due to the introduction of new functionality and new features. For instance, demand may change when an online CD store makes available to customers a function that allows them to listen to samples of the top ten albums. If the navigation structure of a site is modified with the intent of improving customers' experience, the demand to the site may also change. For instance, the introduction of the one-click purchasing process changed customer behavior in the online stores that offered such a capability. Information technology moves fast. And so do the Web applications used by online business. New database management systems, new security software systems, new multimedia software, and new versions of operating systems are examples of software resources usually incorporated to existing sites. In general, new software systems demand additional resources from servers, disks, and networks. These new systems increase the demand at the resource level. In summary, the key to workload forecasting in e-business is understanding the nature and evolution of customers' demands.

12.3   Traffic Bursts

There are two obvious questions that people like to ask about hurricanes: "Is it coming my way?" and "How strong is it?" In electronic business, similar questions arise very often: "Is the site going to receive a burst of hits?" and "How strong will the burst be?" Existing techniques and surveys can be used to answer the first question. But online companies need more information. They need to know how much computing and network capacity needs to be provisioned to support a traffic spike of a given intensity.

Web traffic is quite bursty [4]. Figure 12.2 shows the daily traffic to a real online retailer store. The upper part of the figure shows the hourly volume of hits for a typical week. One observation is that the number of hits to

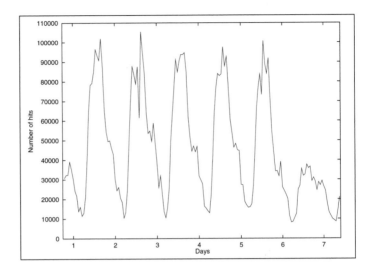

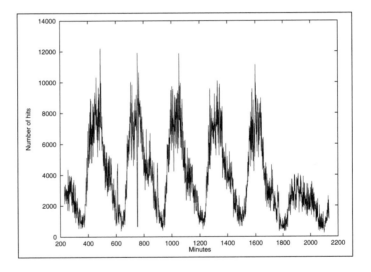

Figure 12.2. Traffic Volume to an E-Tailer Site.

the store is low during the weekend (i.e., days 1 and 7) and surges in traffic occur around 2:00 P.M. A conjecture that could explain this observation is that people spend more time surfing the Web at work than at home because companies have faster connections to the Internet. The graph in the lower part of the figure depicts the number of hits measured in each five-minute interval for the same week. Changing the time scale does not modify the burstiness exhibited by the traffic to the e-tailer store. It is even burstier.

Better forecasting and site preparation can significantly reduce the amount of burst-induced damage to site performance. Although it is difficult to predict erratic usage demands, sites must be prepared for them. An e-business site architecture should be flexible and scalable to support demand spikes. In many cases, it is possible to identify the roots of sudden changes in customer demand and it is also possible to categorize the phenomena that drive bursts of traffic to a site. Once the origins of traffic surges have been identified, it is possible to devise better strategies to handle these surges.

Unpredictable News Events. Web users follow breaking news stories and so does traffic. In the quest for the latest information, Web users may overwhelm news sites. Every time a big event happens (i.e., political scandals, accidents, stock market crashes, and wars), traffic peaks at news and TV sites. For instance, during a stock market crisis when the Dow Jones Industrial Average dove to a very low value, a record volume of shares were traded. Online trading businesses were flooded by visitors seeking quotes and placing trades, creating peaks seven to ten times the average normal trading volumes. These types of events are hard to predict in advance.

Predictable News Events. Surges at specific sites occur because of predictable news events. Natural disasters, such as hurricanes, earthquakes, and storms attract huge numbers of people seeking information from specialized sites. For instance, during the days that followed the announcement of the arrival of a hurricane, the weather sites were clogged with users trying to obtain updates. "We got in just one hour what we typically get in a seven-day period," said the spokesperson for an online weather service. Existing models can predict natural disasters, such as hurricanes and storms, within a few days of their occurrence. Thus, weather-related sites can take advantage of the prediction of some events and prepare for the bursts.

Product or Service Announcement. "We received far more accesses than we had imagined on the Web," said the VP of a software company to explain the performance problems faced by customers who tried to purchase and download the company's popular software. The servers became saturated right after the company started taking orders for the software. An e-business can set the date of a product announcement but cannot know in advance how successful the product will be. For example, the site of an online tax preparation service was shut down in its first week of operation. The company expected 500,000 customers in a period of twelve weeks. However, the site received 220,000 customers in the first week and a surge of customers overwhelmed the system and brought it down. Because a site can be extremely popular during the launch period and dead cold in a month, flexibility in infrastructure should be planned so that resources can be added or removed from the site.

Special Events. Christmas, Valentine's Day, and Thanksgiving always boost e-commerce traffic. This increase in the number of online shoppers is clearly predictable several months in advance. The question is whether the intensity of the bursts can be forecast. Accurate forecasts can be quite valuable when e-business sites are faced with sudden growths in demands. For example, on a Super Bowl Sunday, a dotcom company got 500,000 unique visitors in ten hours after its commercial aired. Although the Super Bowl date, the TV ad, and the expected number of visitors are known in advance, sites are commonly unprepared for post-Super Bowl traffic. In other words, some e-businesses fail to prepare for the traffic generated by their own advertising campaigns.

12.3.1 High Variability

We saw that e-business traffic exhibits a bursty behavior. Bursts refer to the random arrival of requests, with peak rates exceeding the average rates by factors of eight to ten [8], as can be noticed from Fig. 12.2. A practical consequence of burstiness is e-business site management's difficulty in planning the site capacity to support the demand created by load spikes. Spikes can be characterized by the *peak traffic ratio*, defined as the ratio between peak site and average site traffic. In e-business sites, the peak traffic ratio varies according to the nature of the business and can easily reach values up to twenty times the average.

The heavy-tailed distributions and high variability that exist on the Web can also be found in e-business. A study of actual e-commerce logs shows that the algorithm used to identify customer sessions found a significant number of very short sessions and a very small number of long sessions, out of the 628,573 requests analyzed [7]. This is additional evidence of heavy-tailed distributions. The long sessions found in [7] were generated by robot accesses. The graphs in Fig. 12.2 confirm the high variability of the rates for hits/hour and hits/minute.

12.4   Traffic Patterns in E-Business

This section analyzes graphs of traffic patterns derived from actual HTTP logs of a real e-tailer that provided us with sanitized logs. The analysis of patterns of traffic behavior is very useful for predictive purposes. The plots of Figs. 12.2 and 12.3 show different patterns of the daily traffic handled by the e-business site. Figure 12.3 displays some characteristics of customer sessions, defined by a time threshold of thirty minutes. The upper graph of Fig. 12.3 shows the number of active sessions at the beginning of each hour during a typical week. The graph indicates that spikes are smaller than in Fig. 12.2 and that the minimum number of active sessions is around 850. The bottom graph of Fig. 12.3 shows the number of new sessions initiated per hour. As with the other rates, the curve for sessions/hour is bursty, with a peak traffic ratio around seven.

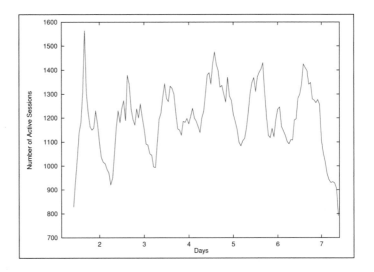

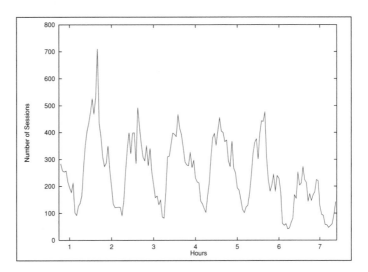

Figure 12.3. Customer Sessions Over Time.

12.4.1 Visual Inspection

Visual representation of traffic to an e-commerce site helps provide insight into the patterns of interaction between customers and the online business. When one aggregates traffic data by summing up and averaging them, precious information can be destroyed. So, before representing a mass of data by simple statistics such as average values and variances, one should visually inspect the data looking for exceptions that could convey important facts about the e-business.

From the visualization of logs of a specific e-business, one is able to carry out traffic pattern analyses. These analyses can provide i) weekly and hourly traffic, ii) peak traffic ratios, iii) number of simultaneous connections, and iv) evolution of the business load, measured by traffic indicators such as requests, sessions, and number of unique visitors per day.

12.5   Forecasting Strategies

The difficulty associated with providing accurate forecasts for electronic business stems from the weak relationship between future and past experience because access paradigms change constantly. For instance, consider the hypothetical case of an online bookstore that has tracked the evolution of its customer base on a monthly basis over several months. The evolution of the customer base can be useful for forecasting future demands as long as the online store does not change its business model. Consider now that the bookstore opens an online mall to sell merchandise ranging from auto parts to shoes. In this new business model, books become just one category of items sold in a large online mall. The history of its customer base may not provide insight into future demands because the new business model may have broken the connections between past and future.

In electronic business, management has to be careful when using forecasting methods [5]. Instead of working with a few planning scenarios that consider high, medium, and low probability events, one should also consider events with very low probability but whose impact on the business could be enormous. This is a consequence of the high variability phenomenon discussed before. Suppose that a company is planning its e-commerce site for the launch of a new game. Management is considering three basic scenarios. The optimistic one assumes 900,000 customers visiting the site in the first day. The most likely scenario predicts 500,000 customers downloading the game in the first day. The pessimistic scenario estimates that no more than 100,000 customers will access the site in the first day. Instead of concentrating only on these three scenarios, which were drawn from numbers collected during previous game launches, management should also be asking questions such as how the site will behave if two million customers visit the site in the first day. Although the probability of getting such a number of customers is considered very low, the consequence of having two million customers would be disastrous if the site did not have enough capacity to handle the load. Therefore, management should prepare for contingencies, such as a huge number of customers trying to download the game.

Forecasting methods can be divided into two approaches, namely quantitative and qualitative. Figure 12.4 illustrates how these two approaches fit in the forecast strategy. Quantitative methods rely on the existence of historical data to estimate future values of the workload parameters. The qualitative approach is a subjective process based on market surveys, judgement, intuition, business plans, expert opinions, historical analogies, commercial knowledge, and any other relevant information. The quantitative approach makes use of forecasting techniques discussed in next section. Values obtained through the use of forecasting techniques should be adjusted by factors, such as peak traffic ratio, obtained by using the qualitative approach.

12.6 Forecasting Techniques

The literature describes several forecasting techniques [9] [10]. In selecting one of them, a few factors need to be considered. The first one is the availability and reliability of historical data. The accuracy and the planning horizon are also factors that determine the forecasting technique. The pattern found in historical data has a strong influence on the choice of the technique. The nature of historical data may be determined through visual

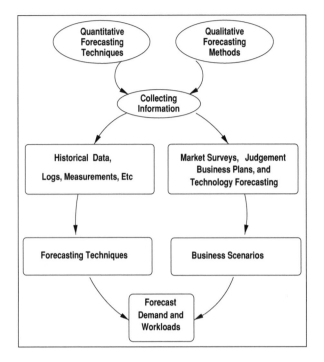

Figure 12.4. A Forecast Strategy Model.

inspection of a plot of the data as a function of time. Data collected in chronological order are called a time series. As displayed in Fig. 12.5, four patterns of historical data can be clearly identified: trend, cyclical, seasonal, and stationary. While the trend pattern reflects a workload that tends to increase (or decrease, in some cases), the stationary pattern does not show any sign of systematic variation (i.e., it exhibits a constant mean). Seasonal and cyclical patterns are similar with respect to the presence of fluctuations. The difference is the periodicity of the fluctuations exhibited by the seasonal pattern.

E-business traffic seasonality is an important element in forecasting and planning. E-business affected by seasonality includes online shopping, sport sites, and financial services. For example, sites for college-age students show a significant decrease in traffic during the summer months. However, as e-commerce expands worldwide, the effects of seasonality may be reduced due

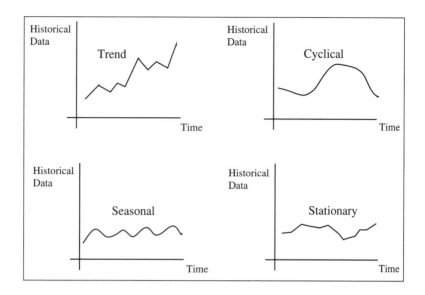

Figure 12.5. Historical Data Patterns.

to the existence of customers in different seasons, such as a customer in the USA and another one in Australia. For the same reason, customers from widely different time zones may provide a more homogeneous traffic pattern over the hours of the day.

The underlying hypothesis of forecasting techniques is that the information to be forecast is somehow directly related to historical data. This emphasizes the importance of knowing the pattern of historical data. Let us now examine in detail some forecasting methods. The most often applied techniques to workload forecasting are moving averages, exponential smoothing, and linear regression. There are many commercial packages (e.g., MS Excel, Matlab, and SPLUS) that implement various forecasting techniques.

12.6.1 Regression Methods

Regression models are used to estimate the value of a variable as a function of other variables. The predicted variable is called the dependent variable, and the variables used to forecast the value are known as independent variables. The mathematical relationship established between the variables can take many forms, such as a polynomial curve (e.g., linear or quadratic). The most commonly used relationship assumes that the dependent variable is a linear function of the independent variables. Regression methods are appropriate for working with non-seasonal data that show a trend. For example, the simple linear regression assumes that historical data exhibit a linear evolution pattern.

12.6.2 Moving Averages

This is a simple forecasting technique that makes the value to be forecast for the next period equal to the average of a number of previous observations. When applied to nearly stationary data, the accuracy achieved by the technique is usually high [9]. In this context, a time series is considered stationary [3] if there is no systematic change in mean and variance. Also any periodic variation should be removed to consider the data stationary. In other words, no trend is shown in the historical data. A disadvantage of simple moving averages is that only one forecast value into the future can be calculated at a time. This technique is appropriate for short term forecasting. The forecast value is given by

$$f_{t+1} = \frac{y_t + y_{t-1} + \cdots + y_{t-n+1}}{n}, \qquad (12.6.1)$$

where

f_{t+1} is the forecast value for period $t+1$;

y_t is the actual value (observation) at time t;

n is the number of observations used to calculate f_{t+1}.

As can be noted from Eq. (12.6.1), a forecast for time $t+2$ cannot be made until the actual value for time $t+1$ becomes known. One problem with this technique is the determination of n, the number of periods included in the average. One should try to select a value for n that minimizes the forecasting error, which is defined by the square of the difference between the forecast and actual values. The mean squared error (MSE) is given by Eq. (12.6.2). Different values of n may be tested to find the one that gives the smallest MSE.

$$\text{MSE} = \frac{\sum_{t=1}^{n}(y_t - f_t)^2}{n}. \tag{12.6.2}$$

Example 12.1

The IT staff of an electronic retailer monitors site traffic every fifteen minutes and calculates average arrival rate of transactions for the period. At the end of the day, the system provides the peak traffic ratio for the day. Also, at the end of the week, management receives a weekly performance report, in which the highest surge in demand is highlighted. From the traffic graphs, management learned that most of the surges occur in the middle of the week. At the end of every week, management analyzes the patterns of evolution of several performance metrics. In order to anticipate problems, management wants to know how high customer surges will be following week.

Table 12.1 shows the maximum peak traffic ratio index for the last eight weeks. Based on the data, we will estimate this index for the next week. To estimate the peak traffic ratio for next week, management decided to use the moving averages technique with the three most recent values in the table. Thus, the peak traffic ratio index for next week is $f = (13.2 + 17.1 + 15.7)/3 = 15.3$.   ■

12.6.3   Exponential Smoothing

Historical trends can be analyzed using the exponential smoothing technique. This technique should be used for non-seasonal data showing no systematic trend. Exponential smoothing uses a weighted average of past observations to forecast the value for the next period. Exponential smoothing is similar to the moving averages technique with respect to the way that both techniques calculate the forecast value. They both make the average of known

Table 12.1. Customer Surge Statistics.

Week Number	Peak Traffic Ratio
1	13.5
2	16.3
3	19.9
4	14.8
5	12.6
6	13.2
7	17.1
8	15.7

observations equal to the forecast value. The difference is that exponential smoothing places more weights on the most recent observations. The motivation for using different weights stems from the hypothesis that the latest observations give a better indication of the near future. Similar to moving averages, this technique is appropriate for data that present little variation and for short term prediction. The forecast value is calculated as

$$f_{t+1} \; = \; f_t + \alpha \, (y_t - f_t), \tag{12.6.3}$$

where

f_{t+1} is the forecast value for period $t + 1$;

y_t is the actual value (observation) at time t;

α is the smoothing weight ($0 < \alpha < 1$).

Example 12.2

An Internet research firm keeps track of the customers (i.e., visitors and buyers) of an online toy store. The size of the customer base is a key information for planning resources and infrastrucure for the store. Past logs indicate that the monthly average number of visits of a customer to the store is 2.7. In addition to the data, management has the following information derived from the Customer Behavior Model Graph (CBMG): the average buy to visit ratio (BV) is 1.87%, the average customer session length is 5.91, and the average number of visits to the home page is 1.21. Except for the home page, each visited page generates one transaction. So, the average number of transactions per visit is 4.7 ($= 5.91 - 1.21$).

Table 12.2 shows the size of the customer base for the first six months of the year. The CIO of the toy store wants to estimate the total volume of transactions to be processed in July. Let us now apply the exponential smoothing technique to the data shown in Table 12.2. The second column of the table shows the actual data and the third column displays the forecast data, obtained through the use of the exponential smoothing technique. We need to calculate the estimated size of the customer base for July from the historical data composed of six observations. Using $\alpha = 0.60$, the estimated size of the customer base for July is $f = 319,987 + 0.60 \times (352,000 - 319,987) = 339,195$. Therefore, the estimated number of monthly transactions is calculate as follows.

$$TotalNumberOfVisits = AvgVisitsPerCustomer \times CustomerBase$$
$$= 2.7 \times 339,195 = 915,827$$

Table 12.2. Evolution of the Customer Base.

Month	Actual Size of the Customer Base	Forecast ($\alpha = 0.6$)
January	354,000	354,000
February	327,000	354,000
March	318,000	337,800
April	356,000	325,920
May	304,000	343,968
June	352,000	319,987

$$\text{TransactionsPerMonth} = \text{AvgTransactionsPerVisit} \times \text{TotalNumberOfVisits}$$
$$= 4.7 \times 915,827 = 4,304,387. \qquad (12.6.4)$$

So, the estimated number of transactions for July is 4,304,387. ∎

12.6.4   Applying Forecasting Techniques

Before performing the forecasting, the selected technique should be validated on the available data. This can be done using only part of the historical data to exercise the model. The remaining data, which correspond to actual values, can then be compared to the forecast values to assess the accuracy of the method. Tests can be made to assess the mean squared error (MSE) of each method under study so that the one that gives the smallest MSE is selected. Future workload can be forecast in two different modes [9]: causal and trend. The causal mode uses customer demands (e.g., the arrival rate of the Search function) as the independent variable and workload parameters (e.g., processor demand) as the dependent variable. For instance, a regression model can be used to estimate the future processor demand of a Web-based catalog application as a function of the number of items existing in the catalog.

12.7   Concluding Remarks

Workload forecasting is a key issue for preparing e-business sites for waves of demand. Forecasting is useful in many ways. It helps system administrators and capacity planners anticipate performance and operation problems and prepare alternative plans to support surges in customer demands. The basic steps to a workload and demand forecasting are:

- Analyzing customer demand variations,
- Understanding the patterns of e-business traffic,
- Evaluating peak-to-average ratio,

- Performing a qualitative-oriented forecasting,

- Selecting the demand and workload parameters to be forecast,

- Analyzing historical data,

- Selecting a forecasting technique,

- Applying the forecasting technique to the historical data,

- Calibrating forecast results,

- Analyzing and validating forecast results.

Bibliography

[1] M. Arlitt and C. Williamson, "Web Server Workload Characterization," *Proc. 1996 SIGMETRICS Conference on Measurement of Computer Systems*, ACM, May 1996.

[2] J. Armstrong, *Long-Range Forecasting*, Wiley, New York, 1985.

[3] C. Chatfield, *The Analysis of Time Series: An Introduction*, Chapman & Hall, Fourth Edition, 1989.

[4] M. Crovella and A. Bestavros, "Self-Similarity in World Wide Web Traffic: Evidence and Possible Causes," *IEEE/ACM Transactions on Networking*, vol. 5, no. 6, pp. 835–846, Dec. 1997.

[5] W. Farrell, *How Hits Happen*, HarperCollins Publishers, Inc., New York, 1998.

[6] B. Huberman, P. Pirolli, J. E. Pitkow, and R. Lukose, "Strong Regularities in World Wide Web Surfing," Science 280, pp. 95–97, 1998.

[7] D. A. Menascé, V. A. F. Almeida, R. C. Fonseca, and M. A. Mendes, "A Methodology for Workload Characterization for E-commerce Servers," *Proc. 1999 ACM Conference in Electronic Commerce*, Denver, CO, Nov. 1999.

[8] J. Mogul, "Network Behavior of a Busy Web Server and its Clients," *Research Report 95/5*, DEC Western Research, Palo Alto, 1995.

[9] H. Letmanyi, *Guide on Workload Forecasting*, Computer Science and Technology, National Bureau of Standards, Special Publication 500–123, 1985.

[10] R. Jain, *The Art of Computer Systems Performance Analysis*, John Wiley & Sons, Inc., 1991.

Part IV
Models of Specific
E-Business Segments

Chapter 13: Business-to-Consumer Case Studies
Chapter 14: Business-to-Business Case Studies

Chapter 13

Business to Consumer Case Studies

13.1   Introduction

This chapter illustrates the use of the quantitative methods presented in the book through several examples in the business-to-consumer segment. First, a hypothetical electronic retailer is described. Then, different planning situations are discussed. In light of the models introduced throughout the book, we show how to tackle the problems and we present their solutions. The goal of the chapter is to guide the reader, in a step-by-step manner, through the model-based solution of a number of e-commerce examples.

13.2   The OnLine Computer Store Problem

Consider an online retailer, called *e-buypc.com*, that sells computer products, software, and electronics to consumers, exclusively over the Internet. This online store offers a large selection of products with detailed product description and pictures to help visitors and customers in the selection and purchasing processes.

The site of e-buypc.com offers a simple and attractive interface to consumers. The shopping process, as shown in Fig. 13.1, is organized around three major steps: 1) Find a Product, 2) Register, and 3) Place an Order. The Find a Product step can be accomplished by two main functions, namely Search and Browse. A third way to select a product is to pick up one of the hot items, which are displayed in the special offer section, located in the *Welcome* page. To place an order, a consumer has to select the product using the Add to Shopping Cart function. Before checking-out, the customer must have gone through the registration process, which sets up an account and provides the customer identification and password. The store uses secure connections for transactions that transmit confidential information. To check out, the customer simply clicks on the Check-Out button to submit the order for the items in the shopping cart. During the check-out process, the store contacts the billing service, which checks with the buyer's bank or credit card company to obtain the credit authorization. Then the billing service informs the store that the transaction is approved and the product delivery process is started. The transaction completes when the customer receives the products purchased. From the customer's perspective, the site is easy to use and efficient. With three clicks, a registered customer is able to perform all the steps required by the purchase process, from product selection to check-out. The site has also a privacy policy clearly stated in the Welcome page.

The store's revenue consists of merchandise revenue and banner advertisement sales. Merchandise revenue is all revenue derived from sales made

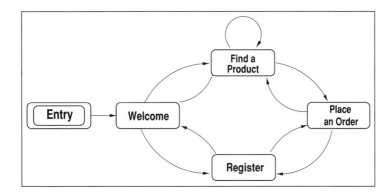

Figure 13.1. CBMG of the Shopping Process of e-buypc.com.

through the site. By letting outside marketers advertise on its Web store front, the online company obtains another source of revenue. Last fiscal year, which ended September 30, generated a merchandise revenue of $94,378,000 and an ad revenue $900,000. Most of the customer base is formed by small to medium businesses and home office customers. This type of customer is substantially less seasonal in buying behavior than consumers who buy gifts, flowers, toys, books, and CDs during holidays. However, the online store wants to increase the number of seasonal customers and attract more traffic to the site. It is common in the Internet economy for online retailers to see surges in traffic during events like the Super Bowl or holidays such as Valentine's Day and Christmas. Increases in unique visitors of about 400% relative to the week before are not uncommon during these special events. Retailers seize the opportunity to attract online shoppers seeking the comfort, ease, and efficiency of buying on the Web. Moreover, the Internet is turning out to be a great advertising medium, particularly for event-driven efforts when advertisers can make pushes tied to e-commerce. Thus, ad sales are becoming an important source of revenue. The e-buypc.com vice-president of operations observed that around 95% of the company's site visitors do not purchase any products. So, the company wants to make money from the traffic.

13.2.1   Planning Situations

Two different planning situations are being addressed by management. In the first case, management wants to know the impact of corporate goals on the site's infrastructure. In the other case, management would like to know how to prepare for a given future scenario. The planning situations are as follows.

- *Assessing the Impact of the Business Goals.*
  Corporate management has set several business goals for the e-buypc.com computer store. Some of these goals are related to stock holders, personnel, and financing. The board of directors set a goal for next year: $130 million of merchandise revenue and $3 million dollars of ad sales. The question management wants to answer is whether the site has an adequate infrastructure to support the increase in revenue without compromising the quality of service.

- *Introducing Digital Downloadable Products.*
  The company will soon be announcing the launch of a new online store that will allow consumers to purchase and download digital products. The company will begin selling high quality downloadable music in MP3 format. Before introducing the new product, management wants to plan the site capacity to adequately support the new business.

13.3   General Guidelines

Before developing the solution for the two planning problems, remember these specific aspects associated with planning e-business projects.

- One of the major performance metrics of e-business sites is the user perceived response time, which can be written as

$$UserResponseTime = ClientTime + NetworkTime + SiteResponseTime.$$

The relative contribution of each component of the end-to-end response time varies for each application and online company because it depends on the complexity of the application, the network infrastructure, and the site's architecture. The network time is a function of the performance of the Internet and is beyond the control of any single company or organization. Thus, end-to-end performance, measured by user response time, cannot be totally controlled as in traditional corporate information systems. Considering that the company cannot manage the Internet, the solution concentrates mainly on the site architecture, its connection to the ISP, and the ISP networking capacity.

- E-commerce sites have frequently been caught by unexpected traffic surges. The unpredictable nature of Internet traffic should always be considered when designing online businesses. Traffic surges may cause e-business companies serious problems, such as a system crash, poor performance, unhappy customers, lost revenue, and bad public perception. To handle traffic surges, companies should size their IT infrastructure taking into consideration peak volumes of transactions and requests.

- E-business activities are essentially real time processes, where performance and availability problems have a high cost for the company. Frustrated visitors can translate into lost customers and lost revenue. Quantitative techniques and models should be used to anticipate problems.

Example 13.1

Suppose an e-commerce site. To analyze the user-perceived quality of service, the administrator relies on two sources of information: i) the site's server access logs and ii) user perceived performance, provided by an outsourced service that shows how end users experience the company's site. In other words, the third party service measures how fast users can download a page from the e-commerce site or execute a business function from their geographic location. How can the administrator use this information to improve the quality service of the online store?

The first step is to set service level goals for the most used and critical business functions available in the company's site. Suppose we set a goal of a 3 sec response time for the Search function. Based on Web server logs and data provided by the service measurement company, we can break down the user response time into three percentages as shown in Fig. 13.2. Then, we can determine what the target number should be for the site response time.

$$\text{SiteResponseTime} = 0.55 \times 3 = 1.65 \text{ sec.}$$

Thus, the site's infrastructure and the application design team should work together to guarantee the above response time goal for the Search function. ■

13.4   A Model-Based Solution Approach

The solution approach presented in this section relies on the reference model for electronic business shown in Fig. 13.3. The model creates a framework for the quantitative approach developed in this book. It also provides a basis for building solutions of planning problems of e-business sites. As described in Section 1.3, the upper blocks focus on the nature of the business and the processes that provide the services offered by the e-business site. The lower blocks concentrate on the way customers interact with the site and the demand they place on the resources of the site infrastructure.

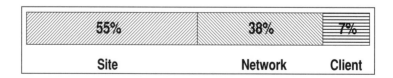

Figure 13.2. User Response Time Components.

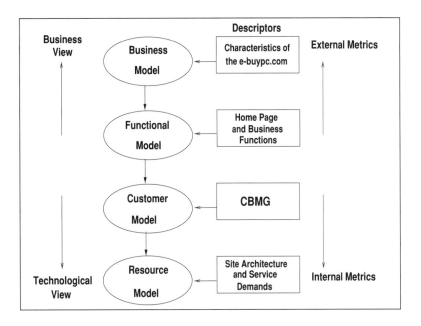

Figure 13.3. Reference Models for e-buypc.com.

The four-layer model requires the following inputs: business quantitative descriptors, functional descriptors, customer behavior patterns, and service demands that characterize the execution of the main business functions. In Section 13.2, the description of the online store allows one to specify the business quantitative descriptors and the functional model. The Customer Behavior Model Graph (CBMG) and the Customer Visit Model (CVM) represent user navigational patterns. To keep the example simple, let us assume the workload of the online store can be represented by a single CBMG, shown in Fig. 13.4.

In fact, an actual workload would be better represented by several CB-MGs, which model different classes of customers with different navigational patterns, as explained in Section 11.4. Even being a simplification, the single CBMG provides us insights on the interaction between a "typical customer" and the online store. Solving the equations for the CBMG of Fig. 13.4 with the methods described in Chapter 11, we obtain the average number of visits

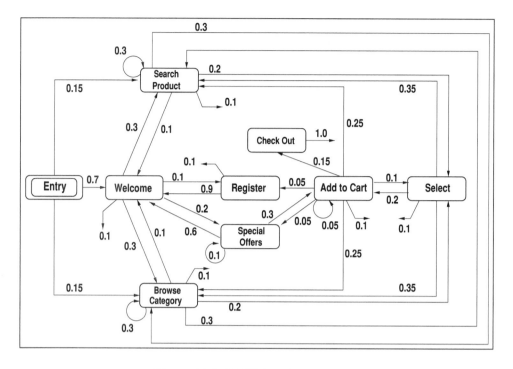

Figure 13.4. CBMG for e-buypc.com.

to each business function (V_i) per session, the average session length and the buy to visit ratio, as displayed in Table 13.1.

13.5   Case 1: Assessing the Impact of Business Goals

The basic problem here is to answer the following question.

> The board of directors has set a goal for next year: $130 million of merchandise revenue and $3 million of ad sales. The question management wants to answer is whether the site has an adequate infrastructure to support the increase in revenue without compromising the quality of service.

To answer this question, we have to calculate the throughput X_0, in transactions/sec, needed to generate $130 million of revenue as well as the average

Table 13.1. Metrics Derived from the CBMG.

Metric	Value
V_{Welcome}	1.172
V_{Browse}	2.583
V_{Search}	2.607
V_{Register}	0.115
$V_{\text{Check}-\text{Out}}$	0.046
V_{Special}	0.250
$V_{\text{Add to Cart}}$	0.304
V_{Select}	1.608
Average Session Length	8.144
Buy to Visit Ratio	4.6%

response time in case the site gets a volume X_0 of transactions. As illustrated in Fig. 13.5, the first question is solved by transforming business goals into performance metrics, such as transaction arrival rates. A queuing network model of the e-commerce site can provide the answer to the question regarding response time.

Relationship Between Traffic and Revenue. To achieve the level of revenue set by the business plans, the online store has to attract more visitors and to increase the number of visitors that buy something. Thus, we have to discover the relationship between traffic and the percentage of customers

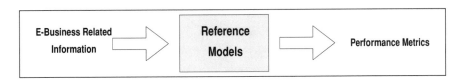

Figure 13.5. From Business Goals to Performance Metrics.

that buy something each time they visit the site. This relation, called buy to visit (BV) ratio or the *conversion rate*, specifies the ratio between the average number of customers who buy from the store and the total number of visits to the Web store. From the functional description of the online store in Section 13.2, we learn that the only function related to merchandise revenue is Check-Out. The next step is to understand the customer navigational patterns and the frequency of Check Out in the patterns.

Understanding Customer Behavior. As described in Chapter 11, the workload processed by the online store site is composed of customer sessions, which can be represented by CBMGs and CVMs. From these two models, we can derive the average session length and the average number of executions of each business function. Thus, we are able to determine the critical functions in terms of load (i.e., the most requested functions) and in terms of revenue (i.e., the functions that generate revenue from sales).

Incorporating Burstiness into Performance Calculations. Traffic bursts have to be considered in the calculation of e-business performance metrics. Indicators of system load and capacity should be adjusted by the peak to average load ratio to account for burstiness. Historical measurement data and market research surveys can provide information to calculate the peak to average ratio for categories of e-retailers as well as for a specific e-business.

Calculating Performance Metrics. We already know that the system throughput (X_0) measures the average number of transactions executed per second. Another metric used for e-commerce is the *revenue throughput*, denoted by X^+ and measured in dollars/sec, generated by completed transactions [3] [5]. The system capacity, measured by the system throughput, can then be calculated as a function of the revenue goal and parameters derived from the workload (i.e., the CBMGs) as

$$\text{RevenueThroughput} = \frac{\text{Sessions}}{\text{sec}} \times \text{BV} \times \text{AverageSale}, \qquad (13.5.1)$$

$$\text{AnnualRevenue} = \text{RevenueThroughput} \times \frac{\text{Seconds}}{\text{Year}}, \qquad (13.5.2)$$

$$X_0 = \frac{\text{Sessions}}{\text{sec}} \times \text{AverageSessionLength}, \qquad (13.5.3)$$

where AverageSale is the average dollar amount generated by a session in which a sale occurs.

We notice from Eqs. (13.5.1)-(13.5.3) that the relationship between traffic and the expected revenue depends strongly on metrics derived from the CBMG. So, the better the workload characterization, the more accurate the performance results. Let us now apply these results to answer the basic problem stated previously.

13.5.1   From Business Goals to Performance Metrics

We notice from Table 13.1 that, on average, every visitor performs 5.19 product searches ($V_{\text{Search}} + V_{\text{Browse}}$). Product searches represent approximately 64% of the transactions generated by every customer session. We also know that only 4.6% of all visits result in purchases. Since search transactions make up the major portion of the workload, we will again make a simplifying assumption and consider that the workload submitted to the online store consists only of Search and Browse transactions. Actually, this simplification does not hurt the model because searches represent the major portion of the load processed by the site.

To translate from the business goal to system throughput, we have to use Eqs. (13.5.1)-(13.5.3). According to Eq. (13.5.2), the revenue throughput X^+ required by e-buypc.com is 4.122 (= 130,000,000 / 31,536,000) dollars/sec. An analysis of the online purchasing behavior of the store's consumers during the past year revealed that they spent an average of $225 dollars per purchase. If we now use the buy to visit (BV) ratio of Table 13.1 in Eq. (13.5.1), we can calculate sessions/sec as

$$\frac{\text{Sessions}}{\text{sec}} = \frac{X^+}{\text{BV} \times \text{AverageSale}}$$

$$= \frac{4.122}{0.046 \times 225} = 0.398 \text{ sessions/sec.} \qquad (13.5.4)$$

Using the value of 8.144 for the average session length, given in Table 13.1, in Eq. (13.5.3), we obtain a system throughput of $X_0 = 0.398 \times 8.144 = 3.241$ transactions/sec.

Now we know that the site of e-buypc.com has to support an average throughput of 3.241 transactions/sec. However, due to burstiness, the site may have a 20:1 peak to average load. So, the capacity needs to be adjusted to handle load spikes and the site must be sized to handle 64.82 transactions/sec (i.e., 3.241×20). However, we have no information about the quality of service of the site. Let us consider in this case that response time is the main indicator of quality of service. So, the last step to complete the answer to the business question is to predict the average response time for a throughput of 64.82 transactions/sec.

13.5.2   Predicting the Site Performance

Performance models of e-business sites can be used to answer some capacity and performance questions. In particular, we want to know the impact of the business goal on the quality of service of the online store. The previous section calculated the throughput needed to achieve the annual revenue of $130 million. The site should be capable of processing at least 62.48 transactions per second. With the current site configuration, what would be the average transaction response time?

Returning to the reference model of Figure 13.3, we have to build a resource model to predict the site performance. A resource model considers the architecture and the configuration of the site in terms of layers that compose the architecture, number of servers of each type, I/O subsystems, and networking infrastructure. Resource usage is derived from the upper layer models. In summary, the resource model is a combination of performance model and workload model. As described in previous chapters, performance models can be based on simulation models or queuing network models. In this example, we use queuing models.

The architecture of e-buypc.com consists of three layers of servers as displayed in Fig. 13.6. The Web servers are on LAN1, the application servers are on LAN2, and the database server is on LAN3. Let us assume that this architecture is considered scalable since any performance goal can be met by adding more hardware resources. Software monitors were used to collect performance measurements at the site. From these measurements, the service demands were computed using methods presented in Chapters 8 and 11. Table 13.2 shows the service demands of a typical Search transaction for the configuration of Fig. 13.6. The service demands for LAN1, LAN2, LAN3, and the external link are 0.49, 0.53, 0.38, and 1.2 msec respectively.

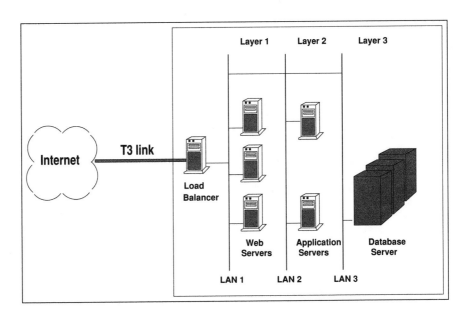

Figure 13.6. IT Infrastructure of the e-buypc.com Site.

Table 13.2. Service Demands (in msec) for the Search Transaction.

Component	Processor	I/O
Web Servers (3)	5.2	9.5
Application Servers (2)	14.0	10.0
Database Server (mainframe)	14.1	31.0

The queuing network model corresponding to the store's site is shown in Fig. 13.7. Considering that the store's site is publicly available on the Internet, we can assume that a very large population of visitors will access the site. Thus, we can only characterize the arrival rate of requests for the business functions, i.e., the transaction arrival rates. The site will be modeled as an open queuing network model, with only one class, composed of Search transactions. The input parameters to the model are the transaction arrival and the service demands at the components of the site (see Chapter 8 for more detail).

Using the techniques introduced in Chapter 9, we solve the open queuing model of Fig. 13.7 for the new arrival rate, which is equal to 64.82 transactions/sec. The system is unable to process this arrival rate because its maximum throughput is given by

$$X_{\max} = 1/D_{\max} = 1/0.031 = 32.26 \text{ transactions/sec.}$$

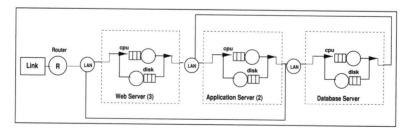

Figure 13.7. Open Queuing Network Model for the e-buypc.com Site.

Because the I/O subsystem (i.e., disks) of the database server has the highest service demand, it is the bottleneck and limits the system scalability. Let us assume that the disk subsystem is replaced by a RAID (Redundant Array of Independent Disks) system four times faster than the original disks of the mainframe. To reflect this change in the site configuration, we modify the I/O service demand for database disks. Thus, the new service demand is

$$D_{\text{RAID}} = \frac{D_{\text{I/O}}}{4} = \frac{31}{4} = 7.75 \ \text{msec}.$$

Again, we solve the model with the new service demand and the calculated response time for a typical search transaction is 0.240 sec, which is considered acceptable by the management of e-buypc.com.

Example 13.2

Let us go back to the problem of e-buypc.com. The second goal set by the board is to have $3 million of ad sales for next year. Is this a feasible goal? Does the site infrastructure support this goal?

Let us revisit some concepts associated with online advertisement. A website that charges $18,000 per banner and guarantees 600,000 impressions has a CPM (Cost-per-thousand-impressions) of $30 (i.e., $18,000/600$). Consider that e-buypc.com charges $12,000 per banner and guarantees 800,000 impressions of the banner. Its CPM equals $15 (= $12,000/800$).

The online store's board of directors defined a policy for placing ads. First, each page must have only one banner. Second, banners will appear only on pages classified as "surfing pages," i.e., Welcome, Browse, and Search. The other pages, called "purchasing pages" must not exhibit ad banners.

To have a revenue of $3 million of ad sales, e-buypc.com has to sell at least 250 (= $3,000,000/12,000$) banners and has to send out two hundred million pages (i.e., $800,000 \times 250$) with banners. To generate that many pages with banners, we need to know the total number of pages that must be sent out to visitors and customers. Again, the CBMG model can help us calculate this number. From Table 13.1, we notice that in each session, surfing pages corresponds to 78.1% of the total number of pages (i.e., (1.172 + 2.583 + 2.607) / 8.144). Thus, to generate two hundred million surfing pages, the site has to process 256,081,946 pages (i.e., 200,000,000 / 0.781).

Considering that each page results from the execution of one business function, we then have the total number of transactions to be processed in one year (i.e., 31,536,000 sec). From these numbers, we calculate the average site throughput needed to support the ad sale revenue.

$$X_0 = 256,081,946/31,536,000 = 8.12 \ \text{transactions/sec.}$$

Table 13.2 displays the service demands for the current configuration of the e-buypc.com site. From Chapter 8, we know that the maximum throughput of a system is limited by the resource with the highest service demand, i.e., equal to $X_0 \leq 1/D_{max}$. Thus, the maximum value for the throughput of the site is 32.25 (i.e., 1/31) transactions/sec, which indicates that the IT infrastructure is capable of handling the number of transactions required by the goal set for ad sales.   ∎

13.6   Case 2: Introducing Digital Downloadable Products

Sales of downloaded music over the Internet are growing exponentially. In its pursue of the online market, e-buypc.com is considering opening an associated store, The Net Music Store, to sell music recordings online. The company plans to sell high quality downloadable music in MP3 format [4]. Before introducing the new product, management wants to plan the site capacity to adequately support the new business. This is a typical initial sizing situation, in which there is little information about the problem. So the solution approach should be guided by simple models with a few input parameters, which capture the most essential aspects of problem.

The reference model of Figure 13.3 is again our starting point for analyzing this sizing problem. A business model can be viewed as a collection of quantitative descriptors that characterize product, service, and information flow between the store and customers. The descriptors of the model are as follows:

- Business pattern: business to consumer,

- Business type: online retailer,

- Product: downloadable music in MP3 format,

- Number of downloads per day: 8,000,

- Estimated number of titles for download: 30,000, of which 7,000 are singles and 23,000 are CDs,

- Sales policy: management decided that the store sells either singles or CDs, but does not sell separate recordings, and it is expected that singles, which have a playing time of ten minutes of music, represent 20% of the sales and CDs, which have a playing time of sixty minutes, represent the rest.

13.6.1 Sizing the Net Music Store: First Cut

In this section, we develop a resource model to obtain a first cut sizing of the online music store infrastructure.

Disk Storage

On average, one minute of music in MP3 format corresponds to 0.3 MByte. Let $Single_s$ and CD_s denote the space required for storing a single and a CD, respectively. Thus, the disk storage requirements for holding the titles offered by the store are calculates as

$$\text{DiskSpace} = 7,000 \times \text{Single}_s + 23,000 \times \text{CD}_s$$

$$\text{Single}_s = 10 \text{ min} \times 0.3 \text{ MB/min} = 3 \text{ MB}$$

$$\text{CD}_s = 60 \text{ min} \times 0.3 \text{ MB/min} = 18 \text{ MB}$$

$$\text{DiskSpace} = 7,000 \times 3 + 23,000 \times 18 = 435 \text{ Gigabytes.} \quad (13.6.5)$$

Server Capacity

Here, we focus on sizing the download server. The architecture of the site consists of three layers: Web servers, application servers, and a download server. Figure 13.8 depicts a node of a CBMG for the music store and the mapping of the Download business function to a CSID.

The question we want to answer now is how many simultaneous download connections the music server should support. The approach to answering the question is to evaluate the average number of connections using Little's Law ($N = X \times R$). To do that, we need to estimate the average duration of a download (R) and the download request rate ($X = \lambda$). The estimated number of downloads per day is 8,000, which yields an average $X = 0.0926$ downloads/sec. Modem bandwidth available on a dial-up connection is 56Kbps. Due to start/stop bit overhead, we assume the effective bandwidth of 5KB/sec. The average size of an MP3 file requested from the music store is

$$\text{FileSize} = \text{Single}_s \times p_{\text{single}} + \text{CD}_s \times p_{\text{CD}}. \tag{13.6.6}$$

where p_{single} and p_{CD} represent the fraction of requested singles and CDs, respectively.

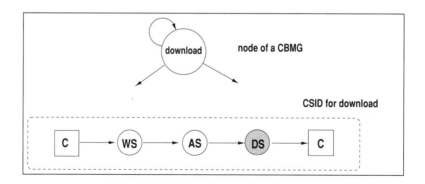

Figure 13.8. From CBMG to CSID.

Assume that $p_{\text{single}} = 55\%$ and $p_{\text{CD}} = 45\%$. The actual values for these probabilities depend on the popularity of the title bought by customers. We can then find the average size of a downloaded MP3 file using Eq. (13.6.6): $9.75 \, (= 0.55 \times 3 + 0.45 \times 18)$ MB. So the time needed to download an average file is

$$R = \frac{9,750 \text{ KB}}{5 \text{ KB/sec}} = 1,950 \text{ sec.}$$

Applying Little's Law, we have that

$$N = X \times R = 0.0926 \times 1,950 = 181 \text{ downloads.} \qquad (13.6.7)$$

Therefore, the server should be sized to support an average of about 180 simultaneous connections. For peak times, this number should be multiplied by the peak to average load ratio.

13.6.2 Evaluating the Impact of the Cable System

The cable system is expected to provide a faster platform for downloading music. Cable modems send and receive data from a TV coaxial cable, typically connecting to a PC via a 10Base-T Ethernet. Download speeds on the coaxial cable are typically 10 Mbps. Uploads are usually in the 0.5 to 2Mbps range. Since the cable bandwidth is shared, if one hundred subscribers are active on a 10Mbps cable, the bandwidth available to each is only 0.1 Mbps. Thus, the effective bandwidth seen by a user depends on how many neighbors are also using the neighborhood cable pipe at the same time. A realistic expectation is around 1 Mbps.

Let us assume that the music store can support 450 shoppers simultaneously. Consider also that each shopper is associated with an open TCP connection. During peak time, all 450 connections are busy. Assuming that all current customers are connected by 56Kbps modems, we would like to know the number of simultaneous shoppers if everyone switched to cable modem. Let us consider that the arrival rate continues to be the same.

From Little's law, we have

$$N = 450 = \lambda \times R, \qquad (13.6.8)$$

where λ is the customer request arrival rate and R is the duration of the connection to download a CD over a dial-up 56Kbps modem. Suppose that the download time substantially dominates the connection time. Let N^{new} denote the new number of simultaneous customers. Considering that $\lambda^{\text{new}} = \lambda$, it follows

$$N^{\text{new}} = \lambda^{\text{new}} \times R^{\text{new}} \qquad (13.6.9)$$
$$R^{\text{new}} = R \times \frac{56,000}{1,000,000}.$$

Then,

$$N^{new} = \lambda \times R \times \left(\frac{56,000}{1,000,000}\right) = 450 \times 0.056 = 25.2. \qquad (13.6.10)$$

So if customers switched to faster connections, the store would be able to receive a higher customer arrival rates and consequently increase its revenue.

13.7   Concluding Remarks

In this chapter, we analyzed two cases in the business to consumer segment using techniques and methods presented earlier in the book. The solution approach presented to solve the case studies relies on the reference model for electronic business introduced in Chapter 1. The four-layer model creates a framework for the quantitative approach developed in this book. It also provides a basis for building solutions of planning problems of e-business sites.

We started the chapter by describing an example of planning situations in an online retail company. Let us go back to the example and reexamine it. An online store, e-buypc.com, decides to increase its revenue and to create an associated store to sell downloadable music. The main problem is to define the site infrastructure that will process the current and expected workloads within the specified service levels. Quantitative techniques and customer behavior model graphs (CBMGs) appear as a means to specify and size the new systems. The steps required to carry out the solution of the two cases are described at length in this chapter. A key issue in e-business planning situations is the model needed to predict the performance of future systems. In our examples, we used simple queuing models to uncover essential aspects of the modifications proposed for the online store.

Bibliography

[1] V. A. F. Almeida, A. Bestavros, M. Crovella, and A. Oliveira, "Characterizing Reference Locality in the WWW," *Proc. Fourth International Conference on Parallel and Distributed Information Systems (PDIS)*, IEEE Computer Society, Dec. 1996, pp. 92–106.

[2] J. Gray and P. Shenoy, "Rules of Thumb in Data Engineering," *Proc. of the IEEE International Conference on Data Engineering*, IEEE, San Diego, CA, April 2000.

[3] D. A. Menascé, V. A. F. Almeida, R. C. Fonseca, and M. A. Mendes, "Resource Management Policies for E-commerce Servers," *Proc. Second Workshop on Internet Server Performance (WISP'99)*, held jointly with ACM Sigmetrics '99, Atlanta, GA, May 1999.

[4] MPEG, http://www.mpeg.org.

[5] D. Willson, "Setting Performance Goals for Duwamish Bookstore, Phase 4," Microsoft Developer Network, Aug. 1999, microsoft.com/library/techart/d4perfgoal.htm.

[6] D. A. Menascé and V. A. F. Almeida, *Capacity Planning for Web Performance: Metrics, Models and Methods*, Prentice Hall, Upper Saddle River, NJ, 1998.

[7] G. Zipf, *Human Behavior and the Principle of Least Effort*, Addison-Wesley, Cambridge, MA, 1949.

Chapter 14

Business to Business Case Studies

14.1   Introduction

Many companies have been able to improve efficiency and reduce costs by integrating their information systems with those of their suppliers and partners. Through the use of Web technologies, suppliers can have access to inventory levels and adjust their production schedules to match the demand. For example, a networking equipment company saves an estimated $500 million a year from improved supply-chain management, online technical support, and online software distribution [4]. A large computer manufacturer has been able to lower its average inventory holdings from thirty-five days to six days in a period of seven years by sharing demand information with its suppliers [5].

In this chapter we describe several B2B processes and discuss, through examples, how capacity planning can be carried out in these environments. We also show the mapping of B2C to B2B processes.

14.2   From B2C to B2B

The board of directors of the online store in Chapter 13 is considering the possibility of generating more computer sales by giving customers the opportunity to configure their machines online and at the same time reducing order processing costs. The board was encouraged by stories that report savings of several million dollars through the reduction of the percentage of misconfigured orders as well as reductions of ninety-six percent in order processing costs [2].

To support sales of made-to-order computers assembled by e-buypc.com, the company will invest in a sophisticated product configuration software that walks customers through product features, analyzes customers' needs, budgets, and time constraints, and only offers components and options that are compatible from a technical standpoint [2]. The new Configure function would allow customers to choose hardware and software options based on technical feasibility constraints. Examples of hardware options include processor type, amount of main memory, hard disk type and capacity, monitor type, and several types of peripherals (e.g., modem, keyboard, CD-ROM drive, DVD drive, tape drive, and speakers). Customers are also allowed to select the software—operating system, office automation, and other application software—to be factory-installed on their machines.

The key to succeeding in customized production is to extend product demand information to suppliers. When a customer clicks on the Buy button, the order is passed to the back-end order fulfillment systems, which update inventory, accounting, and shipping databases [2]. Product demand forecasts should be shared with first-tier suppliers allowing them to adjust their production schedules to match the forecasts and propagate orders and forecasts back through their own suppliers all the way down the supply-chain [3]. Many car manufacturers are working toward streamlining supplier and distribution channels using the Web with estimated savings of 25% of the retail price of a car [1].

14.2.1   Planning Situations

The new situation for e-buypc.com is that they want to give their customers more flexibility in configuring the computers they buy. For that purpose, they will use a configurator software that will allow customers to select feasible configurations and obtain instant price quotes for the machine they configured. The online store also needs to integrate their business processes with those of their suppliers to reduce inventory levels and reduce costs.

The new method of selling computers is summarized in the steps below and is better understood with the help of Fig. 14.1.

1. The customer selects the Configure function.

2. The configurator software is invoked and presents to the customer a page in which options can be selected through a combination of pull-down menus, check boxes, and radio buttons. The options presented depend on information extracted from the parts inventory database and from the customer profile database. For example, if a certain type of processor is not in stock, it will not be presented as a possible option. If the Configure function is being used by a registered user, the configurator customizes the way options are displayed based on the customer's profile. For example, if a customer has shown, in the past, an appetite for computer games and flight simulators, the configurator

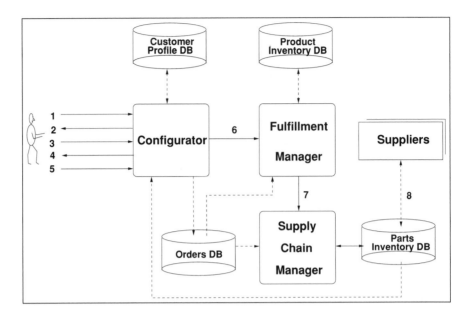

Figure 14.1. Business to Business Process for e-buypc.com.

may emphasize hardware components (e.g., sound cards and graphics accelerators) that will make the use of these games more enjoyable.

3. The customer completes the configuration and requests a price quote.

4. The configurator returns the price of the machine configured by the customer.

5. The customer orders the machine.

6. The fulfillment manager software routes the order to the manufacturing plant, which fills it directly from the supply-chain.

7. The supply manager generates a list of parts needed to fill the customer's order and updates the parts inventory database to reflect the parts committed to fill the order.

8. Suppliers have real-time access to the parts inventory database and to

product and parts demand forecasts. This way, suppliers can decide how fast they should replenish the warehouses of e-buypc.com with parts.

New capacity planning situations have to be considered.

- The board of directors wants to increase annual revenue by $180 million due to the configuration option. They want to know if the site has enough capacity to handle the additional load.

- The sharing of information with suppliers will increase the load on the IT resources of e-buypc.com. The question is whether the site will support the increase in workload intensity.

14.3   Characterizing the New Workload

There are two new types of workloads to be considered in the capacity planning situations described in the previous section. The first workload is due to the new configurator module that runs at the application layer. This workload is generated by B2C interactions. Computer orders generated by these B2C interactions generate B2B interactions due to the supply-chain and fulfillment manager modules.

14.3.1   Configurator Workload

To characterize the workload due to customers who use the new Configure function, we use a Customer Behavior Model Graph (see Fig. 14.2).

From the Welcome page, customers can select the type of computer they want to configure (e.g., desktop or laptop) through the Select Category function. They can then move to the Configure function and interact with the site until they are satisfied with the configuration. At this point, customers

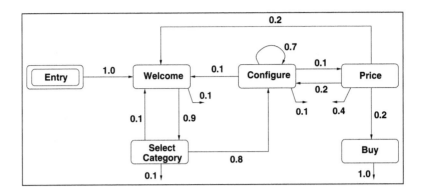

Figure 14.2. CBMG for Customers Who Use the Configure Function.

may invoke the Price function, which computes the price of the selected configuration. Customers can go back and change the configuration or decide to order the machine they just configured by using the Buy function.

Table 14.1 displays the average number of visits to each of the states of the CBMG of Fig. 14.2. The table shows that the Configure function accounts for more than fifty percent of the interactions with the site. The buy to visit ratio (BV) is 8.65%.

We compute now the number of sessions/sec needed to generate the additional revenue of $180 million per year due to the new customization

Table 14.1. Metrics Derived from the CBMG of Fig. 14.2.

Metric	Value
V_{Welcome}	1.622
V_{Select}	1.459
$V_{\text{Configure}}$	4.324
V_{Price}	0.432
V_{Buy}	0.086
Average Session Length	7.924
Buy to Visit Ratio	8.65%

functionality. The desired revenue throughput X^+ is 5.708 (= 180,000,000 / 31,536,000) dollars/sec. Assume that the average value of a computer sale, AverageSale, is \$1,200. Using arguments similar to those of Section 13.5.1, the number of sessions/sec needed to achieve the desired revenue throughput can be computed as

$$\frac{\text{Sessions}}{\text{sec}} = \frac{X^+}{\text{BV} \times \text{AverageSale}}$$
$$= \frac{5.708}{0.0865 \times 1,200} = 0.055 \text{ sessions/sec.} \qquad (14.3.1)$$

Using the value of 7.924 for the average session length from Table 14.1, we obtain a system throughput of $X_0 = 0.055 \times 7.924 = 0.436$ transactions/sec. As discussed in Chapter 13, burstiness considerations dictate that the site be prepared for load spikes. Using a 20:1 peak to average load, we obtain a transaction arrival rate of 8.72 transactions/sec (i.e., 0.436×20). The arrival rate for the transactions generated by the Configure function at peak periods is $0.055 \times 4.324 \times 20 = 4.756$ transactions/sec.

14.3.2 Supply-Chain Integration Workload

The integrated supply-chain model creates new types of transactions. Some are generated by e-buypc.com and some are generated by its suppliers. We concentrate on the transactions generated against the parts inventory database.

- *Update Inventory.* This transaction is generated by the supply-chain manager as a result of orders placed by customers. The parts inventory database is updated to reflect the parts used to fulfill an order. This type of transaction updates a very large number of records. According to Table 14.1 and Eq. (14.3.1), the rate at which these updates occur is sessions/sec $\times V_{\text{Buy}} = 0.055 \times 0.086 = 0.00473$ transactions/sec. Considering the 20:1 peak to average ratio, we obtain an arrival rate of 0.0946 (= 0.00473×20) transactions/sec.

- *Check Inventory.* This type of transaction is a read-only transaction submitted by the various suppliers to check on inventory levels for the parts they supply. There are thirty major suppliers of parts and components for the computers assembled by e-buypc.com. Each supplier checks inventory levels once an hour on average. Thus, the arrival rate of the Check Inventory transactions is $30/3,600 = 0.00833$ transactions/sec.

As seen in this section, B2C functions generate B2B functions (see Fig. 14.3).

14.4   Predicting the Performance

We can use the performance models discussed in Chapters 8 and 9 to answer the capacity planning questions posed in Section 14.2.1. These questions are rephrased below in more precise terms, using the workload intensity parameters derived in Section 14.3.

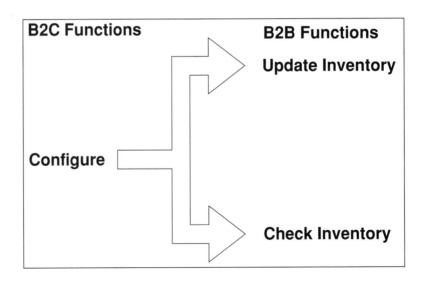

Figure 14.3. Mapping from B2C to B2B Functions for e-buypc.com.

- Will the site be able to support a load of 4.756 transactions/sec generated by the Configure function?

- Will the site support parts inventory updates at a rate of 0.0946 updates/sec and inventory checking queries at a rate of 0.00833 transactions/sec?

The new workloads will share the same IT resources with the already existing workloads.

We need to use a resource model to answer the capacity planning questions. The site architecture is the one depicted in Fig. 13.6. Measurements taken on prototype implementations of the new functions provide service demands at the processors and I/O subsystems of the Web servers, applications servers, and database servers, for the Configure, Update Inventory, and Check Inventory functions. These values are shown in Table 14.2. The table shows that the I/O subsystem of the database server seems to be the bottleneck given its very high service demands. Let us compute the total I/O utilization at the database server. From Chapter 13 we know that the arrival rate of Search transactions is 64.82 transactions/sec and that the I/O service demand at the database server is 7.75 msec. From the Service Demand Law (see Section 8.6.3), we know that $U_{i,r} = \lambda_{i,r} \times D_{i,r}$. The total utilization of a resource is the sum of the utilization of the resource due to all workloads. Thus,

$$
\begin{aligned}
U_{\text{DB-IO}} = {} & \lambda_{\text{Search}} \times D_{\text{DB-IO,Search}} + \lambda_{\text{Configure}} \times D_{\text{DB-IO,Configure}} + \\
& \lambda_{\text{Update Inventory}} \times D_{\text{DB-IO,Update Inventory}} + \\
& \lambda_{\text{Check Inventory}} \times D_{\text{DB-IO,Check Inventory}} \\
= {} & 64.82 \times 0.00775 + 4.756 \times 0.120 + \\
& 0.0946 \times 1 + 0.00833 \times 0.2 = 1.17 = 117\%.
\end{aligned}
\tag{14.4.2}
$$

Thus, the utilization exceeds 100% on the database server I/O subsystem when the new workloads are added. The existing IT infrastructure does

Table 14.2. Service Demands (in msec) for the Configure, Update Inventory, and Check Inventory Transactions.

	Configure	
	Processor	I/O
Web Servers (3)	5.1	9.5
Application Servers (2)	20.3	15.2
Database Server (mainframe)	16.7	120.0
	Update Inventory	
	Processor	I/O
Web Servers (3)	5.1	9.5
Application Servers (2)	20.0	30.0
Database Server (mainframe)	30.5	1000.0
	Check Inventory	
	Processor	I/O
Web Servers (3)	6.5	10.2
Application Servers (2)	25.6	24.5
Database Server (mainframe)	12.3	200.0

not support the new functionality! From Eq. (14.4.2), we can see that the utilization of the I/O subsystem due to Search transactions only is 50.2% ($=64.82 \times 0.00775$) or almost half of the total utilization. Therefore, a viable approach to cope with the new load is to have a dedicated database server to support the databases needed by the new functions (Configure, Update Inventory, and Check Inventory). The I/O utilization of this new database server becomes $4.756 \times 0.120 + 0.0946 \times 1 + 0.00833 \times 0.2 = 66.7\%$.

Figure 14.4 shows the queuing network that represents the new IT infrastruture. Only Search transactions use database server 1 and the other transactions use database server 2. Therefore, the service demand of Search transactions at the CPU and I/O subsystems of database server 2 is zero.

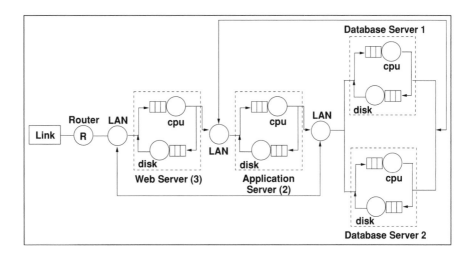

Figure 14.4. Queuing Network for New Configuration.

Similarly, the service demand of the Configure, Update Inventory, and Check Inventory at the CPU and I/O subsystems of database server 1 is zero.

Using a multi-class open queuing network model [6], we obtain the performance metrics with the help of the MS Excel workbook OpenQN.XLS found at this book's Web site (follow link called Chapter 9).

The response times obtained this way are 0.244 sec for Search transactions, 0.464 sec for Configure transactions, 3.147 sec for Update Inventory transactions, and 0.729 sec for Check Inventory transactions. Even though the inventory has to be updated every time a sale takes place, the customer receives a confirmation that the Buy transaction took place before the Update Inventory transaction completes. Therefore, the 3.147 sec of response time due to the Update Inventory transaction does not increase the customer's response time.

14.5 Concluding Remarks

Web-based systems allow suppliers to tap directly into manufacturing and order systems databases in real time. By giving suppliers access to product sales forecasts, manufacturers allow suppliers to adjust their production schedules to guarantee timely delivery of supplies while maintaining inventory levels as low as possible. B2B provides a wealth of opportunities for optimization, cost reduction, better quality of service, customization, and dynamic pricing.

This chapter illustrated, through an example, how B2C interactions affect B2B interactions. The link between customers, manufacturers, and suppliers is the information flow that propagates almost seamlessly, facilitated through the Web. An important lesson of this chapter is that business plans can and should be translated into transaction processing requirements. In other words, one can translate revenue throughput to transactions per second and use performance models to size the capacity of e-business sites. B2C transactions may generate one or more B2B transactions, which need to be taken into account by the performance models.

Bibliography

[1] "At Ford, E-Commerce is Job 1," *Business Week*, February 28, 2000.

[2] K. Cross, "Need Options? Go Configure," *Business 2.0*, February 2000.

[3] S. Donahue, "Supply Traffic Control," *Business 2.0*, February 2000.

[4] "Focus: Cysco Systems, The Paradigm of an e.org," *Strategy & Business*, Booz Allen & Hamilton, First Quarter 2000.

[5] "Focus: Dell's Supply Demands," *Strategy & Business*, Booz Allen & Hamilton, First Quarter 2000.

[6] D. A. Menascé and V. A. F. Almeida, *Capacity Planning for Web Performance: Metrics, Models and Methods*, Prentice Hall, Upper Saddle River, NJ, 1998.

Part V
Summary, Challenges, and Perspectives

Chapter 15: Wrapping Up

Chapter 15

Wrapping Up

15.1 Introduction

The electronic economy can be viewed as having three main components: infrastructure, electronic business processes, and electronic commerce transactions [6]. E-business is any process conducted by an organization over computer-mediated networks. E-commerce consists of any transaction completed over a computer-mediated network that involves the transfer of ownership or rights to use goods or services. Both e-business processes and e-commerce transactions are supported by an infrastructure that includes hardware and software components, telecommunication networks, and people with adequate skills. The continued growth of e-business and e-commerce have increased the demand on computing and communications resources, stressing site's resources and networks to the limit of their capacity. This has resulted, in many cases, in system crashes, degraded performance, deteriorated reliability and security, frustrated customers, and financial losses. At the same time, running and servicing a website to ensure performance and availability involves significant investments and operational costs.

15.2   Summary

The primary purpose of this book is to provide a framework for analyzing and quantifying the impact of e-business and e-commerce situations on the underlying infrastructure. To create such a framework, we organized the book into four major parts. The rationale for each part follows.

Part I: Modeling for E-Business

Our starting point is the definition of a reference model, created for understanding and analyzing e-business and e-commerce issues. The model consists of four submodels, organized into two groups. The top level group focuses on the nature of the business and the processes that provide the services offered online. The business level model and the functional model encompass aspects such as the type of business, type of products, revenue generating schemes, business policies, functions offered to customers, and service level agreements. The low level group concentrates on the way customers interact with the site and the demand they place upon the resources of the infrastructure. The customer model captures the navigational pattern of a customer during a visit to an e-business site. The resource model contains two key components: the workload model and the performance model. The first characterizes the patterns of services required from the site's resources and the second calculates performance metrics of an e-business site.

The four models defined in the first part of the book allow the reader to walk through a specific e-business and to identify quantitative issues needed to develop cost x benefit analyses. The hierarchical organization of the reference model leads to the interchange of parameters and information among the models. As in object orientation, in which each class inherits attributes of the parent class, the reference model allows the lower level submodels to reuse information of the upper level models. Metrics and descriptors are associated with the different layers of the reference model. Three modeling tools are defined to analyze the interaction of customers and online businesses as well as the demand placed on the site's resources by customer requests: 1) the Customer Behavior Model Graph (CBMG), 2) the Customer Visit Model (CVM), and 3) the Client/Server Interaction Diagram (CSID).

Part II: Evaluating E-Business Infrastructure and Services

The common thread among the chapters of Part II of this book is: How does one apply simple analytic models to gain insight into the behavior of e-business services and infrastructure? By breaking down the complexity of an electronic business, one can analyze the functionality of each component and evaluate service requirements. In this part, we analyze several issues related to the infrastructure and services that support electronic businesses. This part offers a quantitative analysis of the security mechanisms used in e-business. Many quantitative examples illustrate the tradeoffs between performance and security. In particular, we analyze how authentication protocols such as the Transport Layer Security (TLS) protocol, a successor of the Secure Sockets Layer (SSL) protocol, affects performance. Payment protocols, such as Secure Electronic Transactions (SET), aim at solving security concerns. We discuss how SET allows for credit card payments to take place over the Internet. SET provides a much higher level of security than SSL or TLS. There is, however, a performance penalty, which we present through the discussion of various numerical examples.

Part III: Capacity Planning for E-Business

In this part, we put together all the techniques needed to carry out capacity planning studies in the context of e-business. We show how to integrate the reference model to the basic steps of any capacity planning process. In other words, we present a model-based methodology that combines business and customer models with workload and performance models. Instead of relying on ad hoc procedures and rules of thumb, this part provides a uniform way of quantitatively analyzing e-business applications. Simple performance models, based on a variant of queuing theory called operational analysis, are used to gain insight and intuition into the behavior of e-business sites. Delays in electronic business transactions have two components: service time and waiting time. Waiting times arise when several requests from customers contend for the use of a finite-capacity hardware or software resources. Detailed analyses of e-business sites can be accomplished by a component-level model, based on queuing networks, in which components are represented by queues. Delays caused by software resources on the execution of e-business requests and transactions are examined here. Good planning and demand forecasting for online business environments are essential to anticipate problems. Demand forecast methods for e-business are included in the set of techniques that comprise part III.

Part IV: Models of Specific E-Business Segments

This part of the book is example-based throughout. We believe that the insight provided by the examples is essential to capture the main idea of this book, i.e., the development of a framework to analyze and understand e-business. We revisit the quantitative methods presented in the book through several examples in the business-to-consumer and business-to-business segments. Different planning situations for a hypothetical e-tailer are discussed in a number of e-commerce examples. B2B processes and transactions are scrutinized through examples. The goal of this part is to guide the reader, in a step-by-step manner, through the model-based solution of a number of e-business examples.

15.3 Perspectives

To understand the challenges that lie ahead of us in the area of e-business, it is worth discussing the ten driving principles of the New Economy [17]:

1. *Matter.* Matter matters less. In the New Economy, a larger percentage of the value of goods is concentrated in intangibles like knowledge, information, services, and software [7].

2. *Space.* The world is the customer and the competitor. In the New Economy, space and geographical boundaries are no longer relevant. The economics of distance has been replaced by the economics of attention [13].

3. *Time.* Time is collapsing. The New Economy thrives on strong and speed-of-light links between people, manufacturers, suppliers, service industries, and governments, and saves us time, which is our scarcest resource [19].

4. *People.* People matter. The New Economy is largely driven by intellectual assets. These assets generate the smart ideas, innovations, and technologies that support electronic commerce [20].

5. *Growth.* Growth is accelerated by the network. Good products spread online with a speed comparable to the biological world. A significant challenge for this hypergrowth is scalability [3].

6. *Value.* Value grows exponentially with market share. In the New Economy, scarcity is no longer the source of perceived value—ubiquity is [14].

7. *Efficiency.* Infomediaries replace intermediaries in the New Economy. As the amount of information and options available on the Web grows exponentially, it is necessary to provide aggregated services, customer assistance, buying and price-comparison tools, and communities of interest. These services are provided by infomediaries [8].

8. *Markets.* Prices in ideal markets reflect all information possibly known about the goods and services being exchanged. Electronic commerce is moving toward the direction of ideal markets and price elasticity is just a click away [18]. Hal Varian predicts that the economic era of posted prices is rapidly coming to an end [16].

9. *Transactions.* Through unprecedented levels of information exchange between individuals and organizations, the New Economy has changed the way buyers and sellers find each other, compare prices and value-added services, and the way businesses optimize business processes and reduce costs [9].

10. *Impulse.* The New Economy is characterized by an infinite number of customized purchasing choices available right at the moment the customer learns about them. The impulse to buy and the purchase itself are now part of the same process [11].

15.4 Challenges

At the business level, challenges involve legal [2], taxation, pricing [1] [10], and privacy issues [12]. At the customer behavior level, it will be necessary to develop techniques and paradigms that enhance the customer's shopping experience [5]. Recommender systems [15] will have to be perfected to provide customized and personalized guidance to online shoppers. Software agents [4] will be acting on the consumer's behalf to locate items in their profiles and find the sites that offer the best conditions in terms of price, delivery time, and return policy. Voice user interfaces will allow people to interact with e-commerce sites hands-free.

The challenges and innovations at the business and customer behavior level will create significant challenges at the resource level. The proliferation of broadband Internet connections to the home, through cable modems or DSL lines, will allow for new types of services and products to be offered, specially in the entertainment business. The consequence will be an increasing demand on e-business sites to deliver more throughput in terms of bits/sec. Also, e-business traffic is increasing at exponential rates. As the number of Internet-ready mobile devices increases, an even higher number of people will shop online. As software agents proliferate, e-business sites will see their capacity stretched to the limit. The access flexibility given by voice user interfaces is bound to increase the number of accesses to e-commerce sites. Ubiquitous computing (PDAs and appliances attached to the Internet) will add an order of magnitude to the number of traffic sources, and will change the characteristics of traffic patterns and demands on e-business sites. Understanding and being able to quantify the impact of these changes on systems is challenging.

Society has been claiming more security in electronic business. As seen throughout the book, security also puts a heavy demand on the computing resources of a site. All of these factors mean one thing: e-business sites are in for a tremendous increase in traffic and demand. E-business sites need to be scalable. Their capacity needs to be planned to face changes in the workload, new functionality, and new business models.

Novel aspects introduced by e-business will also bring challenges. For instance, everything on the web can be recorded. The transactions a customer made, the pages that were visited, the time spent on each one of them, and the banners clicked on. This type of data allows a business to draw customer profiles and to customize services and products. To handle huge masses of data in real time and use them for improving business is also challenging.

With the continued growth of the electronic economy, it will be necessary to train more and more people with adequate skills to understand the problems posed by e-business, e-commerce, and their supporting infrastructure. E-business is a multidisciplinary field that draws from computer science, economics, business, and law. Educating people in an area such as electronic business, with its multiple aspects, is also challenging. Curricula for e-business need to take into account the various levels presented in this book [5]. To grow as a field, electronic business needs a comprehensive library, with articles and books that contribute to the fundamental understanding of its problems. This book is an attempt to move in that direction. It provides models and techniques that allow the reader to grasp a coherent and unified view of electronic business.

We hope you have enjoyed the reading as much as we have enjoyed writing this book!

Bibliography

[1] C. H. Brooks et al, "Automated Strategy Searches in an Electronic Goods Market: Learning and Complex Price Schedules," *Proc. 1999 ACM Conf. Electronic Commerce*, ACM Press, New York, NY, pp. 31–40.

[2] B. N. Grosof, Y. Labrou, and H. Y. Chan, "A Declarative Approach to Business Rules in Contracts: Courteous Logic Programs in XML," *Proc. 1999 ACM Conf. Electronic Commerce*, ACM Press, New York, NY, pp. 68–77.

[3] S. Jurvetson, "Turning Customers into a Sales Force," *Business 2.0*, March 2000.

[4] P. Maes, R. Guttman, and A. G. Moukas, "Agents that Buy and Sell," *Comm. ACM*, vol. 42, no. 3, Mar. 1999, pp. 81–91.

[5] D. A. Menascé, "A Reference Model for Designing an E-Commerce Curriculum," *IEEE Concurrency*, Jan.-Mar. 2000, pp. 82–85.

[6] T. Mesenbourg, "Measuring Electronic Business: Definitions, Underlying Concepts and Measurement Plans," *U.S. Census Bureau*, March 2000.

[7] C. Meyer, "What's the Matter?" *Business 2.0*, March 2000.

[8] W. Mougayar, "Aggregation Nation," *Business 2.0*, March 2000.

[9] S. Mott, "Winning One Customer at a Time," *Business 2.0*, March 2000.

[10] A. Odlyzko, "Paris Metro Pricing," *Proc. 1999 ACM Conf. Electronic Commerce*, ACM Press, New York, NY, pp. 140–147.

[11] R. H. Reid, "The Impulse Economy," *Business 2.0*, March 2000.

[12] J. Reagle and L. F. Cranor, "The Platform for Privacy Preference," *Comm. ACM*, vol. 42, no. 2, Feb. 1999, pp. 48–55.

[13] M. Sawhney, "Making New Markets," *Business 2.0*, March 2000.

[14] P. B. Seybold, "Ubiquity Breed Wealth," *Business 2.0*, March 2000.

[15] J. B. Schafer, J. Konstan, and J. Riedl, "Recommender Systems in E-Commerce," *Proc. 1999 ACM Conf. Electronic Commerce*, ACM Press, New York, NY, pp. 158–166.

[16] M. Schrage, "To Hal Varian the Price is Always Right," *Strategy & Business*, First Quarter 2000.

[17] C. Shapiro and H. R. Varian, *Information Rules*, Harvard Business School Press, Boston, MA, 1999.

[18] Z. B. Singh, "Super Markets," *Business 2.0*, March 2000.

[19] D. F. Spulber, "Clock Wise," *Business 2.0*, March 2000.

[20] D. Tapscott, "Minds over Matter," *Business 2.0*, March 2000.

Glossary of Terms

ACID The basic transaction properties of atomicity, consistency, isolation, and durability.

Active Server Pages A specification for dynamically created Web pages that utilizes ActiveX scripting—usually VB Script or Jscript code. When a browser requests an ASP page, the Web server generates a page with HTML code and sends it to the browser.

Analytic model Set of formulas and/or algorithms used to generate performance metrics from model parameters.

Applet Software downloaded from a server to run on a desktop computer.

Arrival theorem for closed systems The average number of customers seen by an arriving customer to a queue of a closed system is equal to the mean number of customers in the queue in steady-state if the arriving customer were removed from the system.

Arrival theorem for open systems The average number of customers seen by an arriving customer to a queue of an open system is equal to the mean number of customers in the queue in steady-state.

ASP See *Active Server Page.*

Availability Metric used to represent the percentage of time a system is available during an observation period.

Authentication A process by which two parties involved in a dialogue are given a guarantee that they are indeed interacting with whom they think they are interacting.

B2B See *Business-to-Business*.

B2C See *Business-to-Consumer*.

Baggage An extra piece of information carried by messages, which may be used in a reply message.

Bandwidth The amount of data that can be transmitted over a communications link or network per unit of time, usually measured in bits per second.

Basic component Generic unit of work that arrives at a system from an external source.

Benchmarking Process of running a set of standard programs on a system to compare its performance with that of others.

Bottleneck Resource that saturates first as the workload intensity increases. It is the resource with the highest service demand.

Browser A program that allows a person to read hypertext.

Burstiness A characteristic of Web traffic that refers to the fact that data are transmitted randomly with peak rates exceeding the average rates by factors of eight to ten.

Business function Customers interact with an e-business site by requesting the execution of an e-business function. Examples of these functions include Search, Browse, Login, Register, and Pay.

Business-to-Business A category of electronic commerce that includes all transactions made by a company with its suppliers or any other companies.

Business-to-Consumers A category of electronic commerce mainly represented by electronic retailing and covers a large range of commercial sites from online retailing to online financial services to online publishing.

Business model An architecture for product, service, and information flow, including a description of business players, their roles, and revenue sources.

Buy to visit ratio (BV) The average number of sale transactions per visit to the site. The buy to visit ratio is also called *conversion rate*.

C2C See *Consumer-to-Consumer*.

Cache A small fast memory holding recently accessed data designed to speed up subsequent accesses to the same data. Although caching techniques have been most often applied to processor-memory access, they have also been used to store a local copy of data accessible over a network.

Calibration Technique used to alter the parameters (either the input or the output parameters) of a base model of an actual system, so that the output parameters of the resulting calibrated model match the performance of the actual system being modeled.

Capacity planning Process of predicting when future load levels will saturate the system and of determining the most cost-effective way of delaying system saturation as much as possible.

CBMG See *Customer Behavior Model Graph*.

CA Certificate Authority.

CGI See *Common Gateway Interface*.

Ciphertext Scrambled or encrypted text.

Class Concept used in a performance model to abstract the parameters of a workload that are relevant to performance.

Class population Number of customers of a class.

Client Process that interacts with the user and is responsible for implementing the user interface, generating one or more requests to the server from the user queries or transactions, transmitting the requests to the server via a suitable interprocess communication mechanism, and receiving the results from the server and presenting them to the user.

Client/Server (C/S) A computing paradigm is predicated on the notion of splitting the work to be performed by an application between two types of processes— the client and the server. The server accepts requests from a client and returns the results to the client.

Client/Server Interaction Diagram (CSID) A graphical notation with nodes (squares and circles) and directed arcs (arrows) connecting these nodes. Nodes of a CSID represent visits to clients and/or servers during the execution of an e-business function.

Client think time Time elapsed between the receipt of a reply from a server and the generation of a new request.

Click-throughs Measures the percentage of users that not only view an online ad but also click on it to get to the Web page behind it.

Closed model Queuing model of a system with a fixed number of customers who circulate among the system resources. The number of customers in the system at all times is fixed and the number of possible system states is finite.

Clustering analysis Process by which a large number of components are grouped into clusters of similar components.

Common Gateway Interface (CGI) A protocol for processing user-supplied information through Web server scripts.

Common Object Request Broker Architecture A set of standard mechanisms for naming, locating, and defining objects in a distributed computing environment.

Confidentiality Deals with protecting the contents of messages or data transmitted over the Internet from unauthorized people.

Cookies Pieces of information used to identify customers and/or sessions. Cookies are sent by the server to the browser and stored there. The information is sent back to the server on every subsequent request to the server.

Consumer-to-Consumer A category of electronic commerce, also known as costumer-to-customer, that includes transactions between individuals. Usually, this type of transaction occurs in electronic markets formed basically by Web-based auctions.

CORBA See *Common Object Request Broker Architecture.*

Cryptography A technique by which data, called *plaintext*, is scrambled or encrypted in such a way that it becomes extremely difficult, expensive, and time consuming for an unauthorized person to unscramble or decrypt it.

C/S See *Client/Server.*

CSID See *Client/Server Interaction Diagram.*

Customer Behavior Model Graph (CBMG) A graph model, in which the nodes depict the states a customer is in during a visit to an e-commerce site. Arrows connecting states indicate possible transitions between them.

Customer Visit Model (CVM) A set of vectors that indicate the number of times each of the functions supplied by an e-business site is executed.

Database Management System Collection of programs that enable users to create and maintain a database.

Datagram Independent packets of the connectionless organization of the network layer.

Data integrity Related to preventing data from being modified by an attacker.

DBMS See *Database Management System.*

DCOM See *Distributed Component Object Model.*

Delay resource Resource in a queuing network in which no queuing is allowed; only a delay is imposed to the flow of a request.

Demilitarized Zone A zone that is accessible to the outside world.

DES Data Encryption Standard.

Digital envelope A DES-encrypted message along with the RSA-encrypted key used in DES encryption.

Distributed Component Object Model Microsoft's version of an ORB.

Digital Subscriber Line Special hardware technology attached to both the user and switch ends of a line that allows data transmission over the wires at far greater speeds than the standard phone wiring.

Disk array A storage system that consists of two or more disk drives designed to improve performance and/or reliability.

Domain Name Server (DNS) A distributed, replicated, data query service that provides host IP address based on host names.

DMZ See *Demilitarized Zone.*

DSL See *Digital Subscriber Line.*

Electronic Data Interchange (EDI) The inter-organizational, computer-to-computer exchange of structured information in a standard, machine processable format.

Electronic commerce Any form of business transaction in which the parties interact electronically.

Electronic market Allows participating sellers and buyers to exchange goods and services with the support of information technology.

Electronic wallet A helper application or a plug-in to the browser used to store all the information about the credit cards that the customer possesses as well as SET digital certificates for each of these cards.

Exponential smoothing A technique that uses a weighted average of past observations to forecast the value for the next period.

Extensible Markup Language (XML) A specification developed by the W3C designed especially for Web documents. XML allows applications to define their own markup extensions, enabling the definition, transmission, validation, and interpretation of data between applications and between organizations.

FDDI See *Fiber Distributed Data Interconnect.*

Fiber Distributed Data Interconnect (FDDI) A high-speed (100 Mbps) LAN standard, whose underlying medium is fiber optic.

Firewall Mechanism used to protect data and computers from activities of untrusted users.

Flow equilibrium assumption Principle that equates the customer's rate of flow into a system state to the customer's rate of flow out of the system state.

Functional model Describes the functions provided by an e-business site.

Heavy-tailed distribution A random variable X follows a heavy-tailed distribution if $P[X > x] \sim x^{-\alpha}$, as $x \to \infty$ for $0 < \alpha < 2$.

Hits/sec Measures the average number of requests for objects served in one second by a website.

Homogeneous workload assumption All requests that make up the workload are assumed to be statistically identical.

Hypertext Markup Language (HTML) A language that allows authors to specify the appearance and format of multimedia documents, in particular Web documents.

Hypertext Transfer Protocol (HTTP) A protocol used by the World Wide Web that defines how client browsers and Web servers communicate with each other over a TCP/IP connection.

Internet The global set of interconnected networks that uses TCP/IP.

Internet Protocol (IP) The protocol that defines the format of packets used in the TCP/IP protocol suite and the mechanism for routing a packet to its destination.

Internet Service Provider (ISP) A company that provides other companies or individuals with access to, or presence on, the Internet.

Intranet A private Internet deployed by an organization for its internal use and not necessarily connected to the Internet. Intranets are based on TCP/IP networks and Web technologies.

IP See *Internet Protocol.*

ISAPI Microsoft's programming interface between applications and Microsoft's Internet Server.

ISP See *Internet Service Provider.*

IT Information Technology.

Java An object-oriented, distributed, architecture-neutral, portable, multithreaded, dynamic, programming language developed by Sun Microsystems.

Java servlet Server-side applet.

k-means algorithm A clustering algorithm that begins by selecting k points in the space of points, which act as an initial estimate of the centroids of the k clusters. The remaining points are then allocated to the cluster with the nearest centroid. The allocation procedure iterates several times over the input points until no point switches cluster assignment or a maximum number of iterations is performed.

LAN See *Local Area Network.*

Latency The time required to complete a request is the latency at the server. It is one of the components of the client's response time.

Layered Queuing Networks Queuing network models that combine contention for software and hardware components.

Little's Result Fundamental and general result that states that the average number of customers in a system is equal to the product of the arrival rate of customers to the system and the mean time that each customer stays in the system (i.e., the customer's mean response time).

Load-dependent queue Queue whose rate of service delivery is a function of the number of customers in the queue.

Local Area Network A network intended to serve a small geographic area.

Maximum Transmission Unit (MTU) The largest amount of data that can be sent across a given network using a single packet.

Mean Value Analysis (MVA) Elegant iterative technique for solving closed queuing networks. It iterates over the number of customers.

Message digest (MD) A fixed size string generated by a one-way hash function applied to a message.

Model validation Process of verifying if a model accurately captures key aspects of a system.

Model Calibration Process of modifying a model so that it can be validated.

Monitors Tools used for measuring the level of activity of a computer system.

Moving averages A simple forecasting technique that makes the value to be forecast for the next period equal to the average of a number of previous observations.

MP3 The file extension for MPEG, audio layer 3, one of three coding schemes for the compression of audio signals. MP3 files are small and can easily be transferred across the Internet

MSS Maximum segment size.

MTU See *Maximum Transmission Unit*.

Multiclass model Model in which customers may be partitioned into different classes. Each class has unique device service demands and routing behavior.

MVA See *Mean Value Analysis.*

Non-repudiation An attribute of secure systems that prevents the sender of a message from denying having sent it.

NSAPI Netscape's programming interface between applications and Netscape's Web Server.

Object Request Broker A component in CORBA's programming model that acts as the middleware between clients and servers.

Open model Queuing model of a system with no constraints on the size of the customer population. Customers arrive from the outside world, receive service, and exit. Usually, infinite buffer sizes are assumed and the number of possible system states is infinite.

Operational analysis Computer system analysis technique that assumes that the input parameters of the system model are all based on measured quantities.

Operational quantities Set of measurements used by operational analysis relations.

ORB See *Object Request Broker.*

Overhead System resources (e.g., processor time and memory space) consumed by activities that are incidental to, but necessary to, the main tasks. Examples include the operating system overhead involved in user program execution or the extra bits added to a message by a protocol.

Page Views/Day Indicates the number of individual pages served per day.

Payment gateway Also called the acquirer payment gateway, is the interface between the acquirer bank and the banking network that supports authorizations and settlement.

PDA See *Personal Digital Assistant.*

PDU See *Protocol Data Unit.*

Pareto distribution A heavy-tailed distribution with the following cumulative distribution function: $F(x) = P[X \leq x] = 1 - (k/x)^{\alpha}$.

Peak traffic ratio The ratio between peak and average site traffic.

Performance model A system's representation used for predicting the values of performance measures of the system.

Personal Digital Assistant A handheld device that combines computing, telephone/fax, and networking features. Most PDAs are pen-based and incorporate handwriting recognition features. Some PDAs can also react to voice input by using voice recognition technologies.

PK See *Public Key.*

POS Point of Sale.

Potential loss throughput Measures the amount of money in customers' shopping carts that is not converted into sales per second because the customer leaves the site due to poor performance or other reasons.

Protocol A set of formal rules describing how computers interact, especially across a network.

Protocol Data Unit An international standard denomination for packet.

Proxy Server A special type of World Wide Web server that acts as an agent that represents the server to the client and the client to the server. Usually, a proxy is used as a cache of items available on other servers that are presumably slower or more expensive to access.

Private Key A key known only to the receiver of a message.

Public Key A key known to everybody and used to encrypt messages that can only be decrypted with the receiver's private key.

Public key cryptography A cryptographic system in which the public key is known to everybody and is used for encryption. The receiver uses its private key to decrypt messages sent to it.

QNM See *Queuing Network Model.*

Queue Element of a queuing network composed of a resource and its associated waiting queue.

Queue length Number of customers or requests in a queue including the customers in service as well as enqueued customers.

Queuing Network Set of interconnected queues.

Queuing Network Model A collection of single queues arranged in the same configuration as a real system.

RAID See *Redundant Arrays of Inexpensive Disks*.

Redundant Arrays of Inexpensive Disks (RAID) A storage system that provides improved availability and/or performance.

RSA A public key cryptographic algorithm. RSA stands for Rivest, Shamir, and Adleman.

Reliability Measures the rate or probability of occurrence of failures during the processing of services.

Remote Procedure Call (RPC) A paradigm for implementing the client/server model. In general, a program invokes services across a network by making modified procedure calls.

Residence time Total time spent by a request, transaction, or program at a resource.

Response time Time from when a request arrives to a system until the request completes service and exits the system.

Resource model A representation of the various resources of a site that captures the effects of the workload model on these resources. The resource model is also called the IT resource model.

Revenue throughput A business-oriented metric that measures the number of dollars/sec derived from sales from an e-commerce site.

ROT See *Rule of Thumb*.

Round trip time (RTT) A measure of the current delay on a network found by timing a packet bounced off some remote host.

Router A device that uses network layer information and routing tables to forward traffic between networks.

RPC See *Remote Procedure Call*.

Rule of Thumb A method or procedure based on experience and common sense.

Secure Electronic Transactions (SET) A standard payment protocol for safeguarding payment card purchases made over open networks.

Secure Hash Algorithm (SHA) An algorithm to generate message digests developed by the U.S. National Institute of Standards and Technology (NIST) with the assistance from the National Security Agency. It accepts messages that are multiple of 512 bits long and produces a 160-bit output.

Secure Sockets Layer (SSL) A protocol developed by Netscape that offers authentication, confidentiality, and non-repudiation to Web servers and end-users.

Server process Process, or set of processes, that collectively provide services to clients in a manner that shields the client from the details of the architecture of the server's hardware/software environment. A server does not initiate any dialogue with a client; it only responds to requests. Servers control access to shared resources.

Service demand Sum of the service times at a resource (e.g., CPU, disk, or network) over all visits to that resource during the execution of a transaction or request.

Service Level Agreement (SLA) A contract between the service provider (e.g., IT department or ISP) and the end user or business unit. SLAs set specific goals for response time, throughput, overall uptime, and cost.

Service time Time spent at a resource (e.g., CPU, disks, or network) receiving service from it each time a transaction or request visits that resource.

Session A sequence of consecutive requests issued by the same customer during a single visit to an e-commerce site.

SET See *Secure Electronic Transactions*.

SHA-1 See *Secure Hash Algorithm*.

Simple Mail Transfer Protocol The protocol used to transfer e-mail from one computer to another over the Internet.

Simulation model A computer program that mimics the behavior of a system and provides statistics on the performance metrics of the system under study.

Simultaneous resource possession Situation in which a request simultaneously holds more than one resource.

Single-class model Model in which all customers are indistinguishable with respect to their service demands and routing behavior.

SLA See *Service Level Agreement.*

SMTP See *Simple Mail Transfer Protocol.*

SPEC See *Standard Performance Evaluation Corporation.*

SPECweb A standardized benchmark developed by SPEC to measure a system's ability to act as a Web server.

SQL See *Structured Query Language.*

SSL See *Secure Sockets Layer.*

Standard Performance Evaluation Corporation (SPEC) An organization of computer industry vendors dedicated to developing standardized benchmarks and to publishing reviewed results.

Structured Query Language (SQL) The standard language for defining and accessing relational databases.

System monitor Monitoring tools (hardware or software) that collect global performance statistics and do not distinguish among workload classes.

System-level model A model that treats the actual system as a black box.

T1 A term for a digital carrier facility that transmits at 1.544 Mbps.

T3 A term for a digital carrier facility that transmits at 44.736 Mbps.

TCP See *Transmission Control Protocol.*

TCP/IP The protocol suite used in the Internet.

Theoretical capacity Maximum rate at which a computing system can perform work.

Think time Interval of time elapsed since a response is received until a new request is submitted by a customer.

Throughput Rate at which requests depart from the system (measured in number of departures per unit time).

TLS See *Transport Layer Security*.

TPC See *Transaction Processing Performance Council*.

TPC-W A benchmark aimed at evaluating sites that support e-business activities. The business model of TPC-W is a B2C e-tailer that sells products and services over the Internet.

Transaction Processing Performance Council A nonprofit corporation founded to define transaction processing and database benchmarks.

Transmission Control Protocol (TCP) The most common transport layer protocol used on the Internet as well as on Ethernet LANs.

Transport Layer Security (TLS) A protocol that superseded SSL. TLS is now an IETF RFC and contains minor changes with respect to SSL version 3.0.

UDP See *User Datagram Protocol*.

Uniform Resource Locator (URL) A syntactic form used for identifying documents on the Web.

UMTS See *Universal Mobile Telecommunications System*.

Unique visitors Metric that indicates how many different people visited a website during a certain period of time.

Universal Mobile Telecommunications System A third generation of mobile communications systems that shows seamless integration of advanced multimedia services over both fixed and mobile networks.

User Datagram Protocol (UDP) A connectionless protocol that uses the Internet Protocol (IP) to deliver datagrams.

Utilization of a device Fraction of time that a device is busy, or equivalently, the percentage of time that at least one customer is present at the device receiving service.

XML See *Extensible Markup Language*.

WAN See *Wide Area Network*.

Web A common short name for the World Wide Web.

Web server A combination of a hardware platform, operating system, server software, and contents.

Webstone A configurable client/server benchmark for HTTP servers.

Wide Area Network A network, usually built with serial lines, that covers a large geographical region.

Workload characterization Process of partitioning the global workload of a computer system into smaller sets or workload components composed of transactions or requests having similar characteristics, and assigning values that represent their typical resource demand and intensity.

Workload model A representation that mimics the real workload under study. The model describes the workload of an e-business site in terms of workload intensity (e.g., transaction arrival rates) and service demands on the various resources (e.g., processors, I/O subsystems, networks) that make up the site.

World Wide Web (WWW) A client/server architecture that integrates various types of information on the global Internet and on IP networks.

Zipf's Law States that if one ranks the popularity of words (denoted by ρ) in a given text by their frequency of use (denoted by f), then $f \sim 1/\rho$.

Subject Index